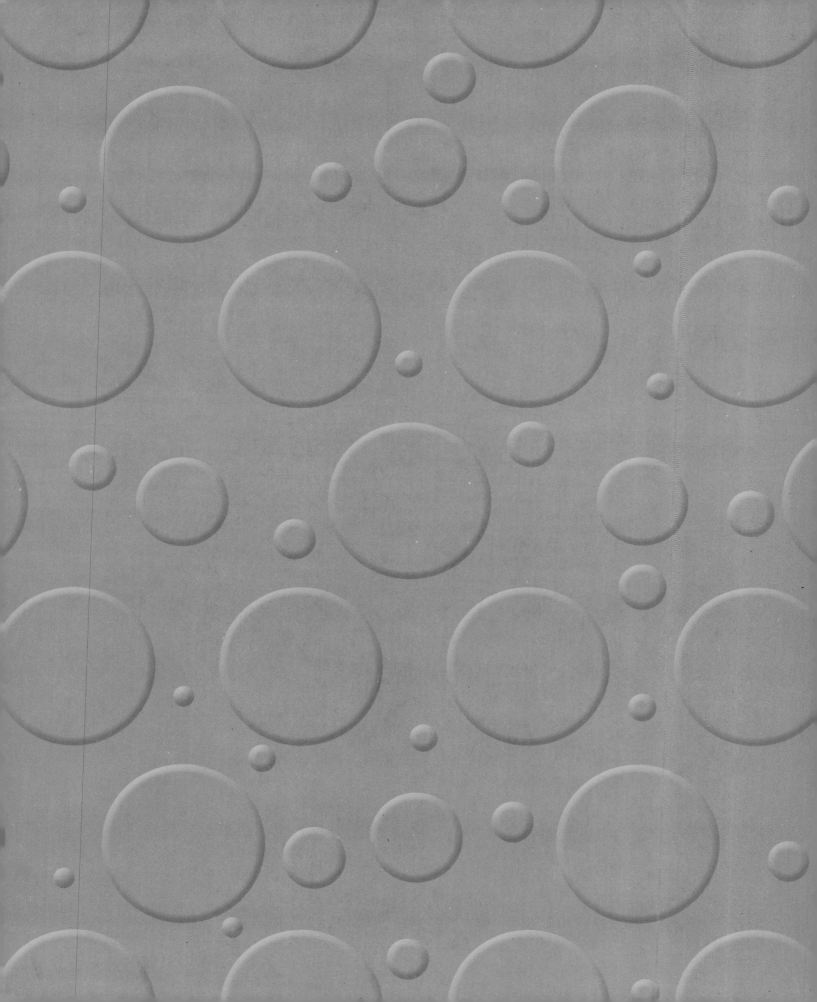

Harcourt
Health and Fitness

 **Harcourt**
SCHOOL PUBLISHERS

Orlando • Austin • New York • San Diego • Toronto • London

Visit *The Learning Site!*
www.harcourtschool.com

CONSULTING AUTHORS

Lisa Bunting, M.Ed.
Physical Education Teacher
Katy Independent School District
Houston, Texas

Thomas M. Fleming, Ph.D.
Health and Physical Education
    Consultant
Austin, Texas

Charlie Gibbons, Ed.D.
Director, Youth and School Age
    Programs
Maxwell Air Force Base, Alabama
Former Adjunct Professor,
    Alabama State University
Health, Physical Education and
    Dance Department
Montgomery, Alabama

Jan Marie Ozias, Ph.D., R.N.
Director, Texas Diabetes Council;
    and Consultant, School Health
    Programs
Austin, Texas

Carl Anthony Stockton, Ph.D.
Dean, School of Education
The University of Texas at
    Brownsville and Texas
    Southmost College
Brownsville, Texas
Former Department Chair and
    Professor of Health Education
Department of Health and
    Applied Human Sciences
The University of North Carolina
    at Wilmington
Wilmington, North Carolina

Printed in the United States of America

ISBN 0-15-337529-9

5 6 7 8 9 10 032 13 12 11 10 09 08 07 06

Chapters

Contents

CHAPTER 1 A Growing and Changing Body 2

CHAPTER 2 Being a Wise Consumer 38

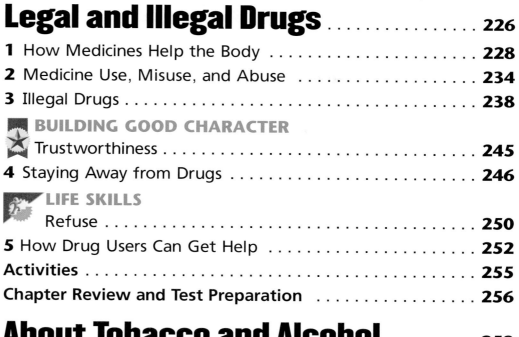

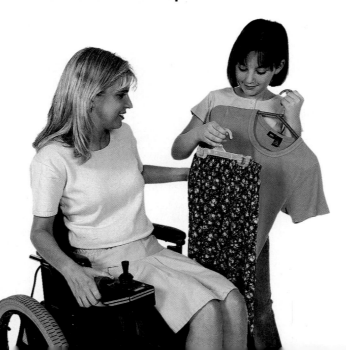

Working Toward a Healthful Community

Reading in Health Handbook

Health and Safety Handbook

Glossary

Index

Why should you learn about health?

You can do many things to help yourself stay healthy and fit. Just as importantly, you can avoid things that will harm you. If you know ways to stay safe and healthy and do these things, you can help yourself have good health throughout your life.

Eating right

Staying active

Getting enough rest

Keeping clean

Why should you learn about life skills?

Being healthy and fit doesn't come from just knowing facts. You also have to think about these facts and know how to use them every day.

These are some important life skills for you to have:

Managing Stress
Finding ways to avoid and relieve negative feelings

Communicating
Sharing ideas, needs, and feelings with others

Making Responsible Decisions
Deciding the most responsible thing to do to avoid taking risks

Refusing
Saying *no* to doing things that are risky and dangerous

Setting Goals
Deciding on specific ways to make improvements to your health and fitness

Resolving Conflicts
Finding solutions to problems in ways that let both sides win

Whenever you see ![LIFE SKILLS] in this book, you can learn more about using life skills.

Building Good Character

Why should you learn about good character?

Having good character is also an important part of having good health. When you have good character, you have good relationships with others and can make responsible decisions about your health and fitness. These are some important character traits:

Caring

Showing kindness and concern for friends, family, and others

Citizenship

Having pride in your school and community and obeying rules and laws

Fairness

Treating others equally, playing by rules, and being a good sport

Respect

Showing consideration for yourself and others

Responsibility

Doing what you are supposed to do, practicing self-control, and completing tasks

Trustworthiness

Being honest, dependable, and loyal

Whenever you see **Building Good Character** in this book, you can learn more about building good character.

What are ways to be a successful reader?

You need good reading skills to do well in school. Here are some tips to help you understand, remember, and use information you read.

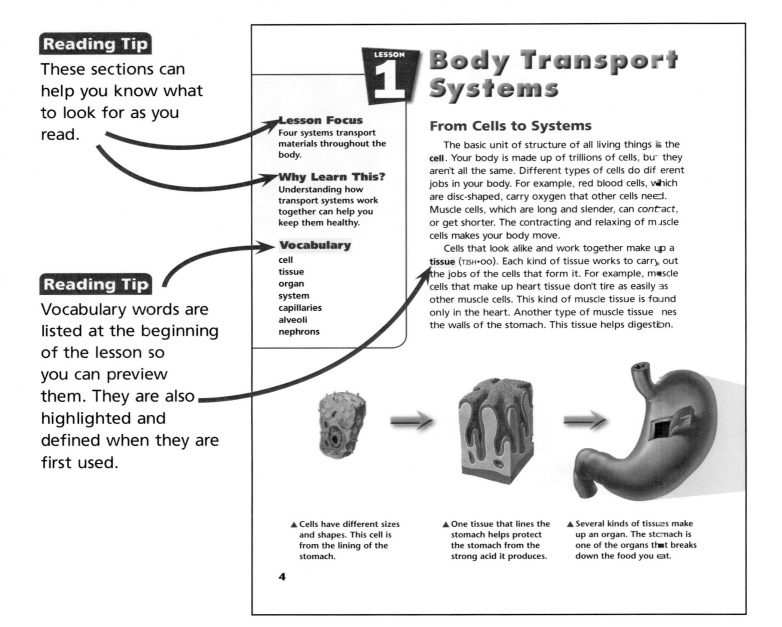

Reading Tip

These sections can help you know what to look for as you read.

Reading Tip

Vocabulary words are listed at the beginning of the lesson so you can preview them. They are also highlighted and defined when they are first used.

LESSON 1

Body Transport Systems

Lesson Focus
Four systems transport materials throughout the body.

Why Learn This?
Understanding how transport systems work together can help you keep them healthy.

Vocabulary
cell
tissue
organ
system
capillaries
alveoli
nephrons

From Cells to Systems

The basic unit of structure of all living things is the **cell**. Your body is made up of trillions of cells, but they aren't all the same. Different types of cells do different jobs in your body. For example, red blood cells, which are disc-shaped, carry oxygen that other cells need. Muscle cells, which are long and slender, can *contract*, or get shorter. The contracting and relaxing of muscle cells makes your body move.

Cells that look alike and work together make up a **tissue** (TISH•oo). Each kind of tissue works to carry out the jobs of the cells that form it. For example, muscle cells that make up heart tissue don't tire as easily as other muscle cells. This kind of muscle tissue is found only in the heart. Another type of muscle tissue lines the walls of the stomach. This tissue helps digestion.

▲ Cells have different sizes and shapes. This cell is from the lining of the stomach.

▲ One tissue that lines the stomach helps protect the stomach from the strong acid it produces.

▲ Several kinds of tissues make up an organ. The stomach is one of the organs that breaks down the food you eat.

4

Check your understanding by answering these questions at the end of each section. These questions also help you practice reading skills. You will see six reading focus skills:

► Compare and Contrast

► Draw Conclusions

► Identify Cause and Effect

► Identify Main Idea and Details

► Sequence

► Summarize

Whenever you see (Focus Skill) in this book, you can learn more about using reading skills.

Reading Tip

Use this section to summarize what you have read, review vocabulary and concepts, and practice writing skills.

Excretory System

The kidneys and bladder are the major organs of the excretory system. This system takes certain wastes from the blood and removes them from the body as *urine*. Urine is collected wastes and water. This job is important because it keeps the right amount of water in the body at all times. It also helps keep wastes from building up in the body. These wastes, in large amounts, are harmful.

As blood passes through the kidneys, **nephrons** (NEF•rahnz) filter out wastes and excess water. Cleaned blood leaves the kidneys and continues through the body. The urine, which contains the wastes, is stored in the bladder until it passes out of the body.

CAUSE AND EFFECT What are the effects of the kidneys' removing wastes and excess water?

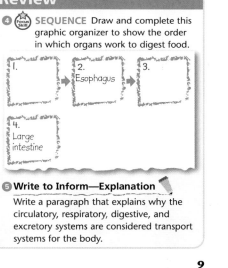

kidneys
ureter
bladder
nephron

In the kidneys, capillaries pass through microscopic filters called nephrons. Materials the body needs are returned to the blood. ▶

Lesson 1 Summary and Review

1 Summarize with Vocabulary

Use vocabulary from this lesson to complete these statements.

Groups of cells make up _____, which make up _____. Groups of these body parts then make up _____. Tiny blood vessels that enable materials and wastes to pass between the blood and body cells are called _____. Gases pass into and out of the blood in the _____ of the lungs. The _____ remove wastes from blood as the blood passes through the kidneys.

2 Critical Thinking Why do you think the air tubes in the lungs branch again and again until they are very small?

3 Why is the removal of wastes by the kidneys important to the body?

4 (Focus Skill) SEQUENCE Draw and complete this graphic organizer to show the order in which organs work to digest food.

1.

2. Esophagus

3.

4. Large intestine

5 Write to Inform—Explanation

Write a paragraph that explains why the circulatory, respiratory, digestive, and excretory systems are considered transport systems for the body.

9

Throughout **Harcourt Health and Fitness**, you will have many opportunities to learn new ideas and skills that will lead to good health.

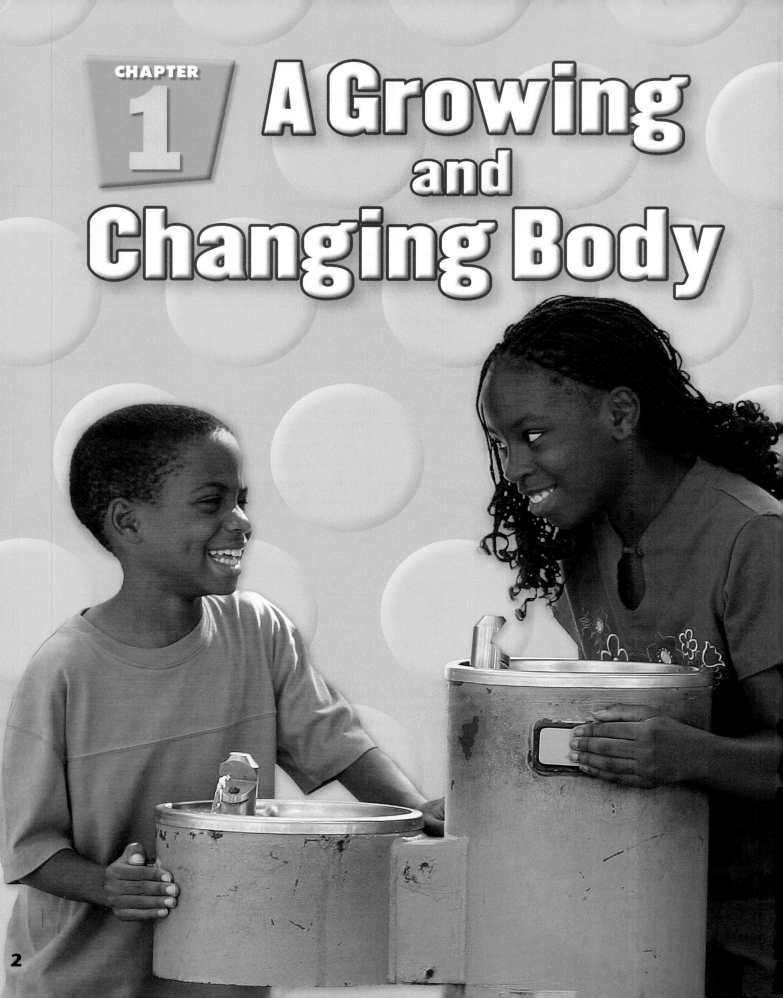

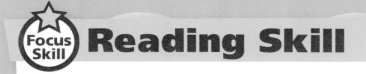
SEQUENCE When you sequence events, you place them in the order in which they happen. Use the Reading in Health Handbook on pages 372–383 and this graphic organizer to help you read the health facts in this chapter.

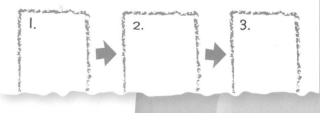

Sequence

1. → 2. → 3.

Health Graph

INTERPRET DATA Sleep patterns change as people grow older. Infants spend most of their time asleep, sometimes as much as sixteen hours each day. Adults, on the other hand, sleep eight hours or less each day. About how long does a ten-year-old child sleep each day?

Hours of Sleep

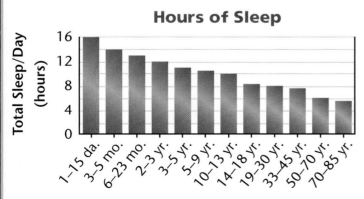

Total Sleep/Day (hours)

16
12
8
4
0

1–15 da. | 3–5 mo. | 6–23 mo. | 2–3 yr. | 3–5 yr. | 5–9 yr. | 10–13 yr. | 14–18 yr. | 19–30 yr. | 33–45 yr. | 50–70 yr. | 70–85 yr.

Age

Daily Physical Activity

Regular physical activity helps keep all your body systems working and growing the way they should.

Be Active! Use the selection, Track 1, **Saucy Salsa**, to get your whole body moving.

Body Transport Systems

Lesson Focus

Four systems transport materials throughout the body.

Why Learn This?

Understanding how transport systems work together can help you keep them healthy.

Vocabulary

cell
tissue
organ
system
capillaries
alveoli
nephrons

From Cells to Systems

The basic unit of structure of all living things is the **cell**. Your body is made up of trillions of cells, but they aren't all the same. Different types of cells do different jobs in your body. For example, red blood cells, which are disc-shaped, carry oxygen that other cells need. Muscle cells, which are long and slender, can *contract*, or get shorter. The contracting and relaxing of muscle cells makes your body move.

Cells that look alike and work together make up a **tissue** (TISH•oo). Each kind of tissue works to carry out the jobs of the cells that form it. For example, muscle cells that make up heart tissue don't tire as easily as other muscle cells. This kind of muscle tissue is found only in the heart. Another type of muscle tissue lines the walls of the stomach. This tissue helps digestion.

▲ Cells have different sizes and shapes. This cell is from the lining of the stomach.

▲ One tissue that lines the stomach helps protect the stomach from the strong acid it produces.

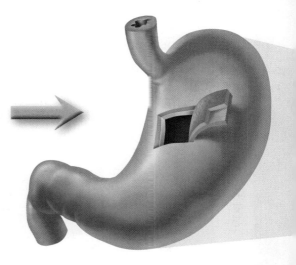

▲ Several kinds of tissues make up an organ. The stomach is one of the organs that breaks down the food you eat.

Many body parts are made up of several tissues. A group of tissues that work together to do a job is called an **organ**. The heart is an organ. It is made up of muscle and other tissues. The heart's job is to pump blood to all parts of your body.

Each organ in your body is part of a body system. A **system** is a group of organs that work together to do a job. The heart, for example, can't *transport*, or carry, blood to all parts of the body on its own. To transport blood to all parts of the body, the heart depends on blood vessels, which are also organs. The heart, blood vessels, and blood make up the *circulatory system*.

Other body transport systems include the *respiratory system*, the *digestive system*, and the *excretory system*. You will learn about each of these systems in this lesson.

Focus Skill SEQUENCE **Beginning with cells, in which order are body systems built?**

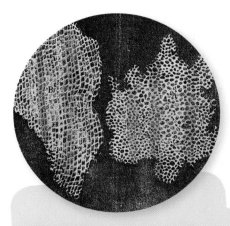

Did You Know?

In the mid-seventeenth century, Robert Hooke, a scientist and inventor, coined the term *cell* after he viewed thin slices of cork through a microscope. The boxlike structure of the cork cells reminded Hooke of the cells, or rooms, of a monastery. The photograph above shows cork cells like the ones Hooke observed.

◀ The stomach is part of a body system that digests food, transfers digested food into the blood, and stores wastes.

Circulatory System

Your body depends on your circulatory system to deliver important materials throughout your body. These materials are carried by blood, which circulates through your body in blood vessels. The circulatory system also helps remove wastes. In other systems, organs such as the lungs and kidneys help the blood get rid of the wastes.

Blood is carried throughout your body by three kinds of blood vessels—arteries, veins, and capillaries. Most arteries carry needed materials, such as oxygen, to body tissues. Most veins carry wastes, such as carbon dioxide, away from body tissues. **Capillaries** (KAP·uh·lair·eez) are tiny blood vessels that connect arteries and veins. Capillaries enable nutrients and oxygen to reach every body cell. They also pick up wastes from body cells.

The foods you eat and the physical activities you do are important in keeping your circulatory system healthy. In Chapters 3 and 4 you'll learn about foods and physical activities that help your circulatory system stay healthy.

COMPARE AND CONTRAST How are arteries and veins alike? How are they different?

Blood circulates throughout your body in one direction. Your heart provides the force to push the blood. Arteries carry blood away from the heart and to all parts of the body. Veins carry blood from all parts of the body back to the heart. ▼

heart

vein

artery

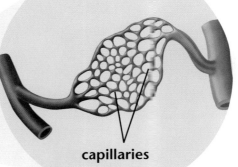

capillaries

▲ Oxygen and nutrients pass from the blood, through capillary walls, and into the cells. Cell wastes pass through capillary walls and into the blood.

▼ Oxygen in the air enters the blood through capillaries that surround the alveoli. Carbon dioxide leaves the blood through these capillaries and enters the alveoli.

nasal passages

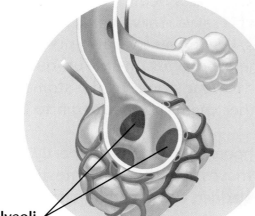

trachea

lungs

alveoli

To keep your respiratory system healthy, don't smoke, and avoid other people's tobacco smoke. Also, avoid air pollutants and get plenty of exercise. ▶

Respiratory System

The respiratory system's job is to take in oxygen, which body cells need, and to get rid of carbon dioxide, a waste gas. Muscles help your respiratory system move gasses into and out of your body.

When you breathe in, air enters through your nose, where it is cleaned and warmed. The air then passes through the windpipe, or *trachea* (TRAY•kee•uh). A branch of the trachea enters each lung.

The lungs are the major organs of the respiratory system. They are filled with air tubes, air sacs, and blood vessels. In each lung the air tubes branch again and again. At the ends of the smallest branches are the air sacs, called **alveoli** (al•VEE•uh•ly).

In the alveoli oxygen from the air enters the blood and carbon dioxide leaves the blood. When you breathe out, carbon dioxide is forced out of your body.

(Focus Skill) **SEQUENCE** **What happens to air right after it enters through your nose or mouth?**

Quick Activity

Write an Explanation Write a paragraph that explains how the circulatory and respiratory systems work together.

Digestive System

The food you eat cannot be used by your body until it is *digested*, or broken down. This is the job of the digestive system. This process begins in your mouth, where food mixes with saliva. Saliva begins breaking down carbohydrates. When you swallow, muscles push the food through the *esophagus* (ih•SAHF•uh•guhs), a long tube that leads to your stomach. The stomach contains acid and other chemicals that begin to break down proteins.

After a few hours in the stomach, partly digested food moves into the small intestine. The gallbladder, the pancreas, and the small intestine itself release chemicals to finish the job. In the small intestine, materials from digested food move into the blood. Undigested food passes into the large intestine. There, minerals and water move into the blood, and solid wastes are stored temporarily.

SUMMARIZE **List the organs of the digestive system, and tell the role of each.**

You can help keep your digestive system healthy by eating a variety of low-fat foods, including fruits, vegetables, and foods made with whole grains. You should also drink plenty of water. ▼

salivary glands

esophagus

liver

pancreas

stomach

small intestine

large intestine

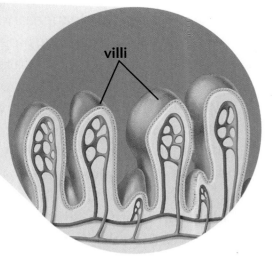

villi

▲ Materials from digested food enter the blood through projections called *villi* in the walls of the small intestine.

Excretory System

The kidneys and bladder are the major organs of the excretory system. This system takes certain wastes from the blood and removes them from the body as *urine*. Urine is collected wastes and water. This job is important because it keeps the right amount of water in the body at all times. It also helps keep wastes from building up in the body. These wastes, in large amounts, are harmful.

As blood passes through the kidneys, **nephrons** (NEF•rahnz) filter out wastes and excess water. Cleaned blood leaves the kidneys and continues through the body. The urine, which contains the wastes, is stored in the bladder until it passes out of the body.

CAUSE AND EFFECT **What are the effects of the kidneys' removing wastes and excess water?**

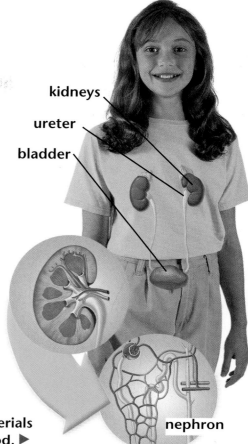

kidneys

ureter

bladder

nephron

In the kidneys, capillaries pass through microscopic filters called nephrons. Materials the body needs are returned to the blood. ▶

Lesson 1 Summary and Review

❶ Summarize with Vocabulary

Use vocabulary from this lesson to complete these statements.

Groups of cells make up _____, which make up _____. Groups of these body parts then make up _____. Tiny blood vessels that enable materials and wastes to pass between the blood and body cells are called _____. Gases pass into and out of the blood in the _____ of the lungs. The _____ remove wastes from blood as the blood passes through the kidneys.

❷ Critical Thinking Why do you think the air tubes in the lungs branch again and again until they are very small?

❸ Why is the removal of wastes by the kidneys important to the body?

❹ (Focus Skill) **SEQUENCE** Draw and complete this graphic organizer to show the order in which organs work to digest food.

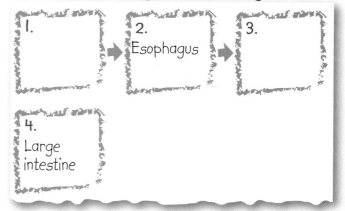

1.

2. Esophagus

3.

4. Large intestine

❺ Write to Inform—Explanation

Write a paragraph that explains why the circulatory, respiratory, digestive, and excretory systems are considered transport systems for the body.

Body Coordination Systems

Lesson Focus

Three body systems coordinate your body's movements.

Why Learn This?

Knowing what the coordination systems do helps you understand how to protect them.

Vocabulary

joint
ligaments
tendons
neurons
reflex action

An adult's skeleton has 206 bones. ▶

Skeletal System

You probably know that your skeletal system is mostly bone, but did you know it is made of other tissues, too? Your outer ear, the tip of your nose, and the ends of many bones are made of *cartilage*. This tough material is softer and more flexible than bone.

Your skeletal system supports your body. It also protects organs, such as the brain, heart, and lungs. The skeletal system's role in helping you move also makes it one of the body's coordination systems. Even the simplest body movements, such as changing positions in a chair, involve the skeletal system and other body systems.

Physical activity is important to the health of your skeletal system. So is eating foods that contain calcium—which helps build strong bones.

SUMMARIZE List three jobs of the skeletal system.

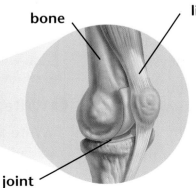

bone

ligament

joint

◀ A joint is a place where two or more bones fit together. Bones are attached at joints by strong bands of tissue called ligaments. Ligaments give joints flexibility for bending and stretching. Muscles also attach to bones near joints.

10

Muscular System

Your skeletal system wouldn't be able to move without your muscular system. The muscles that make your body move are attached to bones. For this reason they are called skeletal muscles. A skeletal muscle has a bulging middle and narrow tendons near each end. **Tendons** are strong, flexible bands of tissue that attach muscles to bones near the joints.

Skeletal muscles work in pairs. When one muscle contracts, it pulls on the bone it's connected to. The bone moves. To move the bone back again, a muscle on the other side of the bone must contract.

You can protect your muscles by warming up and stretching before doing strong physical activity. Be sure to ease out of activity, too, so muscles won't get sore.

CAUSE AND EFFECT **What causes a bone to move?**

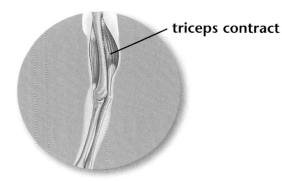

triceps contract

Muscles can pull bones but can't push them. Arm movement requires a pair of muscles—the triceps and the biceps.

biceps contract

The muscles that move the skeleton are *voluntary muscles*—you control them. You have other muscles, such as those in the heart, that you can't control. These are *involuntary muscles.* ▶

shoulder

elbow

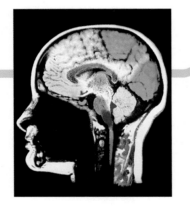

Nervous System

Your nervous system is responsible for your thoughts and your body's movements. It keeps your heart beating and makes sure your lungs take in oxygen. It enables you to see, smell, hear, taste, and touch. Your nervous system lets you learn, remember, and feel emotions. It is important as a system because it controls most of the activities of your body.

Your brain is your body's command center. Different parts of the brain control different body actions. Your spinal cord is a thick bundle of nerve tissue located inside the column of bones along your back. The job of the spinal cord is to transfer messages between your brain and different parts of your body. Nerves that branch from the brain and spinal cord receive information from the environment and send signals to muscles.

Sense organs in your body have nerves that gather information about conditions around you. Your skin, for example, has nerves that sense heat, cold, and pressure. Your eyes detect light, and your

neurons

brain

spinal cord

nerves

The nervous system includes the brain, spinal cord, and nerves. Nerves are bundles of cells, or neurons, which send messages to and receive messages from other neurons. ▶

ears pick up sound waves. Your sense organs provide information to prepare you for most situations.

Most of the time, information from sense organs travels to the brain. The brain receives and analyzes the information. If a response is needed, the brain sends out signals to muscles to take the necessary action.

In some situations, such as the one shown at the right, a response is needed right away. In a case like this, a **reflex action**, or automatic response, involving the spinal cord, but not the brain, may occur.

You can protect your nervous system in several ways. Don't take illegal drugs, and don't take any medicines unless they are given by your doctor or a parent. Eat a variety of healthful foods. Use safety gear when participating in sports.

CAUSE AND EFFECT **What causes a muscle to respond?**

▲ **This girl reacts to the hot pan before she even feels the pain. Nerves in her hand, sensing heat, send a message directly to nerves in her spinal cord that control muscles in her arm and hand.**

Lesson 2 Summary and Review

❶ Summarize with Vocabulary

Use vocabulary from this lesson to complete these statements.

Bones fit together at _____. Bones are attached to one another by _____. Muscles are attached to bones by _____. Messages from the brain travel to muscles through nerves, which are made up of _____. In an emergency, a _____ may occur to prevent injury.

❷ How can you keep your skeletal, muscular, and nervous systems healthy?

❸ Critical Thinking Besides the heart, where might involuntary muscle be found?

❹ (Focus Skill) SEQUENCE Draw and complete this graphic organizer to show the order of events in a reflex action that occurs when someone touches a hot pan.

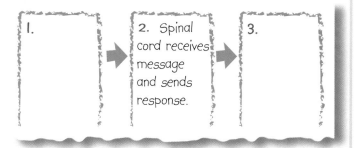

1.

2. Spinal cord receives message and sends response.

3.

❺ Write to Inform—Description

Write a paragraph that describes how the coordination systems work together when you bend your arm.

Growth, Heredity, and the Endocrine System

Heredity and Environment

Is your hair light or dark? Do you play a musical instrument? Are you good at math? Whatever your traits may be, where did they come from?

Heredity and environment combine to affect who you are and the way you grow. **Heredity** (huh·RED·ih·tee) is the passing of traits from parents to children.

You inherited a set of traits, such as your eye color, hair color, and the shape of your nose. Instructions for these traits are carried in your cells. The combination of traits you inherited from your parents affects the way you look and act.

Your parents give you guidance to help you make good choices. Close ties with family and friends enable you to develop your abilities. This helps you grow as a person.

Some inherited traits aren't easily noticed. One of these is the rate at which you grow. No two people grow at exactly the same rate or in the same way.

Your body and some of your talents were determined by your heredity before you were born. However, as you grow, the way your body, talents, and other traits develop also depends on your environment (en•VY•ruhn•muhnt). The **environment** is all the things that surround you every day.

An environment that is good for growth includes clean air to breathe, clean water to drink, nutritious food to eat, and a safe neighborhood to live in. As you get older, you become more responsible for your environment. Healthful choices, such as avoiding the use of drugs, alcohol, and tobacco, encourage growth and help you stay well.

Your parents gave you your inherited traits. They also do their best to provide you with a healthful environment. You will take on more and more responsibility for your development as you grow. Your parents, other trusted adults, and friends will continue, however, to be an influence.

SUMMARIZE **Explain how environment and heredity influence growth.**

Quick Activity

Take a Survey Take a survey to determine how many of your classmates can roll their tongues. This trait is passed from parents to their children.

◄ Has anyone ever said you look like someone else in your family? Inherited traits can make family members look very much alike.

Endocrine System

Heredity and environment affect your growth, but your body's systems actually make growth happen. One system, the *endocrine system*, is especially important in determining how your body grows. The endocrine system sends messages in the form of chemicals throughout your body. The chemicals, called **hormones** (HAWR•mohnz), travel in your blood to the organs and tissues of your body systems.

Hormones are produced by **glands**, or groups of specialized cells. Each gland has certain organs, or target organs, that its hormones act on. The whole endocrine system has many glands. The diagram below shows the locations and roles of several of the body's endocrine glands.

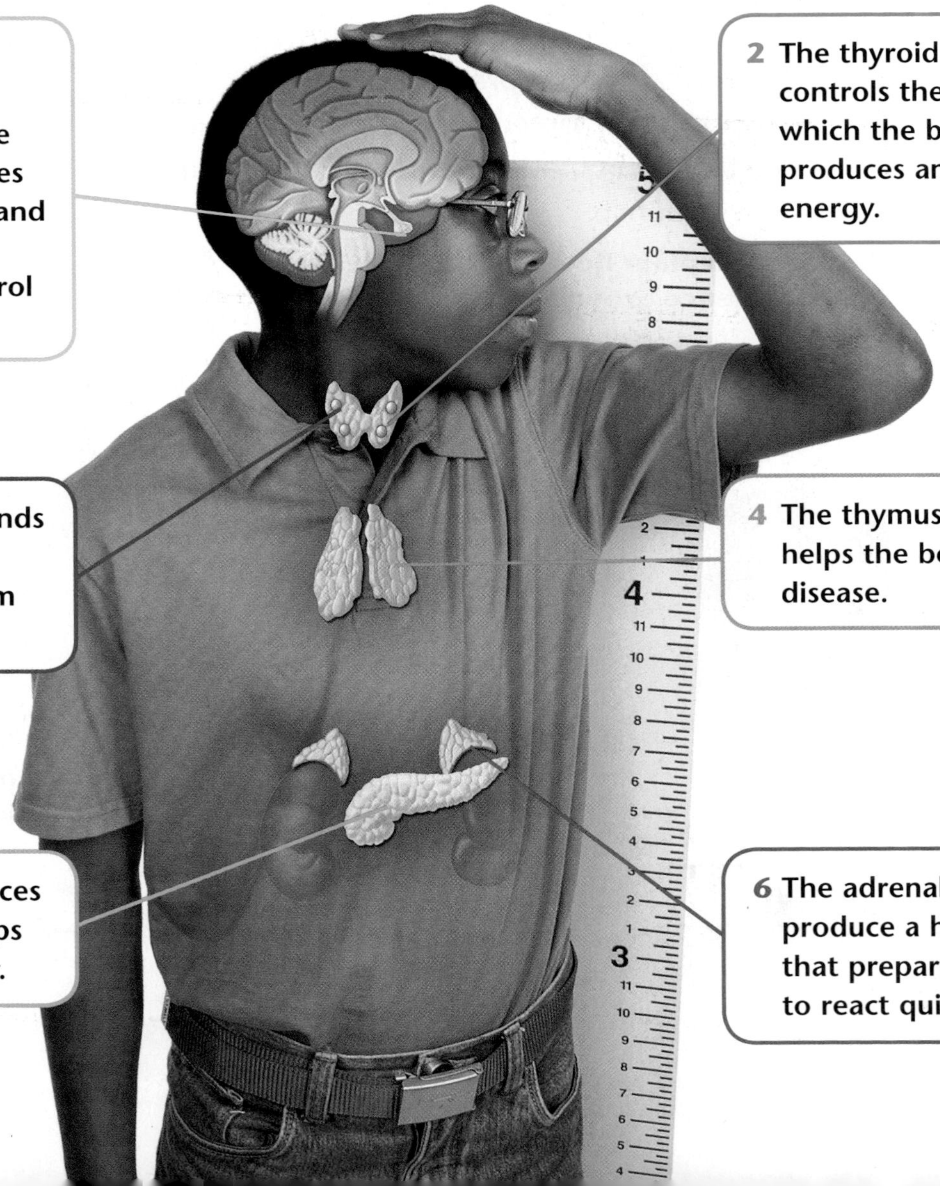

Did You Know?

About one in ten young people experience "growing pains" in their legs. The pains usually happen at night, and the aching can wake you up. Fortunately, growing pains normally do not last long and can be helped by massage, heat, or medication.

1 The pituitary gland (pih•TOO•uh•tair•ee) controls growth. The pituitary is sometimes called the master gland because it makes hormones that control other glands.

2 The thyroid gland controls the rate at which the body produces and uses energy.

3 The parathyroid glands help regulate the body's use of calcium and vitamin D.

4 The thymus gland helps the body fight disease.

5 The pancreas produces a hormone that helps body cells use sugar.

6 The adrenal glands produce a hormone that prepares the body to react quickly.

Hormones cause you to feel thirsty if your body fluids are low. ▼

Most glands make and release several different hormones. Every body function controlled by the endocrine system is controlled by more than one hormone. Hormones work together. If the level of one hormone is too high or too low, the level of another hormone changes to fix the problem.

Several hormones affect body growth. Growth hormone, which is produced by the pituitary gland, controls how much and how fast you grow. It affects the growth of your bones and skeletal muscles. Growth hormone causes the rapid growth that many teenagers experience. Other hormones aid in growth, too.

CAUSE AND EFFECT **What effects do the pituitary, parathyroid, thymus, and thyroid glands have on the body?**

Myth and Fact

Myth: **Sports drinks are better than water if you are really thirsty.**

Fact: Water is just as good as sports drinks for people who are really thirsty. Sports drinks may be better, however, for people who exercise for long periods, such as long-distance runners.

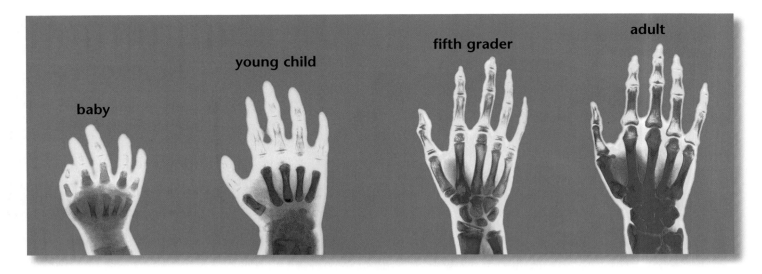

baby

young child

fifth grader

adult

▲ These X rays show the hands of a baby, a young child, a fifth grader, and an adult. Notice how the bones of the hand change from one period of life to the next.

growth plate

How Growth Occurs

You may think of your bones as hard, dry, dead body parts, but less than half of a bone contains hard material. About one-fourth is water. The rest is living tissue.

When you were a baby, your bones contained a lot of soft, rubbery cartilage. Cartilage bends instead of breaking. It helped protect you when you fell as you learned to walk. As you grew older, much of the cartilage hardened into bone. By the time you are twenty-five years old, your bones will be fully developed. Cartilage will remain only in places such as your knees and elbows. In these places cartilage works like a cushion so your bones can easily move against one another.

◀ Growth occurs at a bone's growth plates. In adults, growth plates are replaced with ordinary bone tissue. This change causes bone growth to stop.

Until you become an adult, your bones grow by making new cells. New cells increase the length and thickness of your bones. When you are a teenager, your bones will grow rapidly. They may grow several inches in a year's time.

Your muscles, too, grow in length and thickness. Like bones, your muscles stop getting longer after you become an adult. However, physical activity can make your muscles grow thicker and stronger. Physical activity will remain important for your muscles and bones even after you have finished growing. Throughout adulthood you will need to stay active to keep your muscles strong. The changes in your bones and muscles as they grow over the next few years will enable you to do more physical activities.

COMPARE AND CONTRAST Compare the growth of bones to the growth of muscles.

▲ The exercise this firefighter gets will tire his muscles. When he rests, his muscles will use materials from food for repair.

Lesson 3 Summary and Review

❶ Summarize with Vocabulary

Use vocabulary and other terms from this lesson to complete these statements.

Both _____ and _____ affect the way you grow. The body system most responsible for your growth, however, is the _____. In this system, _____, or groups of specialized cells, produce _____ that cause changes in the tissues of the body. During growth, _____ changes to bone.

❷ What substances should you stay away from to help keep your body healthy?

❸ Critical Thinking How does the function of cartilage in a baby differ from its function in an adult?

❹ (Focus Skill) SEQUENCE Draw and complete this graphic organizer to show how the endocrine system sends a message to a target organ.

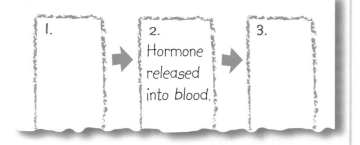

1.

2. Hormone released into blood.

3.

❺ Write to Inform—Explanation

Write a paragraph that explains why it is important to continue exercising throughout life.

19

Growth Comes in Stages

Growth Changes You

Imagine increasing your weight more than two billion times! That's just what you did in the nine months before you were born. You began growing inside your mother's body as a tiny single cell. During the **prenatal** (pree•NAYT•uhl) stage, or the time before birth, the single fertilized cell divided rapidly to form many new cells. These cells developed into different types of cells with different purposes. Your major body organs formed. By the time of your birth, your heart, lungs, stomach, and other organs were working together in systems. You could now live outside your mother's body.

In the prenatal stage, you went through a period of rapid growth, called a **growth spurt**. You went through a similar period during *infancy*, or babyhood. That growth spurt began the day you were born. Throughout infancy, your appearance changed and so did the things you were able to do. At first, you depended on your parents for survival. During your first year, your brain, muscles, and bones grew quickly. Your increased strength made sitting, crawling, and walking possible. You also learned new ways to communicate.

During the prenatal stage, new kinds of cells form and divide over and over again. From a tiny cell no bigger than the period at the end of this sentence, you grew into a baby. ▶

cell division

20

How You've Grown

Growth Stage	Age	Characteristics
Prenatal	Before birth	You grow faster than at any other period in your life. While inside your mother's body, you develop all the body parts you need.
Infancy	Birth to two years	Your body becomes bigger and stronger. You change from an infant into a toddler who can sit up, crawl, walk, and talk.
Childhood	Two years to ten years	Growth is slow but constant. You get taller, stronger, and more coordinated. Your mental, emotional, and social abilities develop. You also develop better problem-solving and communication skills.

▲ Every child grows at his or her own rate.

In time you began to think problems through and do things that you couldn't do before. Infancy prepared you for the next growth stage—childhood. During childhood, your body and mind developed even more. As you grew taller, stronger, and more coordinated, you were able to do things such as dance and twirl, play games and sports, and type on a computer keyboard.

Mental, emotional, and social changes also occurred during childhood. You learned to read. You discovered new interests and skills in a variety of areas. You learned to write and do math. These skills help you communicate with other people. Also during childhood, you began to develop friendships, and you became involved in many kinds of social activities.

MAIN IDEA AND DETAILS **The growth stages on the chart above are three main ideas. List two details for each main idea.**

Information Alert!

Research on Human Growth As scientists develop new techniques for studying the human body, they learn more about changes that happen during each stage of growth.

 For the most up-to-date information, visit The Learning Site. www.harcourtschool.com/ health

Building Good Character

Caring A person who feels that he or she is too far ahead or too far behind in growth may feel awkward and shy in group activities. Name at least two things you could do to help such a person feel at ease in your group.

You Continue to Grow

Like the boy in the picture, you may have noticed that some of your clothes are suddenly too small. Your body is getting ready to enter the next and final growth spurt of your life. The period of rapid growth and development from about age ten to age nineteen is called *adolescence* (ad•uh•LES•uhnts). You enter this period as a child and leave it as an adult.

The physical changing a person experiences during adolescence is called **puberty** (PYOO•ber•tee). Puberty can begin in girls as young as eight years of age and in boys as young as ten years of age. However, everyone enters puberty at his or her own time. During puberty, hormones affect the body not only by increasing growth but also by causing the development of adult characteristics. Some of the changes in your body may seem unfamiliar and odd.

As a teenager, you will also experience mental, emotional, and social growth. Your ability to think and solve problems will increase. You will be better able to use logic and reasoning. Your feelings may become stronger than they were before. Relationships with other people will become more important.

Adolescence is not without its problems, though. You may experience many different *moods*, or general feelings. Your moods may change quickly from great excitement and happiness to anger and sadness.

◀ Physical changes aren't the only changes during adolescence. You'll develop skills to help you deal with the consequences of your actions. You'll also learn to make better decisions about what is right and wrong.

Sometimes, feelings during adolescence are affected by physical changes. When people change physically, they may compare themselves with others. They may think of themselves as too tall, too short, too thin, or too heavy—even if they aren't. Such people have an unrealistic body image of themselves. **Body image** is how you think your body looks. People who develop an unrealistic body image may also feel low in self-esteem. They may become shy or try to change their looks by dieting or changing their hair. Most teenagers overcome an unrealistic body image as they get older.

The physical, mental, and emotional changes you experience during adolescence help prepare you to be an adult. During adolescence you will learn to take on more responsibilities, and you will earn more privileges. Adolescence is sometimes called "coming of age." You grow up and become more independent.

MAIN IDEA AND DETAILS Describe adolescence, and identify the three types of growth people experience during this stage.

▲ Kesha likes the way she looks in a mirror. Her ideals aren't based on movie and TV stars, but on real people.

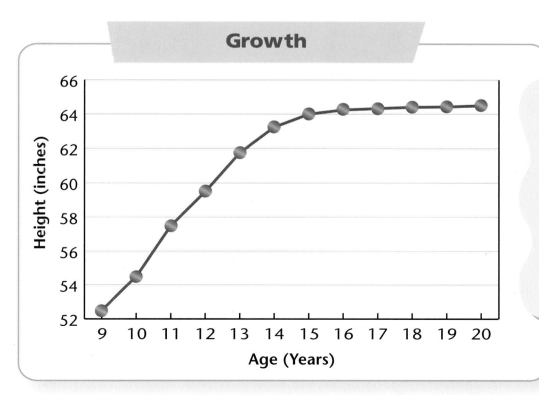

Growth

Height (inches) vs. Age (Years)

Quick Activity

Graphing Growth
This graph shows the growth of one person during adolescence. Start a similar growth chart to track changes in your own growth. If you keep track on a monthly basis, you may be amazed at how quickly you grow.

Becoming an Adult

Although you won't experience physical growth spurts after puberty, you will continue to grow emotionally, mentally, and socially. Entering adulthood, you'll probably continue your education, choose a career, and begin to support yourself financially. You'll develop close personal relationships. You may marry, have children, and take the responsibility of providing a healthful family environment.

As an older adult, you will change physically again. Some of your physical abilities will decline. However, you can help yourself stay healthy and active as an older adult by practicing good habits during all stages of your life. These habits include being physically active; eating healthful foods; getting plenty of rest; and avoiding alcohol, tobacco, and illegal drugs.

▲ As you approach adulthood, you'll change less physically, but you'll "grow" in other ways.

CAUSE AND EFFECT What is the effect of practicing healthful habits during all stages of your life?

Lesson 4 Summary and Review

①Summarize with Vocabulary

Use vocabulary and other terms from this lesson to complete these statements.

During the _____ stage, before birth, there is a(n) _____, or time of rapid growth. The stage after childhood is _____. You experience _____, the physical changing that makes you develop into an adult. Some people have a problem with changes in their appearance and develop an unrealistic _____.

②What kinds of problems do adolescents sometimes experience?

③Critical Thinking What are some ways a person becomes more independent at each life stage?

④ (Focus Skill) SEQUENCE Draw and complete this graphic organizer to show the order of growth stages.

1. → 2. Infant → 3.

4. → 5. Adult

⑤Write to Inform—Explanation

Write a paragraph that explains the similarities and differences between the prenatal stage and infancy.

Trustworthiness

Building a Good Reputation

On the road to becoming an adult, there will be times when your character may be tested. For example, a test of your trustworthiness could be having the honesty to return something valuable that you have found. Making choices that show that you have good character can help you build a good reputation. Here are some tips for building a reputation of trustworthiness.

- **Have the courage to do what is right.**
- **Be honorable.**
- **Live by your principles, no matter what others say.**
- **Follow your conscience.**
- **Always tell the truth.**
- **Be sincere.**
- **Keep your promises.**
- **Be dependable.**
- **Return what you borrow.**
- **Be on time.**
- **Don't repeat gossip or say bad things about others.**

Activity

Make a character map about trust. Write the word *trust* in a circle at the center of a sheet of paper. In each corner of the paper, draw a large box connected to the circle by a line. During one day, take note of all the things you do that show that you can be trusted. Select four of those things, and describe them in the boxes of your map.

Dealing with Adolescence

Lesson Focus

Physical, mental, and emotional changes accompany the growth spurt during puberty.

Why Learn This?

Knowing about the different kinds of changes during puberty will help you appreciate your own growth and development.

Vocabulary

concrete thinking
abstract thinking

Learning New Skills

It's easy to see how your growth spurt during puberty affects you physically. What isn't as easy to see is how it affects you mentally and emotionally.

During adolescence, new cells that are produced and the actions of hormones increase your ability to reason, solve problems, imagine, and invent. You add new thoughts, dreams, and opinions to what you already know. You may find that your interests change often. For the first time, you may become interested in different kinds of music, a team sport, or new hobbies.

Your new interests open doors to new friends, new activities, and new ideas. By following your interests, you add further to your abilities and knowledge. At this stage you are able to understand the value of practice in sports, schoolwork, and music. As your skills increase through practice, so does your self-confidence.

Quick Activity

Listing Interests
Make a list of all the things you did for the first time this year. Include new hobbies, skills, and interests. Then list three new things you might like to try in the next year.

As you enter puberty, you'll notice your mental growth as you discover new ways to accomplish tasks.

When you were younger, you were able to solve problems only by using things around you. For example, you could fit shapes together in a jigsaw puzzle, and you enjoyed sorting blocks by color and size. Solving problems involving real objects that you can see and touch is called **concrete thinking**.

Over the years, your thinking abilities have changed. You've learned ways to analyze and solve more complicated problems. Now you are able to use a more complex kind of thinking, called **abstract thinking**. With abstract thinking, you are able to imagine different solutions to problems.

Your thinking abilities will continue to develop as you enter puberty. You will become even better at identifying problems, thinking about possible solutions, and testing those solutions in your own mind. Using this abstract-thinking process, you will be able to handle even harder problems and learn to share your opinions and ideas with others.

COMPARE AND CONTRAST **How are your present thinking abilities similar to and different from those of a young child?**

ACTIVITY

Life Skills
Communicate

Although she hasn't said anything yet, Sakari is upset about her sister's using her music player without asking. Now her sister has accidentally erased Sakari's favorite song. What "I" message could Sakari use to explain her feelings to her sister? An "I" message is a statement you make in which you use the word *I* to clearly explain your feelings about something.

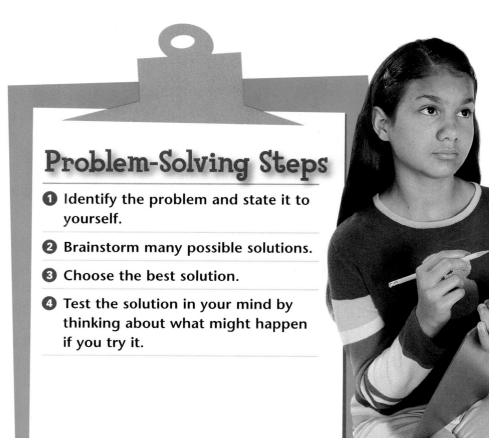

◀ When you are faced with a problem, you may discover that it has more than one solution and that a solution can be reached in more than one way.

Problem-Solving Steps

❶ Identify the problem and state it to yourself.

❷ Brainstorm many possible solutions.

❸ Choose the best solution.

❹ Test the solution in your mind by thinking about what might happen if you try it.

Real-Life Situation
Think of some decisions you made in the past year. Consider how you made each one and if you were satisfied with the results.
Real-Life Plan
Choose one decision that didn't turn out well. Identify some ways to improve the way you make similar decisions in the future.

Handling Feelings and Problems

The road to maturity is exciting, but at times it can be scary. As you grow up, you will have feelings and experiences you've never had before. You will also have important decisions to make and new problems to solve.

At this time of your life, you may be dealing with some personal problems. You may question who your friends are and what kinds of friends you want to have. You may want more independence from your family. New responsibilities may challenge you. Solving personal problems can require a great deal of effort and attention.

During adolescence you will learn how to reason through problems. You will learn that you have many options and that your choices bring both responsibilities and consequences. You will learn to make decisions after carefully weighing several possible outcomes.

As you travel toward adulthood, you will come across many challenges. Some will be like obstacles to get over or around. Other challenges will be rewarding and will be proof of your progress.

Adolescence is also a time when many people develop strong emotions and opinions. You may have mood swings, in which your mood changes often and quickly. You may feel happy one moment and sad the next, and your feelings may be stronger than ever before. As you learn to manage your emotional changes, you will need time to be alone with your thoughts. Talking about your feelings and problems with a parent or other trusted adult can also be helpful.

DRAW CONCLUSIONS Which events will likely be problems to overcome on your way to adulthood?

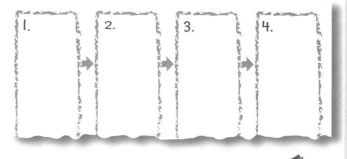

Lesson 5 Summary and Review

❶ Summarize with Vocabulary

Use vocabulary and other terms from this lesson to complete the statements.

When you were younger, you used _____ thinking to solve problems involving real objects you could see and touch. Now you also can use _____ thinking, which helps you see many options during decision making. During adolescence you may experience _____, in which your moods change often and quickly.

❷ Critical Thinking Do you use concrete thinking or abstract thinking when you decide whether to wear a coat to school?

❸ How can the road to adulthood be both difficult and rewarding?

❹ (Focus Skill) SEQUENCE Draw and complete this graphic organizer to show how to apply the steps for solving a problem.

1.	2.	3.	4.

❺ Write to Entertain—Short Story

Write a short story titled "A Day in the Life of a Teenager." In your story, describe how your main character learns to handle a problem.

Resolve Conflicts
with Your Family About Becoming Independent

During adolescence you will start to make decisions for yourself. Some of your decisions may cause conflicts with parents because they are still responsible for your well-being. Using the steps for **Resolving Conflicts** can help you work out disagreements.

Cody's friends plan to go to a movie on a school night. Cody wants to go, too. His mother reminds him that school nights are for homework. What should Cody do?

1 Use "I" messages to tell how you feel.

Mom, I want to go out to a movie tonight.

Not tonight, Cody. It's a school night.

Cody knows that school nights are supposed to be for studying, but he wants to join his friends.

2 Listen to the other person. Consider that person's point of view.

But Mom, all of my friends are going!

You need to do your homework.

Cody and his mom listen to each other. Cody considers his mother's view and understands her rules.

3 Negotiate.

"Let's see how well you do it."

"If I do my homework, may I go?"

Cody offers a solution to satisfy both of them. His mother agrees but has a condition that must be met.

4 Find a way for both sides to win.

"You did a nice job! You may go to the movie."

Cody does his homework—he knows his grades depend on it. His mother knows she has done what is best for Cody. And Cody gets to go to the movie.

Problem Solving

A. Rashawn's father has told Rashawn to mow the lawn on Friday afternoon. At school on Friday, Rashawn learns that all his friends are getting together that afternoon for a basketball game. He wants to play, too, but he knows his father expects the lawn to be mowed.

- Use the steps for **Resolving Conflicts** to help Rashawn handle the situation.

B. Courtney has promised friends they can come to her house on Saturday to watch a movie. However, she knows her sister wants to watch her favorite TV program at the same time.

- How could Courtney handle the conflict in a caring way?

Choices You Make Affect Your Growth

Lesson Focus

Healthful choices about physical activity, diet, rest, and hygiene can make puberty a positive time of growth and development.

Why Learn This?

Information about healthful choices can help you develop a program for taking care of your body.

Vocabulary

hygiene

Personal Health Plan ▶

Real-Life Situation
You're having trouble sleeping because you're worried about a test.

Real-Life Plan
Make a list of things you can do to stop your worrying about the test.

Exercise and Proper Diet Help Your Body Grow

Your body needs special care as it goes through the changes of puberty. Being physically active and eating properly are two important ways to support your growing body.

You probably know that exercise is good for you physically. People who exercise regularly increase their endurance, strength, and flexibility, and they are likely to sleep better. However, you may not know that physical activity is also good for you mentally and emotionally. Exercise helps you feel more confident and enables you to focus better, such as when doing schoolwork. Exercise also reduces emotional stress so

Physical activity is more fun when you work out with a friend and vary the kinds of activities you do. ▶

▲ Eating different types of foods, such as grains, fruits, meats, and vegetables, is the best way to get the nutrients you need. You will learn more about foods in Chapter 3.

that you are better able to solve any problems you might have. You will learn more about the benefits of exercise in Chapter 4.

Eating a healthful diet will supply you with energy and provide you with nutrients to help you grow. The food you eat affects how you look and feel, how well you resist diseases, and how well you perform mentally and physically. Since foods differ in the nutrients they provide, it's important to have variety in your diet. The photograph above shows many healthful food choices.

The amount of food you eat should match your body's needs. Eating too much food and getting too little exercise can make you gain weight. Eating too little food will make you become tired and too thin. Both extremes put your growth and health at risk. By choosing to eat healthfully and to exercise, you show that you are growing up and taking responsibility for yourself.

CAUSE AND EFFECT **What can cause a person to gain weight?**

Consumer Activity

Access Valid Health Information Packaged foods have labels that tell you what the foods are made of and what nutrients they provide. Read the labels of any packaged foods that make up your next few meals. Compare the nutrients they offer.

Other Choices Affect Your Growing Body

Sleep, too, is important to your growth and health. When you sleep, your body has time to recover from its daytime activities. It repairs tissues and releases built-up stress. Much of your body's growth takes place while you sleep.

Taking care of your body also includes making choices about personal **hygiene** (HY•jeen), or cleanliness. As your body changes, perspiration odors and skin problems can make hygiene important. Develop a daily routine you can follow before leaving for school in the morning or before going to bed. You will learn more about the importance of good hygiene in Chapter 2.

MAIN IDEA AND DETAILS Give details to support this statement: Exercise, diet, rest, and sleep affect your growing body.

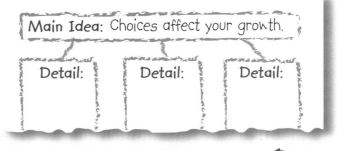

Resting during the day has many of the same benefits as sleeping at night. Find various ways to rest during the day. ▶

Lesson 6 Summary and Review

1 Summarize with Vocabulary

Use vocabulary and other terms from this lesson to complete the statements.

Many _____ you make can affect your growth. _____ reduces stress. Eating a healthful _____ supplies you with energy. Sleep and other kinds of _____ allow your body to recover. Practicing good _____ helps prevent body odor.

2 What are five benefits of exercise?

3 Critical Thinking If you feel tired after school and have only half an hour before soccer practice, what two things might you do to help restore your energy?

4 MAIN IDEA AND DETAILS

Draw and complete this graphic organizer to show the supporting details in this lesson.

Main Idea: Choices affect your growth.

Detail:	Detail:	Detail:

5 Write to Inform—Explanation

Write a paragraph that explains the importance of sleep for a teenager.

ACTIVITIES

Physical Education

Perform a Song Select a song you like that has a strong beat. You can use the song's tune, but write your own lyrics about any or all of the body systems. Or, make up lyrics to go with your own tune. Perform your song as you exercise, skip rope, or bounce a basketball in time with the song's beat.

Science

Research Heredity Do research on heredity. What are some physical characteristics that children inherit from their parents? Can a child have characteristics that grandparents have but parents do not have? Describe your findings in a booklet, and place it in the class library.

Technology Project

With a computer, make a slide presentation about the main parts and the jobs of each body transport system. Present your slides to your family or classmates.

For more activities, visit The Learning Site.
www.harcourtschool.com/health

Home & Community

Communicating Make a poster encouraging teenagers who are having problems to talk with a parent or another trusted adult. Display your poster in your classroom or cafeteria.

Career Link

Endocrinologist Endocrinologists are doctors who specialize in the endocrine system. Suppose you are an endocrinologist. What might you say to an eleven-year-old boy who complains that he has not yet gone through puberty? Write your response in a paragraph.

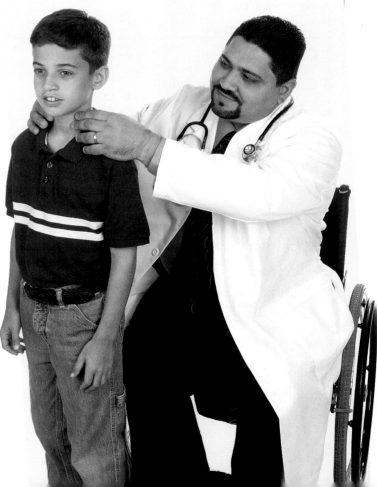

Reading Skill

SEQUENCE
Draw and then use this graphic organizer to answer questions 1 and 2.

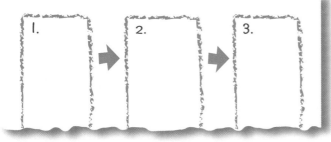

1 Which organ of the circulatory system pumps blood to the rest of the body?
2 Which blood vessels allow oxygen and nutrients to pass through their walls?

Use Vocabulary

Match each term in Column B with its meaning in Column A.

Column A	Column B
3 Groups of organs	A abstract thinking
4 Groups of similar cells	B concrete thinking
5 Bands that connect bones at joints	C heredity
6 Bands that attach muscles to bones	D ligaments
7 Passing of traits from parents to children	E puberty
8 The physical changes during adolescence	F systems
9 Solving problems by using real objects	G tendons
10 Solving problems by imagining solutions	H tissues

Check Understanding

Choose the letter of the correct answer.

11 What are tiny air sacs in the lungs called? (p. 7)
  A alveoli   C nephrons
  B capillaries D blood vessels

12 Blood passes through tiny filters in the kidneys, called _____. (p. 9)
  F neurons   H capillaries
  G nephrons J glands

13 Places where two or more bones meet are called _____. (p. 10)
  A ligaments
  B tendons
  C joints
  D cartilage

14 What is another name for nerve cells? (p. 12)
  F nephrons H alveoli
  G systems   J neurons

15 All the things that surround you every day make up your _____. (p. 15)
  A systems   C hormones
  B environment   D heredity

16 Hormones are produced by _____ in the endocrine system. (p. 16)

F   H

G   J

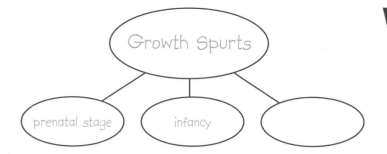

17 Which growth stage is missing from the graphic organizer? (p. 22)
   A adolescence
   B puberty
   C independence
   D adulthood

18 Your _____ is the way you think your body looks. (p. 23)
   F puberty   **H** body image
   G adolescence   **J** privilege

19 Sleep and other kinds of _____ allow your body to recover from the day's activities. (p. 34)
   A nutrition
   B exercise
   C rest
   D hygiene

20 Cleanliness, or _____, involves cleaning your whole body. (p. 34)
   F puberty   **H** perspiration
   G hygiene   **J** relaxation

Think Critically

21 How could a food label be helpful in choosing healthful foods?

22 If you had a problem with your esophagus, which body function would likely be affected?

Apply Skills

23 **BUILDING GOOD CHARACTER**
Trustworthiness You promised to meet a friend to go jogging after school. When you get home, you become interested in a TV show that won't end until after you are supposed to meet your friend. Use what you know about being trustworthy to make a decision about what you should do.

24 **LIFE SKILLS**
Resolve Conflicts You and your father disagree about whether you should get an expensive pair of basketball shoes for the upcoming season. He thinks you will grow out of the shoes too quickly. Use what you know about resolving conflicts to work out a fair agreement with your father.

Write About Health

25 **Write to Inform—Explanation** Explain why you might expect to face new problems during adolescence.

Being a Wise Consumer

DRAW CONCLUSIONS When you draw conclusions, you use what you know and what you read. Use the Reading in Health Handbook on pages 372–383 and this graphic organizer to help you read the health facts in this chapter.

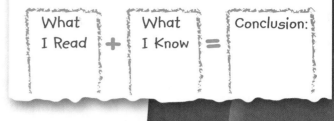

Draw Conclusions

| What I Read | + | What I Know | = | Conclusion: |

Health Graph

INTERPRET DATA Although most dental cavities can be prevented, the graph shows that as children grow older, the number of cavities increases. How does the average number of cavities for twelve-year-olds compare with the number for seventeen-year-olds? What do you think could reduce the difference?

Average Number of Cavities

Number of Cavities vs. Age bar graph: Age 9 = 1 cavity, Age 12 = 3 cavities, Age 17 = 8 cavities.

Daily Physical Activity

One of the easiest ways to take care of your body is to be sure to include some physical activity every day.

Be Active!
Use the selection, Track 2, **Locomotion**, to take care of your muscles and bones.

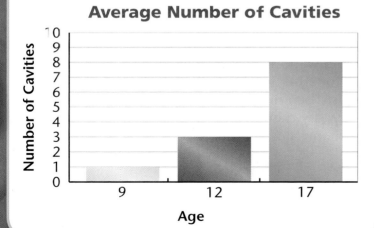

Healthy Skin, Hair, and Nails

Lesson Focus

Taking care of your skin, hair, and nails can help you stay healthy and look and feel your best.

Why Learn This?

Learning about skin, hair, and nails can help you make wise choices about caring for them.

Vocabulary

ultraviolet rays
SPF
hair follicle
oil gland

Caring for Your Skin

You may think of your skin as just a covering for your body. But it's much more than that. Your skin is an organ that protects you from diseases and helps keep body tissues from drying out. Keeping your skin healthy is important. Showering or bathing regularly with soap and water helps remove dirt, germs, dead skin cells, and excess oil from your skin. Use a mild soap to help keep your skin from drying out. You may want to use lotion if you have dry skin.

Wash your hands often to stop the spread of germs that cause illness. Always wash your hands before you prepare food or eat and after you use the bathroom. Wash your hands after you touch items that may have germs on them, such as trash or an animal. If you cough or sneeze into your hands, wash them before you touch anything.

 DRAW CONCLUSIONS Why should you wash your hands after sneezing into them?

◀ Wash your hands carefully. Using soap and warm water, rub your hands together for about twenty seconds. Then rinse your hands well and dry them with a clean cloth or towel.

Sun Dangers

The sun can be more dangerous for your skin than dirt and germs are. The sun gives off invisible waves of energy called **ultraviolet rays** (uhl•truh•vy•uh•lit), or UV rays. These rays cause sunburn and tanning, which are signs that the skin has been harmed. Years of being in the sun can damage your skin, causing wrinkles, loss of stretchiness, and dark spots. Over time, skin damage may lead to skin cancer. If some skin cancers aren't treated early, they can cause death.

It is important to find skin cancer in its early stages. A change in the appearance of a mole or birthmark may be an early indication of skin cancer. Know the simple ABCD rules for possible signs of skin cancer. If you find any of these signs, see a health-care professional.

CAUSE AND EFFECT **What is the effect if the cause is "I spend hours in the sun"?**

Did You Know?

If you are like most kids, you'll spend more time in the sun before you're eighteen years old than you will for the rest of your life. By protecting your skin now, you can greatly reduce your chances of developing skin cancer as an adult.

ABCD Rules for Signs of Skin Cancer

- **Asymmetry** One-half of a mole doesn't match the other half.

- **Border** The edges of a mole are irregular, ragged, uneven, or blurred.

- **Color** The color of the mole isn't the same all over but may have differing shades of brown or black. Sometimes the spot will have patches of red, white, or blue.

- **Diameter** The diameter of the mole is larger than $\frac{1}{4}$ inch or is growing larger.

People with fair skin sunburn especially easily. ▶

41

Sunscreen Protection

When you go outside, it's important that you protect yourself from the sun. Following these precautions will help you stay safe in the sun.

- Cover up. Wear shirts and pants that cover and protect as much of your skin as possible.

- Use a sunscreen with an **SPF**, sun protection factor, of at least 30. Apply the sunscreen 30 minutes before going outside. Be generous when applying the sunscreen to your body. Reapply sunscreen every two hours if you are swimming or sweating. Use lip balm with sunscreen to protect your lips.

- Wear a hat to protect your face, neck, and ears.

- Wear sunglasses to protect your eyes from harmful UV rays.

- Limit your sun exposure. Stay out of the sun between 10 A.M. and 4 P.M., when UV rays are strongest.

Quick Activity

Choose Sun Protection
Do you need a different sunscreen for an afternoon at the beach than you do for bike riding? Write down other items you need for sun protection for both activities.

Sunscreen Protection

SPF	Amount of Protection
0–14	Offers little or no protection from the sun. Not recommended for UV-ray protection.
15–30	Provides some UV-ray protection. The higher the SPF, the more protection. An SPF of at least 30 is recommended.
30+	Recommended for high UV-ray exposure, as in high altitudes and on or near water, sand, or snow.

SUMMARIZE Tell what you should do to protect your body from UV rays when you're outdoors.

Caring for Your Nails

Your nails protect the tips of your fingers and toes. Like hair, nails grow from your skin. Keeping your nails trimmed is important for their appearance and health.

Long nails can break or tear easily, exposing living skin. Dirt and germs can get under your nails even when they are neatly trimmed. To prevent the spread of germs, clean your nails at least once a day. Use warm, soapy water and a nail brush to remove the dirt and germs. Watch for changes in your nails. A change can be a sign of illness.

Don't bite your nails. Doing so can spread germs from your nails to your mouth. Use nail clippers or manicure scissors to cut your toenails and fingernails. Don't cut your nails too short. Making them too short can expose living skin or cause the nail to grow into the skin. Exposing the living skin around a nail can lead to infection. Cut each toenail straight across, just beyond the tip of your toe.

MAIN IDEA AND DETAILS **Give two details to support this statement: Keeping your nails trimmed to the right length is important.**

▲ Biting your nails can lead to infection. Toenails should be cut straight across, not rounded like fingernails.

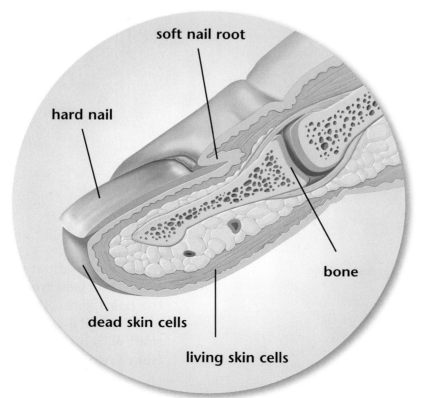

soft nail root

hard nail

bone

dead skin cells

living skin cells

◀ The fingernails you can see are dead cells that grow from living skin cells in the soft nail root.

Real-Life Situation
Combing or brushing your hair is important for looking your best. Suppose a person in your gym class asks to borrow your comb or brush.
Real-Life Plan
Write down what you would say to politely refuse to lend your comb or brush.

Caring for Your Hair

Much of your body is covered with hair. Each hair grows from a pitlike area called a **hair follicle** (FAHL•ih•kuhl). Special cells in the follicle grow to form hair. These cells grow, die, and then harden. The dead cells are forced out of the hair follicle as new cells form. The dead cells stack up, one on top of another, in a long column that makes up the hair shaft. An **oil gland** in each follicle makes oil that coats the hair and spreads over the surface of your skin. The oil makes your hair and skin soft and smooth and keeps it from drying out.

There are about 200,000 hairs on your head. They help protect your scalp from the sun. They also keep you warm in cold weather. Each hair grows from four to seven years and then falls out.

To keep hair looking neat, brush or comb it each day. Brushing gets rid of tangles and spreads oil over the hair shafts. Brushing once a day is usually enough to keep your hair healthy. Comb your hair often throughout the day to keep it looking neat.

Grooming is important, but don't share combs or

Although it may appear healthy, the part of the hair that you can see is actually dead. Only the hair follicle is alive. ▼

hair shaft

oil gland

hair follicle

▲ A hair grows about 6 inches in a year from the hair follicle. The oil gland coats the hair shaft with oil to keep it from drying out.

44

brushes with friends. Head lice can be passed from person to person by sharing items that are used on the head.

Shampooing your hair keeps it clean. Talk with a parent about how often to wash your hair. If your hair is naturally oily, you may need to wash it every day. If your hair is dry, you can wash it less often. A parent can help you find a shampoo that works well with your hair type.

Comb your hair gently after shampooing. Gentle combing helps keep wet hair from being damaged. Unless your hair is very curly, let it dry a little before combing. To make your hair easier to comb, use a small amount of conditioner to coat the hair shafts.

Letting your hair dry naturally is best. Electric dryers can make your hair brittle, causing it to break. Curling irons, hot rollers, and hot combs damage hair, too. If you want to dry and style your hair, use a blow-dryer on a warm setting. Brush your hair gently as you blow-dry it.

CAUSE AND EFFECT
What might happen if you blow-dry your hair every day?

Myth and Fact

Myth: **Brushing your hair one hundred strokes a day will make your hair healthier.**

Fact: Brushing your hair too hard and too often will cause the hair shafts to weaken and break.

About 200,000 hairs grow on your head. They protect your scalp from the sun and cold weather. ▶

Personal Hygiene

Before and during puberty, hormones will cause changes in your body. For example, your oil glands will release more oil, which may cause pimples called *acne*.

Acne forms when a pore becomes clogged with oil, dead skin cells, and bacteria. The bacteria grow in the blocked pore. The pore may swell and become red, forming a pimple. To remove excess oil and control acne, wash your face often with soap and water. If you do get acne, it's not your fault. Acne develops because of changes caused by hormones.

You may also notice that you sweat more than you did when you were younger and that the sweat has an odor. These changes are normal and are also caused by hormones. Daily bathing and using a deodorant or an antiperspirant can help control body odor and excess sweating.

SEQUENCE Tell how a pimple forms.

▲ Hormone changes may cause coarse hair to grow on your body during puberty. Ask a parent before using a razor to remove unwanted hair.

Lesson 1 Summary and Review

❶ Summarize with Vocabulary

Use vocabulary and other terms from this lesson to complete these statements.

The sun gives off _____, which can damage your skin. Sunscreen with a(n) _____ of 30 is recommended for all skin types. Hair grows from a pit in the skin called a(n) _____. Your skin and hair are protected from water loss by oil from _____. _____ and _____ control body odor and excess sweating.

❷ Why do you need your skin?

❸ Critical Thinking What should you do if a mole on your body is growing larger and its border is irregular?

❹ (Focus Skill) DRAW CONCLUSIONS Complete this graphic organizer to draw a conclusion about the importance of washing your hands.

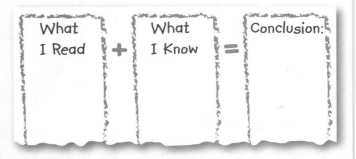

| What I Read | + | What I Know | = | Conclusion: |

❺ Write to Inform—Explanation

Some classmates are making fun of a boy who has acne. Write a paragraph to explain why the acne isn't the boy's fault.

Respect

Develop Self-Confidence

Almost everyone would like to have the same self-confidence that many of their favorite celebrities have. But for some people, being confident isn't easy, especially when they're in front of others. To be confident, you must respect yourself. Here are some tips to help you respect yourself and develop self-confidence:

- **Always look your best. The extra time you spend on grooming will boost your confidence.**
- **Use antiperspirant or deodorant to control sweating and body odor.**
- **Keep your hair clean and neatly combed.**
- **Take care of your teeth and gums to prevent cavities, gum disease, and tooth loss.**
- **Wash your face with soap and water to control acne. See your doctor for acne cleansers and creams, if necessary.**
- **If you are asked to speak in front of an audience, prepare notes about what you're going to say. Practice giving your presentation in front of a mirror, making eye contact with a pretend audience. Avoid reading to the audience from your notes.**

Activity

Speaking in front of an audience can be frightening. Ask your teacher if you may read your favorite short story aloud to the class. Practice the tips above to help yourself gain confidence.

Healthy Teeth and Gums

Kinds of Teeth

Taking care of your teeth is important to your smile and to your health. Your first teeth started coming in when you were a baby. These teeth, called primary teeth, continued to come in during childhood. As you lost your primary teeth, they were replaced by permanent teeth. Permanent teeth have to last the rest of your life. If one is lost, no tooth will replace it.

By your late teens, you will have thirty-two teeth. This includes four "extra" molars in the back of your mouth. These molars are sometimes called wisdom teeth. Your wisdom teeth may not appear until you are an adult, or maybe not at all.

 DRAW CONCLUSIONS Why is taking care of your permanent teeth important?

The shape of each tooth is well suited to its function. *Incisors* have sharp edges for cutting food. The pointed *cuspids* are good for tearing food. *Molars* and *bicuspids* have flat surfaces for grinding food. ▶

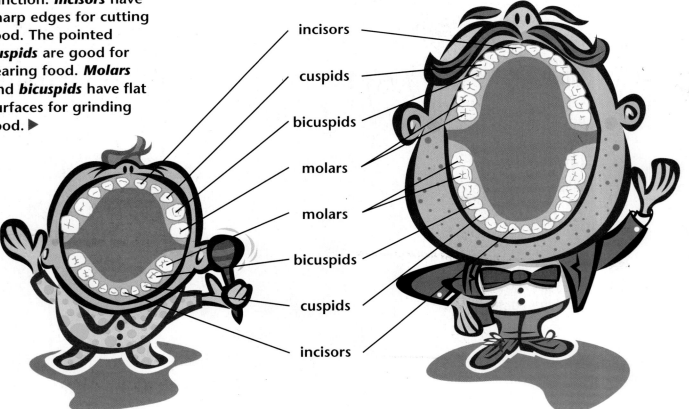

incisors
cuspids
bicuspids
molars
molars
bicuspids
cuspids
incisors

Caring for Your Teeth and Gums

Teeth are made up of three layers. Each tooth has a hard, protective *crown* made of *enamel*. Under the crown is a softer material called *dentin*. Dentin makes up most of the tooth. The *pulp* contains blood vessels that nourish the tooth. It also contains nerves that sense pain and temperature. The *root* anchors the tooth in the jaw. The teeth are surrounded by soft tissue—the gums.

Brushing and flossing remove food and bacteria from teeth and gums. Floss your teeth at least once a day before brushing. Brush your teeth at least twice a day after eating. Use a soft-bristled toothbrush and toothpaste that contains fluoride. *Fluoride* is a mineral that helps protect teeth. Your toothbrush and toothpaste should have the American Dental Association (ADA) seal.

SEQUENCE **Name the layers of a tooth in order, starting with the outermost layer.**

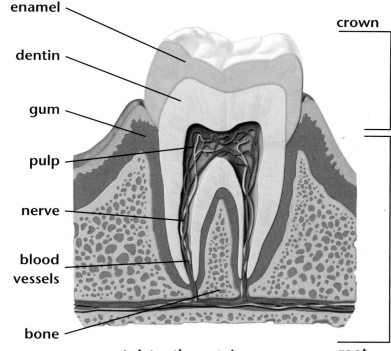

enamel
dentin
gum
pulp
nerve
blood vessels
bone
crown
root

▲ A tooth contains several layers of tissue.

Brushing and Flossing

Brush using short, back-and-forth strokes. To brush along the gumline and the inner surfaces of your back teeth, angle the toothbrush. To clean the inner surfaces of your front teeth, use the tip of the toothbrush. Also brush your tongue.

Cut a piece of floss about 18 inches long. Wrap it around your middle fingers. Insert the floss between two teeth. Gently rub the side of each tooth, moving away from the gumline, with up-and-down motions. Unwind a clean piece of floss, and repeat to clean between all teeth.

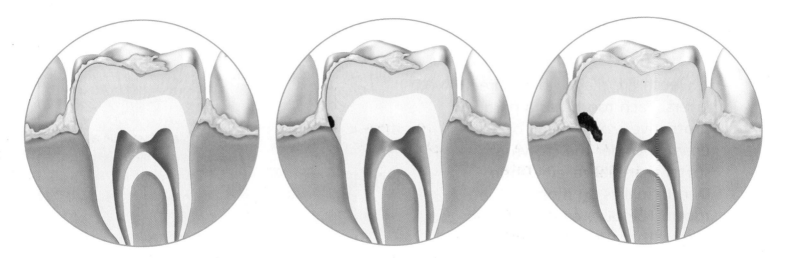

▲ Regular visits to the dentist can catch dental problems. The tooth at the left is covered with plaque. The center tooth shows the beginning of a small cavity. The tooth at the right has a large cavity. See page 390 for what to do in a dental emergency.

Dental Problems

Everyone—including you—has bacteria in his or her mouth. These bacteria make a sticky substance called **plaque** (PLAK), which coats your teeth. When the bacteria in plaque break down sugars in the foods you eat, acids form. These acids make holes, called cavities, in your tooth enamel. If a cavity isn't treated, the hole spreads through the dentin to the pulp and then to the root. A dentist treats a cavity by removing the damaged portion of the tooth. The dentist then fills the hole with a hard material, and the tooth is saved.

Plaque can cause other problems, too. If plaque is allowed to remain on the teeth, it forms a hardened material. This material can cause **gingivitis** (jin·juh·VYT·is), a gum disease in which the gums become red and swollen. Untreated gingivitis can develop into a more severe form of gum disease, in which the gums weaken and pull back from the teeth. Teeth may then fall out. Brushing and flossing can stop gingivitis in its early stages.

CAUSE AND EFFECT Tell how plaque can affect your teeth.

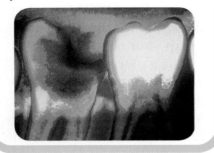

Orthodontia

You may know someone who wears a *dental appliance*—a device that straightens crooked teeth. Some people wear braces, usually for several years, to straighten teeth. After the braces are removed, a person may wear another dental appliance, called a retainer, at night. The retainer keeps the teeth from moving out of place.

The straightening of crooked teeth is called **orthodontia** (awr•thuh•DAHN•shuh). Straightening teeth makes them easier to clean and helps prevent cavities and gum diseases. Straightening can also prevent uneven wear of the teeth. Orthodontia helps ensure that your teeth will last a lifetime.

COMPARE AND CONTRAST
Tell how braces and a retainer are alike and different.

ACTIVITY

Life Skills
Make Responsible Decisions
Anna is hungry for a snack but knows she won't be able to brush her teeth right away. At a food stand, she sees caramel corn, ice cream, taffy, and fresh fruit. Help Anna decide which snack is best. Write your choice based on what you know about dental care.

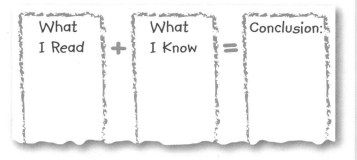

◄ Cleaning the teeth carefully while wearing braces is very important.

Lesson 2 Summary and Review

❶ Summarize with Vocabulary

Use vocabulary and other terms from this lesson to complete the statements.

Babies have _____ teeth. Older children and adults have _____ teeth. Bacteria cause a sticky substance called _____ to form on your teeth. When acids attack the teeth, _____ form. Crooked teeth can be corrected by_____.

❷ Why is taking care of your teeth and gums important?

❸ Critical Thinking Why should you floss before you brush?

❹ (Focus Skill) DRAW CONCLUSIONS Complete this graphic organizer to draw a conclusion about taking care of your teeth.

What I Read	+	What I Know	=	Conclusion:

❺ Write to Inform—How-To

In your own words, tell how to floss and brush your teeth.

Care of Your Eyes and Ears

Lesson Focus

Vision and hearing are important senses that tell you about the world.

Why Learn This?

Knowing how your eyes and ears work can help you protect your vision and hearing.

Vocabulary

farsighted
nearsighted
astigmatism
decibels

How You See

When you wake up in the morning, the first thing you probably do is open your eyes and look around. Your eyes are organs that sense light and let you see the world around you.

When you look in a mirror, you can see several parts of your eye. The *cornea* (KAWR•nee•uh) is a clear covering that protects the eye. The black-looking *pupil* in the center of your eye is surrounded by the colored *iris* (EYE•ris). Muscles in the iris control the size of the pupil. This determines how much light enters your eye. Using the diagram below, trace the path of light through your eye.

Your body has several built-in ways to protect your eyes. The bones of your skull protect the eyes from injury. Eyelashes keep out dust and other particles. Your eyelids close if anything comes near your eyes. And tears flush away particles that enter the eye.

 DRAW CONCLUSIONS How does the iris control the amount of light that enters the eye?

1 The *cornea* protects the eye and helps focus light entering the eye.

2 Light enters the eye through the *pupil.*

3 The *iris* adjusts the amount of light entering the eye.

4 The *lens* bends light rays so that images focus on the retina.

5 Light-sensing cells in the *retina* change light into nerve signals.

6 The *optic nerve* carries messages from the eye to the brain.

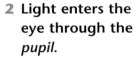

Vision Problems

Many people don't have perfect vision. A **farsighted** person can see things that are far away, but things that are nearby look blurry. For other people the opposite is true. A **nearsighted** person can see things nearby, but objects far away are blurry. For people with **astigmatism** (uh•STIG•muh•tiz•uhm), the cornea or lens of the eye is curved unevenly. Everything looks blurry to people with astigmatism.

Eye exams are important to ensure that your eyes are healthy and working well. Be sure to cooperate with vision checks at school. If you wear glasses, it's important to have your eyes rechecked every two years; more often if there is a family history of eye disease or if you wear contact lenses. Also, have a parent take you to an eye doctor anytime you have a problem seeing.

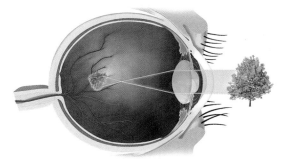
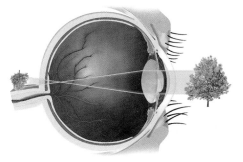

If you are nearsighted (above), the image will focus in front of the retina. If you are farsighted (below), the image will focus behind the retina.

CAUSE AND EFFECT What may be the cause if everything you see on the chalkboard appears blurry?

If your eyes feel tired or you get headaches when using a computer, tell a parent. You may need to see an eye doctor. ▶

Caring During a science experiment, students are using hot liquids, glassware, and chemicals. Montel is surprised that some classmates remove their goggles when the teacher isn't looking. List two things that Montel can do to encourage his classmates to wear their safety goggles.

Protecting Your Vision

Although your body has ways to protect them, your eyes can still be damaged. If you play sports, fast-moving objects can hit your eyes. You should wear safety goggles for protection. You should also wear them when you work with sharp objects, hot liquids, or household cleaners. All of these things can seriously damage your eyes. If you're around someone who is cutting grass, sanding wood, or pounding nails, wear safety goggles to protect your eyes from dust and flying objects.

The UV rays that damage your skin can damage your eyes, too. Even on partly cloudy days, wear sunglasses to protect your eyes. The darkness of the tint is not a good indicator of UV protection. Look for sunglasses with a label stating that they block all UV rays.

SUMMARIZE Name five situations in which you should wear safety goggles.

People mowing their lawns should protect their eyes, ears, and skin by wearing safety goggles (below), ear plugs, a hat, and sunscreen. ▶

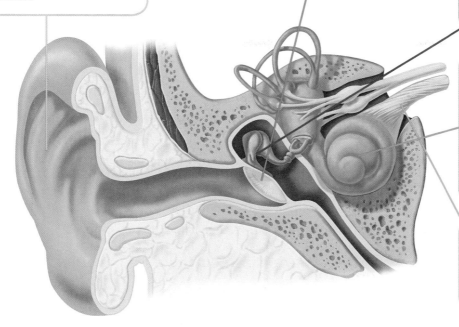

1 The outer ear directs sound waves into the *ear canal.*

2 Sound waves cause the *eardrum* to vibrate.

3 Vibrations cause the *hammer* to move the *anvil,* which moves the *stirrup.*

4 The moving stirrup causes fluid in the *cochlea* to vibrate. Hairlike cells lining the cochlea move, changing the vibrations into nerve signals.

5 The *auditory nerve* carries the signals to the brain, where they are interpreted as sound.

How You Hear

Your ears collect sound waves, process them, and send nerve messages to your brain. This enables you to hear sounds. The outer ear collects sound waves and directs them into the ear canal. There, sound waves make the eardrum vibrate. The vibrations are passed to three small bones in the middle ear. As the bones move, fluid in the inner ear vibrates. Tiny hairlike cells turn the vibrations into nerve signals. These signals are carried to the brain, where they are interpreted as sound. Trace the path of sound in the diagram above.

Like your eyes, your ears have some built-in protection. Most of the ear is within the skull and so is protected by bone. In the ear canal, glands produce a waxy material that traps dirt before it can reach the internal ear parts.

Tubes lead from your middle ear to your throat. These tubes drain fluid that collects in your ears and help keep air pressure the same on both sides of the eardrum. This protects the delicate eardrum and keeps your ears working well.

SEQUENCE Describe the path, as a series of ordered steps, that sound takes through the ear.

Did You Know?

Did you ever feel your ears "pop" when you were riding in an airplane or in an elevator? This feeling was caused by pressure building up in your ears. The popping occurred when the tubes that run between your ears and your throat opened up to relieve the pressure. This is your body's way to prevent ear damage.

Earmuffs and earplugs can reduce the sound level that reaches your ears. You should use ear protection when you're around loud noises.

Protecting Your Hearing

Like your eyes, your ears are delicate organs. Follow these guidelines to take care of your ears and protect your hearing.

- Be careful when you wash your ears. Wash only the outside of your ears.
- Never put anything into your ear canals. Small objects, including cotton swabs, can damage your ears.
- Ask a parent if you think your ear canals need to be cleaned. You may need an appointment with a doctor or nurse to clean them.
- If something gets stuck in your ear, don't try to get it out yourself. You may push the object deeper into your ear. A doctor should remove the object.

Loud sounds can harm your ears by damaging the tiny hairlike cells in the cochlea. If these cells are damaged, you could lose part of your hearing. The body can't replace these cells, so the damage may be permanent. The best way to protect your hearing is to avoid loud sounds as much as possible. Keep your television, stereo, and other sources of sound at a reasonable volume. You should also cooperate during hearing tests at school.

Health & Technology

Audiometry Many schools conduct hearing tests to measure a student's ability to hear the sounds of human speech. Sounds differ in pitch—highness or lowness. An audiometer measures your ability to hear sounds (tones) of different pitches. During the test, you wear headphones. The person conducting the test will check both ears. When the test is complete, you'll know if you can hear speech the way you should.

Hearing tests can determine if you have a hearing loss. A doctor can prescribe a hearing aid if there is a serious hearing loss.

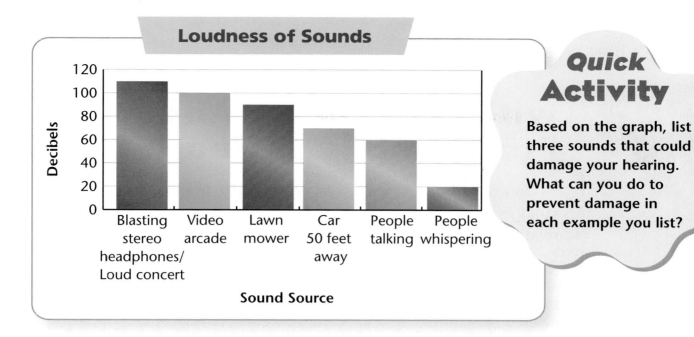

Loudness of Sounds

Decibels (y-axis): 0, 20, 40, 60, 80, 100, 120

Sound Source (x-axis): Blasting stereo headphones/ Loud concert, Video arcade, Lawn mower, Car 50 feet away, People talking, People whispering

Quick Activity

Based on the graph, list three sounds that could damage your hearing. What can you do to prevent damage in each example you list?

The loudness of sounds is measured in units called **decibels** (DEHS•uh•buhlz). Over time, any continuous sound at or above 85 decibels can damage your ears.

Focus Skill **DRAW CONCLUSIONS** Name two things you do for which you should wear ear protection.

Lesson 3 Summary and Review

1 Summarize with Vocabulary

Use vocabulary and other terms from this lesson to complete these statements.

A person who is _____ clearly sees things that are far away, but nearby things look blurry. A person who is _____ clearly sees things that are nearby, but faraway things look blurry. Everything looks blurry to a person who has_____. The loudness of sound is measured in _____. Cells in your eye that sense light are in the _____.

2 How can you protect your eyes from UV rays?

3 Critical Thinking Name three things that would appear blurry to you if you were farsighted.

4 Focus Skill DRAW CONCLUSIONS Complete this graphic organizer to draw a conclusion about taking care of your ears.

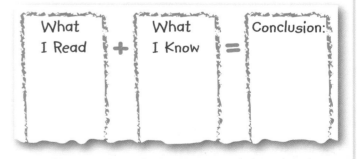

What I Read + What I Know = Conclusion:

5 Write to Express— Solution to a Problem

Write how you would solve the problem of your brother playing music too loudly.

Communicate
with Your Family About Protecting Your Hearing

You communicate every day with family, friends, and strangers. Learning to do this better can improve your relationships with others. You can use the steps for **Communicating** to help you communicate more effectively.

Kayla has won front-row tickets to a rock concert. She knows that the music will be loud and her dad will be concerned about protecting her hearing. How can Kayla communicate with her dad about the concert?

1 Understand your audience.

"Wow! Great tickets!" thinks Kayla. But she wonders how she'll tell her dad that they're sitting in the front row. He'll tell her it's bad for her hearing.

2 Give a clear message. Use a respectful tone of voice.

I've never had tickets for the front row *before*. What if we wear earplugs?

Kayla calmly and respectfully explains to her dad why she wants to sit in the front row. Then she makes a suggestion.

3 Listen carefully, and answer any questions.

That's a good idea, but if it's still too loud, will you agree to leave?

Yes.

Kayla listens to her dad telling her about leaving if the music is still too loud.

4 Gather feedback.

Enjoying the concert, Kayla?

Kayla asks her dad how the earplugs are working for him. "They're working great," he replies. "They make the concert enjoyable."

Problem Solving

A Roberto shares a room with his older brother. His brother likes to play loud music in their room. Roberto's ears ring after he leaves the bedroom when his brother is playing his music.
   • Use the steps for **Communicating** to help Roberto work out this problem with his brother.

B When Susie's dad mows the lawn, the noise is very loud. Susie is afraid that the noise will damage her dad's hearing.
   • Explain how Susie can respectfully share her concerns with her dad. Describe solutions she might suggest.

Being a Health Consumer

Lesson Focus

As a consumer you make choices about products and services that can affect your health.

Why Learn This?

Learning to read labels carefully and to analyze advertisements can help you become a wise health consumer.

Vocabulary

health consumer
ingredients

Sources of Health Information

Do you help choose your own brand of health-care products, such as soap, shampoo, and toothpaste? If you do, you are a **health consumer**, a person who buys and uses health products or services. Getting good information about products is an important step in making good choices as a health consumer. You also need to know how to compare and evaluate products. Having these skills will help you choose the best products for you and avoid wasting money.

When you gather health information, it's important to choose information that is reliable. Some of the information available to you contains myths. Myths are ideas that are thought to be true by some people but are actually false. Advertising can be one source of health myths.

Your library has books and magazines with information about health. To get facts rather than myths, look for books written by health-care professionals. ▼

Books, posters, newsletters, videos, and magazines about health are sources that can contain reliable health information. ▶

Good
FITNESS
STOP
cravings
24 hours
a day
Your
HEALTH
All a
HE
Eating for
GOOD
HEALTH
What everyone needs
to know

Advertisements appear in many places, including on television, in magazines, on the Internet, on the radio, and in newspapers. Their purpose is to make you want to buy a product, whether it's the best one for you or not. The information in advertisements may be true, false, or misleading. It's important to use reliable sources to determine the truth. That way you can make wise buying choices.

In addition to the sources pictured on these pages, your family is a good source of health information. Health-care professionals are also good sources. Your doctor, dentist, pharmacist, and school nurse can give you and your parents reliable information for making wise consumer choices.

Other good sources of consumer information are magazines published by consumer groups. Consumer groups test and rate health products, such as soaps, hand lotions, shampoos, and sunscreens. Newsletters that are produced by health organizations sometimes rate health products, too.

DRAW CONCLUSIONS **Why might an article from a toothpaste company be a poor source of information about which toothpaste to buy?**

Information Alert!

Health information changes as new health studies and new medicines are introduced.

For the most up-to-date information, visit The Learning Site. www.harcourtschool.com/health

Organizations such as the American Heart Association and the American Cancer Society have pamphlets that contain reliable health information. ▼

Learning from Product Labels

Most health products have detailed labels. The label on the front of a product usually gives the product name, a brief explanation of what the product does, and the amount of product in the package. Since this front label shows on the store shelves, manufacturers often include advertising there. Remember to carefully evaluate the information presented in advertising. The toothpaste and shampoo labels on these pages show information that usually appears on the front of a product.

The label on the back of a product often includes additional information. That label includes a full explanation of what the product does. You should still be careful when reading the label on the back. It may also contain advertising that may or may not be true.

Also shown on labels is the list of **ingredients** (in•GREE•dee•uhnts), or the things that are in the product. Some products, such as toothpastes and dandruff shampoos, provide health benefits. The ingredients that provide the benefits are listed on the labels as active ingredients.

Myth and Fact

Myth: **Certain shampoos can revive lifeless hair.**

Fact: The only living parts of your hair are the cells in the hair follicles deep in your scalp. The strands of hair that you see are all dead. Nothing can make them "come alive."

Toothpaste containing fluoride provides a health benefit. The ADA seal tells you the product is approved by the American Dental Association. ▶

Quick Activity

Analyze Labels Make a table with two columns. Label one column *Advertising Claims* and the other *Useful Information*. Analyze the labels on several bottles of shampoo. Then write information from the labels into the table.

Reading the list of ingredients can be important if you have allergies to soaps, perfumes, dyes, flavorings, or other materials. If you read the label, you can avoid using products with ingredients that may harm you.

Most labels give directions for using the products. You may not need directions for some products, such as shampoo. For other health products, such as medicines, it's important to follow the directions very carefully. Failing to follow the directions may be harmful to your health.

Some labels contain product warnings. The warnings contain information that may save your life. It's important to read and follow all product warning information carefully.

SUMMARIZE List the information that is included on health product labels.

Advertisers try to keep the names of their products in front of you as much as possible. That way, the products will be familiar to you and you might choose them when the time comes to buy. ▶

Analyzing Advertisements

Ads appear all around you—in magazines and newspapers, on radio and TV, on the Internet and billboards. You even see ads on T-shirts, backpacks, and drinking cups. Advertisers may use easy-to-remember songs to remind you of their products. They might use catchy logos or slogans to grab your attention. Advertising can have a strong influence on you. But if you know the tricks advertisers use to get your attention, you can make good buying choices.

One trick of advertisers is to try to convince you that everyone is using their products. The message is that you should use the products, too, if you want to be popular. Some advertisers use famous people to tell you why you should buy certain products. Advertisers hope that you'll trust the good things the famous people say about the products.

Another trick advertisers use is to make you think that their products are good buys. They may offer free gifts or tell you that buying their products will save you money. Don't be fooled by these tricks. Check what the advertisers are saying to see if the products really are bargains.

Don't be fooled by advertising tricks. Use common sense to evaluate products. Consider a product's cost, features, quality, and safety, and listen to the advice of others. Before you buy something, ask yourself these questions: "Do I really need this product? Will it do what I want it to do? Is the price reasonable?" If you can answer *yes* to all of these questions, you're probably making a wise choice. If you answer *no* to any of the questions, you should think again before buying the product.

Parents and health-care professionals can help you decide whether you really need a product. They may suggest different products. They also may suggest stores that have lower prices for the products you are considering. By listening to the advice of informed consumers, such as your parents, and by using common sense, you can become a wise health consumer.

MAIN IDEA AND DETAILS **Give three details to support this idea: Some advertisers use tricks to get consumers to buy their products.**

Advertisers use celebrities to promote their products. People trust celebrities because they feel they know them. This advertiser wants you to believe you can be a celebrity, too, if you visit Dr. Capps. ▼

I got my famous smile from Dr. Capps!

New Sources of Health Information

The website of the CDC, or Centers for Disease Control and Prevention, has accurate health information. ▼

Today you can get reliable health information with the click of a mouse. The Internet enables you to quickly find the answers to many health questions. But anyone can put information on the Internet, so you must make sure that the source you use is reliable. Unreliable sources may give wrong or even dangerous health information. Websites hosted by the government and by hospitals, universities, and professional organizations are the most reliable.

Remember that even reliable sites aren't designed to answer all health questions. They can't replace the advice that you get from a parent, your doctor, or other health-care professional.

SUMMARIZE Tell why evaluating health information on the Internet is important.

Lesson 4 Summary and Review

1 Summarize with Vocabulary

Use vocabulary and other terms from the lesson to complete the statements.

A _____ buys or uses health products or services. A person who is allergic to certain things should check the lists of _____ that are on the health-care products he or she uses. Ideas that are thought to be true by some people but are actually false are known as _____. Ingredients that provide medical benefits are known as _____.

2 Why do you think some advertisers use misleading information instead of reliable health information?

3 Critical Thinking What sources could you use to find reliable information about the benefits of adding fluoride to toothpaste?

4 DRAW CONCLUSIONS Complete this graphic organizer to draw a conclusion about the importance of being a wise consumer.

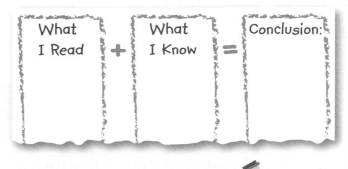

| What I Read | + | What I Know | = | Conclusion: |

5 Write to Entertain—Poem

Write a poem that tells about the tricks advertisers use to get consumers to buy their products.

ACTIVITIES

Math

Calculate Savings Your favorite shampoo is on sale in two different sizes. The 12-ounce bottle is $4.49, and the 8-ounce bottle is $3.19. Which size is less expensive per ounce? How much less?

Science

Show How Sound Travels Research sound to find out how sound waves travel. Then make a visual display to show what you learn.

Technology

Tell About Dental Lasers Dental lasers are replacing drills in some dentists' offices. Lasers can be used to treat cavities with less pain and noise than a drill. Lasers are used for gum surgery, too. Find more information about dental lasers. Then make a video, a slide presentation, a poster, or a brochure about this new technology.

GO ONLINE For more activities, visit The Learning Site. www.harcourtschool.com/health

Home & Community

Identify Noise Pollution Make a list of loud noises that you hear in or around your home. Talk with your parents or, with your parent's approval, community leaders about possible ways to reduce any dangerously loud noise. If it can't be reduced, identify ways to protect your hearing from this noise pollution.

Career Link

Orthodontist Orthodontists are dentists who specialize in straightening teeth and correcting other problems of the mouth. Suppose you are an orthodontist. Make a brochure for your patients to explain the importance of orthodontia to good dental health. In the brochure, explain the importance of cleaning your teeth carefully while wearing braces.

Chapter Review and Test Preparation

Focus Skill — Reading Skill

DRAW CONCLUSIONS

Draw and then use this graphic organizer to answer questions 1–3.

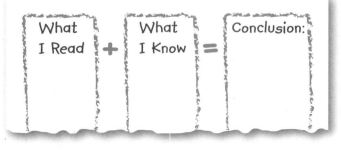

1 Write what you read in this chapter about the sun's effects on your body.
2 Write what you already knew about the sun's effects on your body.
3 Write a conclusion you can draw from this information.

Use Vocabulary

Use vocabulary and other terms from this chapter to complete the statements.

4 If left untreated, _____ can lead to serious gum disease that may cause tooth loss.

5 A sticky substance called _____ forms naturally on your teeth.

6 The correction of crooked teeth is called _____.

7 The loudness of sound is measured in units called _____.

8 All images are blurry for a person with _____.

9 A(n) _____ person can see things clearly that are far away.

10 Ideas thought to be true but which are actually false are called _____.

Check Understanding

Choose the letter of the correct answer.

11 Which of the following would a health consumer purchase? (p. 60)
  A deodorant   C candy bar
  B compact disc   D ice-cream bar

12 Invisible rays given off by the sun are called _____. (p. 41)
  F sonic rays   H tanning rays
  G sound waves   J ultraviolet rays

13 The _____ release oil that coats your hair and your skin. (p. 44)
  A hair shafts   C hair follicles
  B hair surfaces   D oil glands

14 Hair grows from pitlike areas in your skin, called _____. (p. 44)
  F hard nails   H hair follicles
  G bones   J retinas

15 The term *SPF* means _____. (p. 42)
  A sound protection factor
  B sun protection factor
  C silent protection factor
  D saving protection factor

16 Which of the following would **NOT** be used for sun protection? (p. 42)

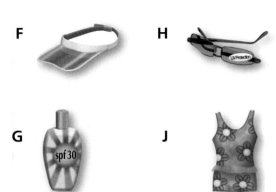

F   H

G   J

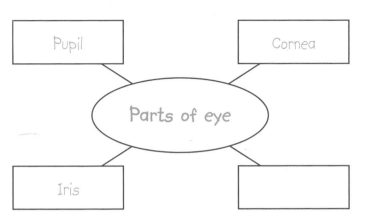

17 Which word or phrase is missing from the graphic organizer? (p. 52)
A follicle
B shaft
C auditory nerve
D retina

18 The top part of a tooth, as shown in the diagram, is called the _____. (p. 49)

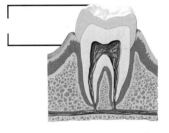

F root
G dentin
H pulp
J crown

19 Which of the following is **NOT** part of the ear? (p. 55)
A optic nerve
B auditory nerve
C cochlea
D hammer

20 The coiled tube in your inner ear is known as the _____. (p. 55)
F stirrup
G anvil
H Eustachian tube
J cochlea

Think Critically

21 Suppose your doctor tells you to use a face wash that contains benzoyl peroxide. At the drugstore, you see several face washes. How can you be certain that the one you choose contains benzoyl peroxide?

22 You want to floss your teeth every day, but you keep forgetting. What type of cue could you use to remind you to floss at the same time every day?

Apply Skills

23 **BUILDING GOOD CHARACTER**
Respect You have been asked by a youth group to give a presentation on skin care. Apply what you know about respect and developing self-confidence to tell how you would prepare for your presentation.

24 **LIFE SKILLS**
Communicate Your sister likes to listen to her favorite CDs with her headphones. The music is so loud that you can hear it across the room. How can you communicate a responsible way for her to listen to music?

Write About Health

25 **Write to Inform—Explain** Identify a variety of consumer influences, including advertising methods, that affect the buying habits of you and your classmates. Write a paragraph to explain how these influences affect your buying decisions.

CHAPTER 3

Foods for Good Nutrition

onions

kale

tomatoes

pears

eggpla

plu

Focus Skill Reading Skill

COMPARE AND CONTRAST When you compare things, you tell how they are alike. When you contrast things, you tell how they are different. Use the Reading in Health Handbook on pages 372–383 and this graphic organizer to help you read the health facts in this chapter.

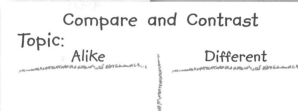

Compare and Contrast
Topic:
Alike   Different

Health Graph

INTERPRET DATA Americans eat a lot of fruits and vegetables. At least five servings a day are recommended for good health. What is the difference in the percent of people who eat the least amount of fruits and vegetables and the people who eat the greatest amount?

Fruit and Vegetable Consumption

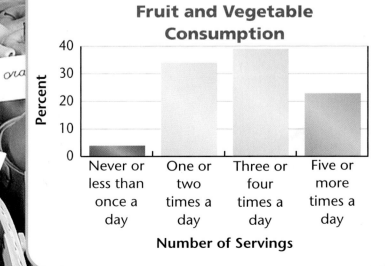

Percent (y-axis): 0, 10, 20, 30, 40

Number of Servings (x-axis): Never or less than once a day | One or two times a day | Three or four times a day | Five or more times a day

Daily Physical Activity

Eating the right foods in the right amounts is one way to stay healthy. Being physically active is another way.

 Be Active!
Use the selection, Track 3, **Late for Supper**, to use some food energy.

Food—Fuel for the Body

Food As Fuel

Your body is a little like a car. A car needs fuel to run, and so do you. While most cars use gasoline as fuel, the human body uses food. Burning fuel releases energy the car uses to run. A car doesn't need to change gasoline into another form in order to release this energy. Your body is different. It must *digest*, or break down, food before it can use the nutrients food contains.

Nutrients (NOO•tree•uhnts) are substances in food that provide your body with energy. Nutrients also provide building materials the body needs for growth, repair, and daily activities.

Breaking down food is your digestive system's main function. When your digestive system breaks down food, it releases several kinds of nutrients. These include carbohydrates, fats, and proteins.

 COMPARE AND CONTRAST How are your body and a car alike? How are they different?

Your car needs fuel (gasoline) to run. Your body's fuel is food. ▶

Digestion

Let's follow a bite of a turkey sandwich to discover how your digestive system breaks down the sandwich into nutrients your body needs. Digestion begins in your mouth. Your teeth chew the bite into smaller pieces. Your saliva contains **enzymes** (EN•zymz), chemicals that help break down foods to release nutrients. Different enzymes are needed to digest different foods.

After you swallow, the food mass moves toward your stomach. There, the partly digested food is squeezed and churned. And more nutrients are released from your bite of sandwich.

Next, the food mass moves into the small intestine, where more enzymes finish the job of digestion. Now the nutrients are ready to move into your bloodstream and into your body cells. Anything that cannot be digested passes into your large intestine.

SEQUENCE List the parts of your digestive system in the order that food moves through them.

Did You Know?

The small and large intestines are like long hoses connected to each other. In an adult, the small intestine is about 23 feet long and 1 to 2 inches wide! The large intestine is about 5 feet long. It's called the large intestine because it is wider than the small intestine. It is about $2\frac{1}{2}$ inches across.

1 Enzymes in your saliva begin to break down starch in the bread.

2 In your stomach, acid begins to break down the meat in the sandwich.

3 Additional enzymes complete digestion in your small intestine. Then nutrients pass into your blood. You can review this process on page 8.

Carbohydrates and Fats

Most of the energy your body needs comes from nutrients called carbohydrates. The **carbohydrates** (kar•boh•HY•draytzs) we eat most are sugars and starches.

Some foods, such as syrup and hard candy, are nothing but sugar. Many other foods, including fruits, some vegetables, and milk, contain sugars along with other nutrients. Starches are made of many sugars linked together. Beans, breads, and pasta are all rich in starches. During digestion, your body breaks down starches into sugars.

The nutrients that contain the most energy are **fats**. Plants, animals, and people store excess energy as fats. Butter, margarine, and oils are mostly fats. Most *junk-food* snacks, such as chips, cookies, cakes, and chocolate, have lots of fat. Foods such as meats, nuts, and milk products also contain fats. But unlike junk food, these foods also contain other important nutrients.

DRAW CONCLUSIONS Which food would supply more energy—a handful of raisins or a handful of peanuts? Why?

◀ What nutrients give these kids the quick energy they need to play basketball?

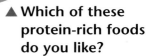

▲ Which of these protein-rich foods do you like?

Proteins

You've certainly grown a lot since you were a baby. You can thank nutrients called proteins for most of this growth. **Proteins** (PROH•teenz) are the building blocks of your body. Your body uses proteins to build and repair cells.

Remember that your body can store extra energy in the form of fats. Your body cannot store extra protein. It needs a new supply every day. You get proteins just as you get carbohydrates and fats—from the foods you eat. Some foods have more proteins than others. Meat, fish, eggs, and milk products are all good protein sources. Dried beans and peas, nuts, and grains also contain proteins.

DRAW CONCLUSIONS **Why do you think a child needs more protein than an adult?**

Quick Activity

Research Fat Find out how the amount of fat in different kinds of milk is indicated on the milk bottle or carton. What do the numbers mean? Make a table comparing the number of fat grams in different kinds of milk.

Vitamins and Minerals

In addition to carbohydrates, fats, and proteins, there are other nutrients that your body needs in smaller amounts. **Vitamins** (VYT•uh•minz) are nutrients that help your body perform specific functions. They are essential to life. Some vitamins help your body use other nutrients. Other vitamins help keep parts of your body strong and healthy. Your body cannot make most vitamins. It has to get them from foods you eat.

Minerals (MIN•uhr•uhlz) are another kind of nutrient, helping your body to grow and work. Minerals help keep your bones and teeth strong, help your body release energy from food, and keep your cells working well. The photographs below show foods that are rich in different vitamins and minerals.

⭐ (Focus Skill) **COMPARE AND CONTRAST** **Name two ways in which calcium is similar to vitamin A and two ways it is different.**

Vitamin A keeps your skin and eyes healthy. It is found in yellow and orange vegetables, tomatoes, and leafy green vegetables.

Vitamin B₁ is needed to release energy from nutrients. It is found in meats, fish, whole-grain breads, and some beans.

Vitamin C helps keep your blood, gums, and teeth healthy. It is found in citrus fruits, strawberries, and tomatoes.

Iron keeps oxygen moving throughout the body and protects against infection. It is found in meats, leafy green vegetables, beans, dried fruits, and nuts.

Calcium builds strong bones and teeth, helps muscles work, and helps blood clot. It can be found in milk, milk products, and broccoli.

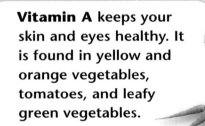

Phosphorus builds strong bones and teeth and helps cells function. It is found in meat, poultry, dried beans, nuts, milk, and milk products.

Water and Fiber

Water is the nutrient your body needs most. You need water to digest food, to transport nutrients to your cells, and to build new cells. Water helps keep your body temperature stable. It also helps remove carbon dioxide, salts, and other wastes from your body.

You get some water from the foods you eat, but you get most of the water you need from drinks like water, milk, and juice. To stay healthy, most people need six to eight glasses of water each day.

Fiber is another part of a healthful diet. Your body needs fiber to help move other foods through the digestive system. Fresh vegetables, fruits, and whole grains are all high in fiber.

MAIN IDEA AND DETAILS **What are two important things water does for your body?**

Whole-grain cereals, like shredded wheat, have more fiber than processed cereals. ▼

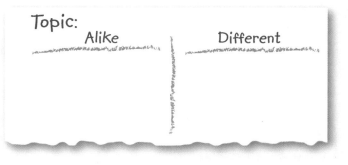

Lesson 1 Summary and Review

1 Summarize with Vocabulary

Use vocabulary from this lesson to complete the statements.

Nutrients with a lot of energy are _____ and _____. Nutrients called _____ are used to build and repair cells in your body. Your body cannot make most _____. Your blood needs iron, a _____, to carry oxygen throughout your body.

2 What are the main uses of nutrients in your body?

3 Critical Thinking Why is water a nutrient, even though most of the water you take in doesn't come from food?

4 COMPARE AND CONTRAST Draw and complete this graphic organizer to show how carbohydrates and proteins are alike and different.

Topic:

Alike	Different

5 Write to Inform—How-To

Describe how a person could design a weekly menu that includes all the necessary nutrients every day.

The Food Guide Pyramid

Lesson Focus

The Food Guide Pyramid groups foods with similar nutrients and shows how many servings from each food group the average person should have each day.

Why Learn This?

You can use the Food Guide Pyramid to help you plan a balanced diet.

Vocabulary

nutritionist
Food Guide Pyramid
serving

Milk, Yogurt, and Cheese Group includes foods such as low-fat milk, yogurt, cottage cheese, and hard cheese.

Vegetable Group includes foods such as corn, carrots, broccoli, lettuce, and tomatoes.

Bread, Cereal, Rice, and Pasta Group includes foods such as rice, bread, tortillas, pasta, and cereals.

The USDA Food Guide Pyramid

Fats, Oils, and Sweets Group includes foods such as potato chips, doughnuts, mayonnaise, candy, butter, and oil.

Meat, Poultry, Fish, Dry Beans, Eggs, and Nuts Group includes foods such as salmon, eggs, mixed nuts, chicken, steak, and peanuts.

Fruit Group includes foods such as strawberries, apples, pineapple, cantaloupe, blueberries, and plums.

People who work in supermarkets arrange similar foods together so they are easy to find. Nutritionists do something very similar but for a different reason. A **nutritionist** is a scientist who studies nutrition and healthful diets. Look at the **Food Guide Pyramid**, which is a tool to help you eat a balanced diet. It was prepared by nutritionists at the United States Department of Agriculture (USDA).

If you look carefully, you will see that the nutritionists grouped each food with other foods that have similar nutrients.

They arranged the groups in a pyramid form so that you can quickly see how many servings from each food group you should eat every day. A **serving** is the measured amount of food recommended for a meal or snack. Generally, you should eat more servings per day of foods near the base of the pyramid than foods near the top.

MAIN IDEA AND DETAILS **What two kinds of information does the Food Guide Pyramid give you?**

Information Alert!

Nutrition As scientists learn more about nutrition and health, the USDA Food Guide Pyramid may change.

GO ONLINE For the most up-to-date information, visit The Learning Site. www.harcourtschool.com/health

A Balanced Diet

Your body needs the right amounts of different nutrients each day to stay healthy. You get those nutrients by eating a balanced diet. The foods in each group of the USDA Food Guide Pyramid contain similar nutrients. That means you can substitute one food for another in the same group. For example, instead of meat, you could eat fish or eggs. You get many of the same nutrients in fish and eggs as you do in meat.

The number of servings from each food group are suggested for children ages 7–12.

Bread, Cereal, Rice, and Pasta Group

Foods in this group are made from grains, such as wheat and rice. Grains contain carbohydrates, protein, fiber, minerals, and vitamins. You should eat six to nine servings daily from this group. A serving is one slice of bread, 1 cup of dry cereal, or $\frac{1}{2}$ cup of cooked pasta.

Fruit Group

Fruits contain carbohydrates, including sugar, fiber, vitamins, and minerals. You should eat two to four servings daily from this group. A serving is one apple, one small banana, or fifteen grapes.

Vegetable Group

Vegetables contain many vitamins and minerals. Many vegetables also contain fiber and carbohydrates, such as starch. You should eat three to five servings daily from this group. A serving is $\frac{1}{2}$ cup cooked vegetables or 1 cup of salad or raw vegetables.

Meat, Poultry, Fish, Dry Beans, Eggs, and Nuts Group

These foods contain protein, fats, vitamins, and minerals. You should eat two to three servings daily from this group. A serving is 3 ounces of cooked meat, poultry, or fish (about the size of a deck of cards), one egg, or a handful of nuts.

Milk, Yogurt, and Cheese Group

This group is sometimes called the dairy group because all of these foods are made from milk. Milk products contain a lot of carbohydrates, protein, fats, and minerals. You should eat three servings daily from this group. A serving is 8 ounces of low-fat milk, 8 ounces of yogurt, or $1\frac{1}{2}$ ounces of cheese.

Fats, Oils, and Sweets Group

These foods contain a lot of carbohydrates (sugars) and fats, but not many other nutrients. You should eat only small amounts of foods from this group, and not every day.

By eating a variety of foods from each food group every day, you will be eating a balanced diet. You will be giving yourself the nutrients you need for energy and for your body to grow and repair itself. Just be careful to limit the amount of fats and sweets you eat.

SUMMARIZE **Name the six food groups, and give examples of at least two foods from each group.**

Personal Health Plan

Real-Life Situation
You're going to a restaurant, and you want to make sure you choose healthful foods.

Real-Life Plan
List two things you can do to make sure you choose healthful foods from a menu.

81

Life Skills

Make Responsible Decisions
Using the USDA Food Guide Pyramid, review the types and amounts of foods people should eat each day. Use the guidelines to write a menu of meals for yourself for one day. Remember to include foods that you like, and leave out those that you are not allowed to eat.

Planning Meals

You can use the USDA Food Guide Pyramid to plan a healthful snack when you get home from school. A healthful snack would include foods from several of the food groups, except the Fats, Oils, and Sweets Group.

When planning your snack menu, think about what you ate for breakfast and lunch. Think about what you might eat for dinner. Check the number of servings recommended on each level of the pyramid. Design your snack so that it gives you more of the foods you might not get enough of during the rest of the day.

The menu below shows what Keya's mother has planned for dinner each night. Which food groups are represented in the menu? Which food groups are missing?

COMPARE AND CONTRAST **Suppose you aren't allowed to eat the same foods for your after-school snack two days in a row. What menu could you make up so that your snack on Tuesday includes the same food groups as your snack on Monday?**

Planning meals helps you eat a balanced diet. ▼

Weekly Menu

Monday	baked chicken, green beans, mashed potato
Tuesday	fish, chips, corn, tomatoes
Wednesday	chicken salad, carrots, bread
Thursday	meatloaf, salad, peas, bread
Friday	soup and salad, lima beans
Saturday	pasta with meat sauce, spinach, bread
Sunday	turkey, mashed potatoes, beets

Jennie's friend is coming for lunch. What if she can't eat what Jennie has chosen? ▶

Quick Activity

Lunch menu The lunch Jennie prepared for herself and a friend included a peanut butter sandwich made with whole-wheat bread. But her friend is allergic to peanuts. What kind of sandwich could Jennie substitute for the peanut butter one?

Lesson 2 Summary and Review

1 Summarize with Vocabulary

Use vocabulary and other terms from this lesson to complete the statements.

The _____ was prepared by USDA _____ to show how a person might plan a balanced _____. It tells how many _____ from each food group people should eat every day.

2 Which food group contains foods you should choose least often?

3 Critical Thinking What foods could you substitute for a friend who doesn't eat meat?

4 (Focus Skill) COMPARE AND CONTRAST Draw and complete this graphic organizer to show how the Vegetable Group and the Bread, Cereal, Rice, and Pasta Group are alike and different in terms of nutrients.

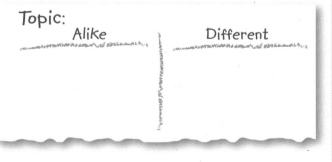

Topic:

Alike	Different

5 Write to Inform—Explanation

List the foods you like to eat, and explain whether they make a balanced diet or not.

Eating Healthfully

Portion Control

Almost everyone who eats in a fast-food restaurant has been asked this question: "Do you want to supersize that?" Supersizing means adding more food—sometimes a lot more—for a little extra money. Every time you supersize a meal, you are eating two or three or more additional servings of food. The items that are most often supersized are those that you should be eating less of, such as fries, soft drinks, and shakes. These often lack important nutrients.

You need to eat a variety of foods to get all the nutrients your body needs. But you also need to control the size of the portions you eat. **Portion control** means limiting the number of servings you eat and the sizes of the servings. Without portion control, you may gain more weight than is healthy. In the United States, more than 15 percent of preteens are greatly overweight. Being greatly overweight as an adult is called *obesity*. Obesity can double the chances of getting diseases such as diabetes and heart disease.

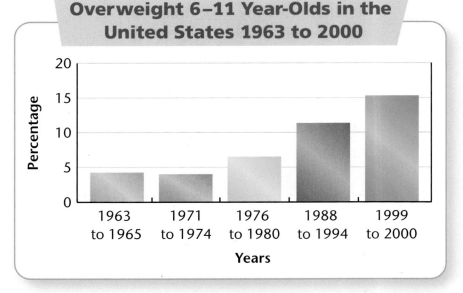

Overweight 6–11 Year-Olds in the United States 1963 to 2000

Obesity isn't the only problem related to portion control. As they grow, many teenage girls think they are overweight, whether they really are or not. To avoid gaining weight, some eat smaller or fewer servings than their bodies need to stay healthy.

About 5 percent of young women develop a serious eating disorder called anorexia (an•uh•REKS•ee•uh). **Anorexia** is excessive dieting and, at times, *self-starvation*. Starvation means not eating at all. Anorexia causes poor general health, low blood pressure, heart problems, bone weakness, and even death.

▲ Low self-esteem sometimes causes young women to "see" themselves as overweight, even when they are not.

COMPARE AND CONTRAST How are serving size and portion control alike? How are they different?

Consumer Activity

Analyze Media Messages
Do advertisements for supersize portions make people want to eat more? Ask ten of your classmates if they supersize meals when eating at fast-food restaurants, and why or why not. Write their responses in a table.

All the foods we eat provide calories for daily activities. ▼

Energy Balance

To keep your body at a healthy weight, you must balance the calories you take in with the calories you use up. **Calories** are a measure of the amount of energy in a food. All three nutrient groups—carbohydrates, fats, and proteins—contain calories. Your body can use these nutrients for energy. Carbohydrates and proteins have the same number of calories—about 4 per gram of food eaten. Fat has about 9 calories per gram.

When you take in more calories per day than you need, your body changes the excess calories into fat, and you gain weight. If you use more calories per day than you take in, your body uses stored fat for energy, and you lose weight. The ideal, called **energy balance**, is to take in the same number of calories as you use. Energy balance keeps you from gaining weight or losing weight. The best way to keep your body at a healthy weight is to combine good eating habits with regular exercise. You will learn more about the benefits of exercise in Chapter 4.

Chicken Soup

Calories Used per Hour

Activity	Calories Used
Walking	155
Swimming	345
Basketball	430
Running	455

SUMMARIZE **What is the best way to keep your weight the same as it is now?**

Athletes can usually eat a lot because they use more calories than the average person. ▶

Quick Activity

Calorie Intake and Energy Use Your body burns calories all the time, but some activities use more calories than others. The table shows how many calories a 100-pound person uses doing a variety of activities. Suppose you eat a 750-calorie dessert. Calculate how long you would have to walk or swim to use up those extra calories.

Lesson 3 Summary and Review

1 **Summarize with Vocabulary**

Use vocabulary from this lesson to complete the statements.

The amount of energy in food is measured in _____. Taking in and using the same amount of food energy is called _____. Gaining or losing weight is often the result of poor _____. Supersizing meals can cause weight gain, which can lead to health problems. Excessive dieting, or _____, is also unhealthful.

2 Why is portion control important?

3 **Critical Thinking** What might happen to your muscles if you exercise a lot but don't take in enough calories?

4 (Focus Skill) **COMPARE AND CONTRAST** Draw and complete this graphic organizer to show how obesity and anorexia are alike and different.

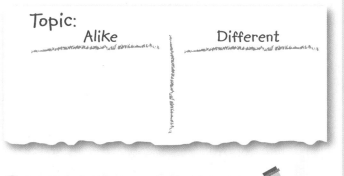

Topic:

Alike	Different

5 **Write to Inform—Explanation**

Research, then explain why someone shouldn't gain or lose weight too quickly.

87

Influences on Food Choices

Family, Friends, and Culture Affect Food Choices

The United States is full of people who came here from other countries and brought their foods with them. The cultures of your parents and grandparents influence your food choices the most. How can the country where your family came from influence what you eat?

Family members can influence the foods you eat, too. Suppose you have an older brother whom you admire. You might want to imitate his food choices. Or, if you don't get along with him, you might choose foods that are different from those he chooses. The same is true of your classmates. The way you feel about them might make you go along with or reject their food choices. No matter what kinds of foods you choose, you should make sure they are healthful.

Many restaurants offer foods of different countries. Which kinds of foods do you like? Why? ▶

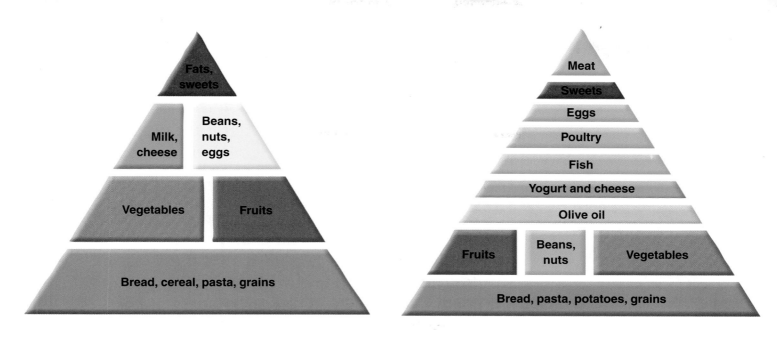

Fats, sweets

Milk, cheese

Beans, nuts, eggs

Vegetables

Fruits

Bread, cereal, pasta, grains

Meat

Sweets

Eggs

Poultry

Fish

Yogurt and cheese

Olive oil

Fruits

Beans, nuts

Vegetables

Bread, pasta, potatoes, grains

▲ People who don't eat meat can still have a healthful diet. A *vegetarian food pyramid* includes foods such as beans that replace meats, poultry, and fish.

▲ The *Mediterranean food pyramid* reflects foods eaten in countries like Spain, Italy, and Greece. It has more fish than meat.

People's diets are also influenced by their environments. In some places, people eat the wild plants and animals that live in the area. Some people eat the crops they grow and the meat of the animals they raise. People who live in coastal areas tend to eat more seafood than people who live far from the sea. How does the place where you live influence what you eat?

A person's values can also influence what he or she eats. For example, vegetarians choose not to eat meat. Some people don't eat meat because they are against the killing of animals or because of their religious beliefs. How do your personal values affect what you eat?

MAIN IDEA AND DETAILS **Give two reasons why one person's diet might be different from another's.**

Quick Activity

Compare Pyramids Compare sources of protein and serving sizes in the USDA Food Guide Pyramid and one of the pyramids above. Colors show similar food groupings. Then make a table of any differences.

Seasons Affect Food Choices

Do you like a hot bowl of soup or maybe a cup of hot chocolate on a cold winter day? A cool salad and an ice-cold glass of milk might be better if the weather is hot and humid. People often eat different foods depending on the weather. What foods do you like in different kinds of weather?

People used to eat different things during different seasons, too. Your parents and grandparents had to wait for late summer to find fresh corn in the market. They could buy canned or frozen corn in the winter, but not fresh. Some foods, like apples and potatoes, are easy to keep fresh. But strawberries, blueberries, tomatoes, and peppers spoil easily. So why can we find all these fruits and vegetables in most supermarkets all year? Look carefully at the labels on these foods and you will find the answer.

Many of these foods are grown in countries like Mexico, Panama, and Brazil, where it's warm all year.

SUMMARIZE Why don't seasons influence a person's choice of foods much anymore?

When the weather is cold, you probably choose hot foods, like soup. ▼

When the weather is hot, you might eat fresh fruits and vegetables that don't need to be heated. ▶

Freezing, drying, canning, vacuum-packing, smoking, and salting are methods of preserving food. ▼

Food Packaging We can eat certain foods all year because of preservation methods such as canning and freezing. Food irradiation is a method of preserving food and killing germs that cause spoilage and disease. This helps some fresh fruits, meats, and vegetables last longer and be safer to eat. The technology for this process was developed to treat foods eaten by astronauts on early space missions.

Cost and Unit Price Affect Food Choices

Foods imported from other parts of the world usually cost more than those produced locally. This may influence what people eat. For example, peaches grown in Chile may be available in February, but they may be too expensive for most families. So, they may buy frozen or canned peaches instead.

Unit price, or the cost of a certain amount of a food, may also influence choice. Suppose a 10-oz can of Brand A peas costs $0.60, while a 12-oz can of Brand B costs $0.66. Which is the better buy? The unit price of Brand A is $0.06/oz, while the unit price of Brand B is $0.055/oz. Brand B is more economical and may be the choice of many shoppers.

Unit pricing also allows shoppers to choose the most economically sized package of the same brand. Buying a half-gallon of juice, for example, is usually less expensive per ounce than buying two quarts.

Unit pricing enables shoppers to choose foods and other products that are more economical. ▼

41.5¢ per ounce Unit price	Retail Price
	$2.49
	pint of Strawberries
096253	6 ounces net weight

DRAW CONCLUSIONS Which is more economical—a 6-oz box of cereal for $2.49 or a 12-oz bag of the same cereal for $4.89?

Emotions Affect Food Choices

Often, people who feel stress or who are upset are likely to eat unhealthful foods. Some people eat large amounts of food or they eat junk food, like chips, cookies, and ice cream when they are upset. These kinds of foods are sometimes called *comfort foods,* because people think eating them makes them feel better. Other people stop eating altogether when they are upset or stressed.

Unfortunately, it won't help your feelings to eat lots of food, to eat junk food, or to eat nothing at all. Eating a balanced diet is more likely to make you feel better. The nutrients provided by the right amounts of healthful foods help you deal with stressful situations.

Even when you're feeling fine, you might choose foods because of some emotion. For example, if your grandma always makes pizza when you visit, you might enjoy having pizza with your friends because it reminds you of the fun you have at your grandma's.

 COMPARE AND CONTRAST **What two opposite changes in eating habits can occur when a person is upset?**

Personal Health Plan ▶

Real-Life Situation
Suppose you're feeling upset about something and don't feel like eating.
Real-Life Plan
Make a menu of well-balanced meals for days when you aren't feeling well. Use your plan when you need it.

▼ What foods do you eat when you're having fun?

Hearth Baked to Perfection

Health Concerns Affect Food Choices

Your food choices can be affected by how your body reacts to certain foods. If you have a food allergy, you probably become ill if you eat the food you are allergic to. A **food allergy** (AL•er•jee) is a bad reaction to a food that most other people can eat. Food allergies can give people rashes, upset stomachs, and headaches. Sometimes food allergies interfere with breathing. People who have severe allergic reactions to certain foods can even die.

Some foods contain chemicals that change the way the body functions. For example, caffeine is a chemical that speeds up body activity. It can make you jittery and keep you awake at night. Caffeine is found in coffee, tea, chocolate, and many soft drinks. You should either avoid foods that have caffeine or limit the amount you eat or drink.

Illnesses can also influence people's food choices. For example, people with diabetes must keep track of the carbohydrates they eat. People with heart disease should limit the amount of fats they eat. And people with high blood pressure should avoid salty foods.

A number of different foods, including peanuts, strawberries, shellfish, and milk, may cause allergies. If you discover that you are allergic to certain foods, you should avoid those foods.

If you are already healthy and want to stay that way, you should eat a healthful diet. Eat a wide variety of foods so you get all the nutrients you need. Avoid foods high in sugar, fat, and salt. Be aware of the amounts of food you eat, too. Too much of a good thing can still be bad for you. Follow portion size guidelines. However, don't cut out something altogether unless you are allergic to it. You still need carbohydrates, fats, and proteins—just not in large amounts.

CAUSE AND EFFECT **Identify three possible effects of caffeine on a person's body.**

▲ Strawberries and peanuts can cause food allergies.

Lesson 4 Summary and Review

❶ Summarize with Vocabulary

Use vocabulary and other terms from this lesson to complete the statements.

If you break out in a rash after eating a certain food, you may have a _____. _____ is a chemical found in some foods and drinks that can make you jittery. People who have _____ should limit the amount of carbohydrates they eat.

❷ Give an example that shows how unit price can influence a person's choice of foods.

❸ Critical Thinking Why is it a bad idea to eat large amounts of healthful foods?

❹ (Focus Skill) COMPARE AND CONTRAST

Choose two countries whose foods you eat. Draw and complete this graphic organizer to show how the foods of these countries are alike and different.

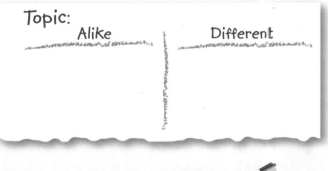

Topic:

| Alike | Different |

❺ Write to Inform—Explanation

Describe how your family influences your food choices.

94

Responsibility

Self-Control

As you grow older, you must take more and more responsibility for your health. This includes choosing healthful foods. It also includes practicing self-control. With self-control you can choose portion sizes that are right for you.

When you look at three popcorn containers at a theater refreshment stand, you might be tempted to get the biggest one. Even if you aren't very hungry, the smell may be tempting you. Or maybe it's the price—the biggest one might cost only a little more than the medium size.

But is the biggest container the most healthful for you? Popcorn is made mostly of carbohydrate. On its own, popcorn is a healthful snack. But at most theaters, popcorn is cooked in fatty oil and covered with butter and salt. Too much carbohydrate, oil, butter, and salt are not good for you.

Activity

Suppose you are the person at the theater refreshment stand. What should you do? You can ask for the popcorn without butter and salt, or you can have just a little of each. You can buy the small container or you can share the larger one with a friend. Write about and explain a healthful choice.

Food Labels and Advertising

Food Labels Provide Information About Nutrition

What's in a box of macaroni and cheese? You might think it's just macaroni and cheese. In fact, even something as simple as macaroni and cheese is made up of many different ingredients. **Ingredients** (in•GREE•dee•uhnts) are all the things that make up a food. What are the ingredients in macaroni and cheese? Look at the label on the following page to find out.

On every box of macaroni and cheese—and on every packaged food—there is a Nutrition Facts label. It tells you how big a serving size is and how many servings are in each package. It also tells you how many calories a serving contains and the nutrients that are in every serving. The label even tells you how much of each day's recommended nutrients one serving provides.

You can learn a lot about what you are eating by reading the Nutrition Facts labels on packaged foods. ▶

Nutrition Facts

Serving Size 2.5 oz
(70g/about 1/3 Box)
(Makes about 1 cup)
Servings Per Container about 3

Amount Per Serving	In Box	Prep*
Calories	260	410
Calories from Fat	25	170

	% Daily Value***	
Total Fat 2.5g**	4%	28%
Saturated Fat 1.5g	8%	23%
Cholesterol 10mg	3%	3%
Sodium 560mg	23%	31%
Total Carbohydrate 48g	16%	16%
Dietary Fiber 1g	4%	4%
Sugars 7g		
Protein 11g		

Vitamin A	0%	15%
Vitamin C	0%	0%
Calcium	10%	15%
Iron	15%	15%

*Prepared with Margarine and 2% Reduced Fat Milk.

**Amount in Box. When prepared, one serving (about 1 cup) contains an additional 16g total fat (3.5g sat. fat), 190mg sodium, and 1g total carbohydrate (1g sugars).

***Percent Daily Values are based on a 2,000 calorie diet. Your daily values may be higher or lower depending on your calorie needs:

	Calories:	2,000	2,500
Total Fat	Less than	65g	80g
Sat Fat	Less than	20g	25g
Cholest	Less than	300mg	300mg
Sodium	Less than	2,400mg	2,400mg
Total Carb		300g	375g
Dietary Fiber		25g	30g

INGREDIENTS: ENRICHED MACARONI PRODUCT (WHEAT FLOUR, NIACIN, FERROUS SULFATE [IRON], THIAMIN MONONITRATE [VITAMIN B1], RIBOFLAVIN [VITAMIN B2], FOLIC ACID), CHEESE SAUCE MIX (WHEY, WHEY PROTEIN CONCENTRATE, MILKFAT, MILK PROTEIN CONCENTRATE, SALT, SODIUM TRIPOLYPHOSPHATE, CITRIC ACID, SODIUM PHOSPHATE, LACTIC ACID, CALCIUM PHOSPHATE, YELLOW 5, YELLOW 6, ENZYMES, CHEESE CULTURE)

Serving Size tells you how much to eat to get the calories and nutrients listed.

Servings per Container is equal to the total amount of food in the package, divided by the serving size.

Calories tells you how much energy you get from eating one serving.

Lists amounts of protein, fats, carbohydrates, sodium, sugar, cholesterol, and fiber per serving.

Percent Daily Value shows how much of an adult's daily need for a nutrient is met by one serving.

Lists vitamins and minerals in the food, including those in the food naturally and those that are added.

Ingredients includes the main ingredients as well as any additives and preservatives.

The Nutrition Facts label also tells you what nutrients are in the food. Many of the ingredients in the macaroni and cheese, such as wheat and milk, are on the Food Guide Pyramid. Some, like calcium and vitamin D, are also nutrients. Other ingredients are additives and preservatives.

Additives (AD·uh·tivz) are things food manufacturers add to foods. Some additives, such as sugar, are nutrients. Other additives, such as salt and food coloring, change the way a food tastes or looks. Manufacturers sometimes add vitamins and minerals to restore the nutritional value of a processed food.

Preservatives (pree·ZERV·uh·tivz) are chemicals added to foods to keep them from spoiling. By law, additives and preservatives must be listed as ingredients on food labels.

You can use the information on food labels to compare different foods or to compare different brands of the same food. You can also use it to decide how much of a food you should eat at one time. It is important to read the label if you are on a special diet or are allergic to any foods. Nutrition Facts and ingredients lists can help you choose foods that are good for you.

SUMMARIZE What kinds of information are shown on food labels?

Ads make you more aware of products. However, they may not give you much information about the products.

Advertisements Influence Food Choices

Do you watch television, read magazines, or look at billboards along the highways? If so, you've probably seen ads for foods. Have you ever seen a food ad and then really wanted that food? If so, the ad did its job.

Many ads appeal to your emotions. They try to make you think that eating certain foods will make you feel good. An ad could show a group of children having fun while eating pizza. A movie star might tell you how good a hamburger tastes. Or a sports star might suggest that drinking a certain juice will make you more like him or her. Some food products have prizes inside the packages. People may buy the product just to get the prize. Advertisers use these "tricks" to get you to buy.

Some ads make claims about the healthfulness of a food. An ad might say the food is low in fat, high in fiber, or sugar-free. While it is against the law to lie in an advertisement, ads can still be misleading. For example, many foods labeled "low-fat" are still high in calories if they contain extra sugar in place of some of the fat. Food packages can also claim to offer health benefits that have not been proved.

If you prefer to eat foods without additives or preservatives, you might choose products labeled "all natural." But be careful. Having no additives or preservatives doesn't mean that a food is good for you. For example, some potato chips are labeled "100 percent natural." But the potatoes are still fried in oil and contain a lot of fat and salt. It's true that salt and oil are natural. But too much salt in your diet can increase your blood pressure, and too much fat can lead to heart disease.

Just remember that food ads and food packages are designed to make you want to buy the foods. If you look carefully at the Nutrition Facts labels, you can decide for yourself what foods are healthful if eaten in the proper amounts.

MAIN IDEA AND DETAILS What is an ad designed to do, and how does it do it?

ACTIVITY

Building Good Character

Respect Not everyone can eat the same foods. Some people avoid certain foods for health reasons. Others avoid foods for personal reasons. If you went to a friend's house and couldn't eat what was being served, how would you tell your friend politely? Write down two things you could say.

Lesson 5 Summary and Review

1 Summarize with Vocabulary

Use vocabulary and other terms from this lesson to complete the statements.

The _____ in a package of food are written on the _____ label. Sometimes, manufacturers put things in foods to improve how the foods look or taste. These things are called _____. To keep a food from spoiling, a food manufacturer might add one or more _____.

2 On a Nutrition Facts label, what does the information under Percent Daily Value tell you?

3 Critical Thinking Why might the label "100 percent natural" on a packaged food be misleading?

4 (Focus Skill) COMPARE AND CONTRAST Draw and complete this graphic organizer to show how the food labels of two cereals can be alike and different.

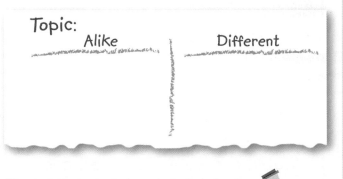

Topic:
Alike   Different

5 Write to Inform—Description

Describe an ad that might persuade your classmates or friends to buy a particular food product.

Make Responsible Decisions
About Fast Food

Suppose you're at a fast-food restaurant for dinner. You got up too late to eat breakfast this morning. Then you had pizza and a cola for lunch. Now you want to order the supersized double cheeseburger special. Follow the steps for **Making Responsible Decisions** about eating a more healthful dinner.

1 Find out about the choices you could make.

2 Eliminate any choices that will make you sick or are against your family rules.

You could order the special—double cheeseburger, fries, and large cola. Or, you could order a grilled chicken sandwich, a green salad, and a banana smoothie.

You like cola, but you have already had one today. Fries are your favorite, but your parents allow you to have only one serving per week.

3 Imagine the possible results of each choice.

The cheeseburger and fries are high in fat and the cola contains sugar. The chicken has less fat, there are vegetables in the salad, and fruit in the smoothie.

4 Make the decision that is right for you.

You order the grilled chicken sandwich, salad, and smoothie.

 **Problem Solving**

A. Joanna needs a lot of energy for track practice, but she isn't sure what she should eat at the coffee shop.
- Use what you know about the steps for **Making Responsible Decisions** to help her choose healthful foods.

B. Jerry's mom prepares three healthful meals every day. She gives him fruits and raw vegetables for snacks. This afternoon Jerry wants to go to the Burger House with his friends.
- What should Jerry order to show that he is trustworthy when eating away from home?

101

Food Preparation and Safety

Food Poisoning

You probably wouldn't think of eating uncooked chicken or eggs. They just don't taste good. But there are more important reasons for not eating uncooked foods. Eating certain uncooked or undercooked foods can cause food poisoning. **Food poisoning** is an illness caused by eating foods containing harmful germs.

Germs get into foods from soil, water, air, and people who haven't washed their hands. Germs also spread from one food to another. Suppose you use a knife to cut some uncooked chicken. Then you use the same knife to cut a sandwich. You could transfer germs from the chicken to the sandwich.

Food poisoning can cause stomach cramps, nausea, and diarrhea. Some forms of food poisoning are very dangerous and can even cause death.

CAUSE AND EFFECT How can someone working in a kitchen spread germs to the food?

◀ Uncooked chicken should never be cut on the same board or with the same knife as other foods.

Proper Storage Keeps Foods Safe

Germs are everywhere. You can't get rid of them all. The important thing is not to let germs multiply. When germs in food multiply, the food starts to look odd, smell unusual, and taste bad. It has spoiled. The way to keep foods from spoiling is to store them correctly.

Germs multiply rapidly at room temperature but more slowly at low temperature. That's why it's important to store cooked foods and all meats, milk, and eggs in a refrigerator. Covering foods like breads and cereals by wrapping them or putting them in containers can help keep them from spoiling. Although vegetables and fruits don't spoil quickly, storing them in a refrigerator keeps them fresh.

Different foods spoil at different rates. Even in a refrigerator, uncooked meat spoils in a few days. Milk will last for about a week, and cheeses and eggs last for several weeks. Juices, vegetables, and most fruits will last much longer. Freezing foods keeps them safe much longer. See also page 391.

▼ Different foods need to be stored in different parts of the refrigerator.

COMPARE AND CONTRAST **What foods spoil the fastest in the refrigerator? The slowest?**

Store cooked foods in plastic containers or wrapped in plastic.

Keep meat, poultry, and fish in the coldest part of the refrigerator. Store them wrapped.

Store eggs and milk in their original cartons. Throw away any cracked eggs. Don't keep eggs or milk on the refrigerator door.

Store fruits and vegetables in a vegetable crisper or in unsealed plastic bags.

Prepare a Safe Meal

Think about everything you've touched today. Think about all the other hands that have touched those things. There are hundreds of places you could have picked up germs. To prevent food poisoning when you prepare food, remember these four rules:

- Clean, clean, clean!
- Separate—don't contaminate!
- Refrigerate properly!
- Cook thoroughly!

Clean, clean, clean!

The first and most important thing to do before you prepare a meal is to wash your hands. Do this before you touch anything. Use warm water and plenty of soap, and scrub for twenty seconds. Make sure to clean under your fingernails and between your fingers. After you wash your hands, dry them with a clean towel. Make sure countertops are clean and dry.

Preparing foods carefully makes it less likely that they will have germs that make you or your family ill. ▼

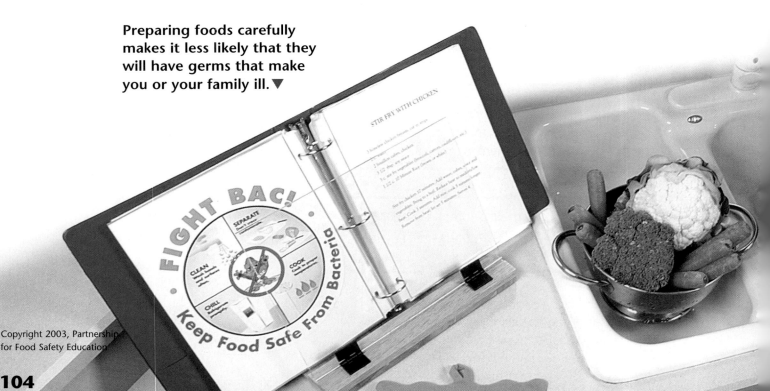

Before preparing or eating fresh fruits or vegetables, wash them thoroughly. This will help get rid of germs as well as any chemicals that were used to kill insect pests. After eating, wash dishes and set them out to dry. If you use towels to dry dishes, always use clean ones.

Separate—don't contaminate!

Raw meat, poultry, seafood, and eggs are the foods most likely to carry harmful germs. After you handle these foods, wash your cutting board and utensils thoroughly with hot water and soap. *Never* cut fruits or vegetables on a surface where you have had raw meat, poultry, seafood, or eggs.

Refrigerate properly!

Keep cold foods cold until you use them. If you are going to cook a food that is frozen, thaw the food in a refrigerator or in a microwave, not on a countertop.

Never leave food that needs to be refrigerated sitting at room temperature for more than two hours.

◀ Why is it important to wash your hands and anything used with raw meat?

▲ Cooking foods completely will reduce the risk of getting food poisoning. Most germs are killed by heat.

Cook thoroughly!

Cooking kills most harmful germs in food. But foods that are not cooked all the way through can still cause food poisoning. To be safe, cook eggs until the yolks are hard. Cook meat and poultry until they are no longer pink inside.

Finally, remember that your eyes, nose, and taste buds are there to protect you. If something looks odd, smells unusual, or tastes bad, throw it out. If you follow these guidelines, you will reduce the chances of getting or causing food poisoning. You can review more tips for kitchen safety in the Health and Safety Handbook, pp. 392–393.

(Focus Skill) **COMPARE AND CONTRAST How do high and low temperatures fight food poisoning in different ways?**

Lesson 6 | Summary and Review

❶ Summarize with Vocabulary

Use vocabulary and other terms from this lesson to complete the statements.

Pains in your stomach with cramps, _____, and _____ might be signs that you have _____. Refrigeration and freezing slow the growth of _____ that can make foods spoil, while sitting out at room temperature speeds up their growth.

❷ Critical Thinking What is the worst thing that can happen to a person who gets food poisoning?

❸ At what kind of temperature do germs multiply fastest?

❹ (Focus Skill) COMPARE AND CONTRAST

Complete this graphic organizer to show how high and low temperatures affect the growth of germs in ways that are alike and different.

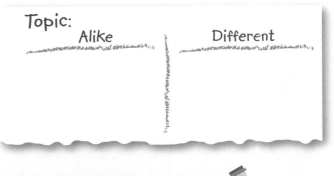

Topic:

Alike	Different

❺ Write to Inform—How-To

Describe a method to prevent germs from spreading from a piece of uncooked chicken to a piece of cooked chicken.

ACTIVITIES

Physical Education

Carbo-Loading Athletes prepare in many ways for long-distance races called *marathons*. The winner will run for more than two hours without stopping. In addition to training, a marathon runner may do something before a race called carbo-loading. Find out what carbo-loading is, and write a paragraph explaining it.

Science

In the Body Use a sheet of poster board to make an outline of a body. Then cut out photos or drawings from magazines and newspapers of foods that represent the six nutrient groups. Paste these on the poster board, and write a short caption explaining the ways in which each nutrient helps the body.

Technology Project

Compare Nutrients Different foods contain different amounts of nutrients. Nutrients and their amounts are listed on the nutrition labels. Using a computer, make a table that compares the nutrients of three similar foods. If a computer is not available, make a poster.

 For more activities, visit The Learning Site.
www.harcourtschool.com/health

Home & Community

At School Many school cafeterias provide menus in advance. Study next week's menu for your school cafeteria. If a menu isn't available, keep a journal of what is served each day for one week. Look at the USDA Food Guide Pyramid on pages 78–79. Add up the number of lunch foods that fit into each group. Then describe ways the foods can be used as part of a balanced diet.

Career Link

School Dietitian School dietitians plan meals for school lunches. They prepare nutritious menus for schoolchildren, making sure students get a balance of the nutrients they need. Suppose you are the dietitian for your school. Prepare a series of menus for one week of school lunches. Be sure to use the information you have learned in this chapter as you prepare your menu.

Reading Skill

COMPARE AND CONTRAST

Draw and then use this graphic organizer to answer questions 1 and 2.

Topic:

Alike	Different

1 Write at least two ways in which a piece of whole-wheat bread and a lump of sugar are alike.

2 Write at least two ways in which a piece of bread and a lump of sugar are different.

Use Vocabulary

Match each term in Column B with its description in Column A.

Column A	Column B
3 A nutrient such as calcium or iron	**A** calorie
	B preservative
4 A measure of the energy in food	**C** additive
	D mineral
5 A condition resulting from extreme dieting	**E** fat
	F anorexia
6 Something added to a food to keep it from spoiling	
7 Something put in food to make it more nutritious	
8 Nutrient at top of Food Guide Pyramid	

Check Understanding

Choose the letter of the correct answer.

9 An enzyme ____. (p. 73)
A holds energy needed by your body
B is a carbohydrate
C helps release energy from food
D causes food poisoning

10 Digestion begins in the ____. (p. 73)
F stomach   **H** small intestine
G esophagus   **J** mouth

11 If calcium is missing in a person's diet, the person might ____. (p. 76)
A have difficulty seeing at night
B have soft bones
C have swollen gums
D have digestion problems

12 The base of the USDA Food Guide Pyramid is made up of ____. (pp. 78–79)
F fats, oils, and sweets
G fruits and vegetables
H bread, cereal, rice, and pasta
J meat, poultry, and fish

13 Which of these foods would your grandparents **NOT** have found in a supermarket in winter? (p. 90)
A apples   **C** steak
B fresh corn on   **D** fish
    the cob

14 If you were trying to add protein to your diet, which of these foods would be the best to eat? (p. 75)

F    **H**

G   **J**

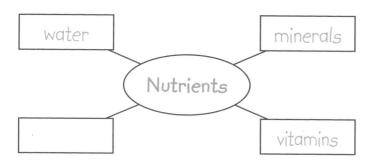

water   minerals

Nutrients

vitamins

15 Which nutrient is missing from the graphic organizer? (pp. 74–77)

   A fats   **C** carbohydrates

   B proteins   **D** all of these

16 Which of the following will you **NOT** find on a Nutrition Facts label? (pp. 96–97)

   F protein   **H** carbohydrate

     content   content

   G fat content   **J** water content

17 At which of the following temperatures will germs grow fastest? (p. 103)

   A 5°F (freezer)   **C** 68°F (room)

   B 40°F (refrigerator) **D** 150°F (dishwasher)

18 Eat chicken only if it is cooked so thoroughly that the inside is no longer _____. (p. 106)

   F red   **H** white

   G pink   **J** orange

19 In a refrigerator, which of the following foods spoils fastest? (p. 103)

   A uncooked meat **C** milk

   B hard cheese   **D** pasteurized juice

Think Critically

20 You slice a peach, a piece of chicken, and a tomato, in that order, with the same knife without washing it. Only the people who eat the chicken, the tomato, or both get food poisoning. Explain how this could happen.

21 Your doctor says your bones are too soft. What question about your diet might your doctor ask? Why? What might he or she suggest you do to make your bones stronger?

22 You see a TV commercial advertising a breakfast cereal. Your favorite basketball player is shown in the background dunking the ball into the basket. How would this affect the way you think about the cereal? Would you be more tempted to buy it? Why or why not?

Apply Skills

23 **BUILDING GOOD CHARACTER**

   Respect You are invited to dinner at a friend's home. You and your friend have the chore of cleaning up after dinner. You notice that a plate of leftover meat is sitting on the countertop. Your friend suggests you play some games now and leave the meat where it is. How can you show good self-control in this situation?

24 **LIFE SKILLS**

   Make Responsible Decisions You learn from some friends about a new diet. It's supposed to make you lose 10 pounds in a week. Do you decide to try it? Why or why not?

Write About Health

25 **Write to Inform—Explanation** Explain why reading Nutrition Facts labels is important to your health.

CHAPTER 4

Keeping Fit and Active

IDENTIFY MAIN IDEA AND DETAILS

The main idea is the most important thought in a passage. Details tell about the main idea. They tell *who*, *what*, *when*, *where*, *why*, and *how*. Details help you understand the main idea. Use the Reading in Health Handbook on pages 372–383 to help you read the health facts in this chapter.

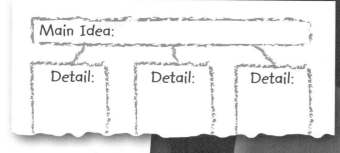

Main Idea:

Detail: | Detail: | Detail:

Health Graph

INTERPRET DATA These are the results of a recent study that looked at the relationship between physical activity and body weight. Based on the graph, list three facts about physical activity, eating, and weight. Do you think the trends shown will change in the near future? Why or why not?

Health Behaviors and Obesity in Teenagers

Percentage Change over 20 Years

- 15.0%
- 10.0%
- 5.0%
- 0%
- -5.0%
- -10.0%
- -15.0%

Obesity

Food Consumption

Physical Activity

Daily Physical Activity

Along with good food choices, some physical activity every day will help keep your muscles, bones, and heart healthy.

 *Be Active!*

Use the selection, Track 4, **Jam and Jive**, to give your heart a workout.

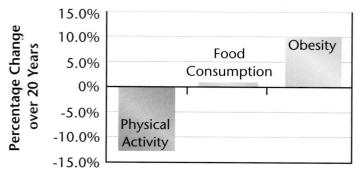

111

Being Active and Fit

Sleep, Activity, and Food

Have you ever thought about things that keep you healthy and fit? Tanisha was interested in how sleep, activity, and food help keep people fit. She went to her teacher with an article on healthful lifestyles. The article said that a healthful lifestyle should include a proper amount of sleep, physical activity that is fun and is done most days of the week, and wise food choices. Tanisha asked if her class could form a group she called the SAFE club to promote good health and physical fitness. *S* stands for *Sleep*, *A* stands for *Activity*, *F* stands for *Food choices* that are healthful, and *E* stands for *Every day*. Her teacher thought it was a great idea.

Your body needs all parts of the SAFE routine. The first part, sleep, is important in several ways. When you sleep, body tissues work to build new cells, repair old cells, and help fight infections.

Healthful foods provide energy to help you do activities longer. ▶

▲ These girls and their dogs help one another stay physically active.

PERSONAL HEALTH PLAN ▶

Real-Life Situation
Studies show that fifth graders do best in school if they get nine hours of sleep each night. Suppose because of soccer practice, homework, and TV, you sleep only seven hours.
Real-Life Plan
Write a plan for changing your schedule so you can get more sleep.

A lack of sleep can cause you to have trouble thinking clearly. It also can make you feel tired. A wise choice is to get plenty of rest before school, because sleep helps you do your best.

To be healthy and fit, your body needs physical activity. **Physical activity** is using your muscles to move your body. There are many reasons why physical activity can improve health. Activities such as walking, biking, swimming, and running can help keep your bones, muscles, and heart healthy and help you maintain a healthful weight.

Your body also needs good food. Good food choices are important decisions to learn to make. The foods you choose can affect your weight and your energy level.

Remember: To be physically fit and healthy, your body needs these things—sleep, activity, and good food every day. Healthful living should be a habit. It needs to be part of your daily life.

MAIN IDEA AND DETAILS List the main ways you can become fit. Include three things you can do to maintain your health.

Did You Know?

A person who has trouble sleeping can go to a sleep clinic for help. The person sleeps there for a night or two as part of a test to determine why he or she does not sleep normally.

113

▲ Hiking with your family is a fun way to stay physically active.

The Benefits of Physical Activity

Being physically active has many benefits. Suzanne joined the SAFE club. She thought she was watching too much television and playing too many video games. She made a personal health plan that included biking, inline skating, and keeping a journal to record her TV watching.

For one month, Suzanne exercised and watched less TV. Then she made a list of the benefits to her of being physically active. At the next meeting of the SAFE club, she shared the list.

- Being physically active helped me reach a healthy weight.
- I feel that exercise has helped me build stronger muscles and bones. It's also helped me do physical activities for a longer period of time.
- Exercise has improved my self-esteem because I can do things I couldn't do before.
- I feel more relaxed and can better handle stressful situations at home and at school.

CAUSE AND EFFECT What changes did Suzanne see in herself after she joined the SAFE club?

Consumer Activity

Equipment You don't need to spend a lot of money to be fit or to have fun. Many activities require little more than comfortable shoes and loose-fitting clothes. List the things people actually need for some physical activities.

Quick Activity

List Safety Needs Pick an activity you like to do. List the safety equipment you need for it. Also list the rules you need to follow to stay safe.

▼ Boating is a fun activity you can do with friends. Many communities rent small boats and offer instruction on how to use them.

Overcoming Barriers to Physical Activity

Some people can't do some physical activities because they face physical challenges. But everyone can be active. People just may need to make a change in their activities so they can do them.

For example, Saul couldn't run with his friends because he was in a wheelchair. Saul talked to his physical education teacher. His teacher encouraged him to become more active using his wheelchair. He also suggested that Saul and his friends try swimming together. Saul found several new activities to enjoy with his friends and to help him stay fit.

DRAW CONCLUSIONS **Saul stayed fit by using his wheelchair and by swimming. What conclusion can you draw about fitness and physical challenges?**

◀ List some of the barriers this person has overcome to do this activity.

Lesson 1 Summary and Review

❶ Summarize with Vocabulary

Use vocabulary from this lesson to complete the statement.

_____ is using your muscles to move your body.

❷ Why is sleep important to your health? About how many hours of sleep does a person your age need each night?

❸ Critical Thinking How can making good food choices be an important part of your plan for keeping physically fit?

❹ (Focus Skill) MAIN IDEA AND DETAILS Draw and complete this graphic organizer to show some benefits of physical activity.

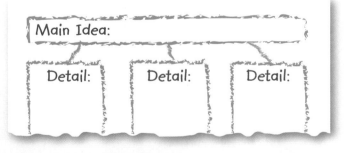

Main Idea:

Detail: | Detail: | Detail:

❺ Write to Inform—Description

Make up a story about Phil Fit, a boy in the SAFE club at his school. Write about a day in the life of Phil. Include sleep, physical activities, and good food choices.

Fairness

Play by the Rules

Any game or activity is more fun when all the players respect each other and follow all the rules. When players cheat, the game becomes pointless and players lose respect for each other.

Here are some rules to follow when you play any game:

- **Always listen for instructions when you receive the signal to stop. This may be the most important rule to ensure a fun game.**

- **If you're not familiar with the rules of a game, ask questions or ask for an explanation.**

- **Show respect for other players by not fighting or arguing. Players receive penalties for those behaviors.**

- **When someone breaks a rule, politely tell him or her or your coach.**

- **Understand the consequences of breaking a rule.**

- **If a rule is broken, team members should discuss the problem so it won't happen again.**

- **Learn how to properly care for equipment.**

Activity

Make a list of the important rules for your soccer team. Ask your teacher or coach to help you rank the rules in order of importance. Then list the rules in order of how often they are broken. Show the list to the soccer team. At the end of the season, compare your lists.

It's important to be fair and play by the rules at all times. ▶

117

How Exercise Helps Your Body Systems

Lesson Focus
Being physically active makes you stronger, helps you feel good, and improves your self-image.

Why Learn This?
Learning about the benefits of physical activity can help you exercise regularly.

Vocabulary
cardiovascular fitness
aerobic exercise
anaerobic exercise

Exercise Helps Your Respiratory System

Regular exercise, such as swimming and biking, helps your entire respiratory system. Your respiratory system includes all the parts of your body that work to get oxygen into your blood and carbon dioxide out of it. Look at the diagram of the respiratory system, on page 119. Find the *diaphragm* (DY•uh•fram). It is a large, flat muscle that separates your lungs from the organs in the lower part of your body. When you breathe in, your diaphragm contracts and moves down. This pulls air in through your nose, down your *trachea*, and into your lungs. When you breathe out, your diaphragm relaxes and moves up. This pushes air out of your lungs.

The diaphragm does most of the work of breathing. The rest is done by your ribs and the muscles around them. As you breathe in, muscles move your ribs up and out to the side. Then, as you breathe out, your ribs

Swimming uses a lot of energy, making you need a lot of oxygen. ▶

move back down and in. Like all muscles, your diaphragm and the muscles around your ribs get stronger with regular exercise.

Recall from Chapter 1 that when air enters your lungs, it goes into *alveoli*. In those tiny sacs oxygen enters your blood. Your blood then carries the oxygen to all the cells of your body. Body cells use oxygen to convert the nutrients from the food you eat into energy. During that process body cells produce carbon dioxide. This waste gas travels to your lungs. Then it is breathed out.

When you exercise, your body needs a lot of energy and produces a lot of waste. Your lungs need to take in more oxygen and get rid of more carbon dioxide, so you breathe more deeply and more often. As you take deep breaths, the alveoli open up. When you exercise regularly, the alveoli stay open most of the time. This makes your lungs take in extra oxygen each time you breathe.

SEQUENCE Write the steps by which oxygen gets into the blood.

PersoNAL HeaLth PLaN ▶

Real-Life Situation
The more you do a physical activity, the easier it becomes. Suppose you sign up to run in a 5-kilometer (5K) race to be held in three months.
Real-Life Plan
After talking with your physical education teacher, write a step-by-step plan for training that would enable you to complete the race.

The diaphragm and the muscles around your ribs become stronger with exercise.

ribs

muscles

diaphragm

Exercise Helps Your Circulatory System

Exercising regularly helps your circulatory system stay healthy. Exercise strengthens your heart, a muscle that pumps blood to all the cells of your body. When you exercise, your heart beats faster. More oxygen and nutrients are carried to your body's cells.

Regular exercise also reduces the amount of fat in your blood. Fat can build up on the inner walls of arteries. This reduces the flow of blood to body organs. It can also cause serious problems in the circulatory system, such as heart attacks and strokes.

Cardiovascular fitness (kar•dee•oh•VAS•kyoo•ler) is the good health of the circulatory system, including a strong heart. When your heart is strong, you can be active for a long time without getting tired. A strong heart pumps more blood with each beat. When you are resting, it beats more slowly, pausing longer between beats.

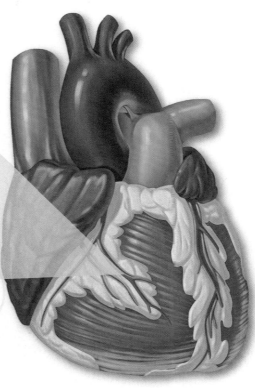

Notice the differences between a healthy artery (above) and one clogged with fat (below).

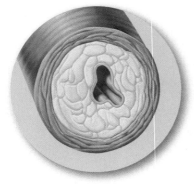

Clogged arteries in the heart can cause chest pains and heart attacks.

Aerobic exercise (air•OH•bik) increases your heartbeat rate for a period of time. This helps build cardiovascular fitness. Aerobic exercise includes bicycling, jogging, and swimming. As you do this kind of exercise, you also breathe harder and faster. Your muscles receive all the oxygen they need to keep working. You should do aerobic exercise at least three times a week for at least twenty minutes at a time. Aerobic exercise also can reduce stress. If you feel angry, sad, or bored, aerobic exercise can help lift your mood.

Not all types of exercise build cardiovascular fitness. In **anaerobic exercise** (an•er•OH•bik), the muscles work hard for a short time. They use the oxygen they already have faster than it can be replaced. Sprinting and rowing as fast as you can are examples of anaerobic exercise. Anaerobic exercise builds muscle strength.

COMPARE AND CONTRAST How are aerobic exercise and anaerobic exercise different? What does each help build?

Myth and Fact

Myth: More children are overweight now than in the past because kids today eat more.
Fact: Over the last twenty years, young people have been eating only 1 percent more food but have become 13 percent less active physically.

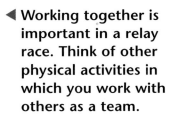

◀ **Working together is important in a relay race. Think of other physical activities in which you work with others as a team.**

The Activity Pyramid

The activity pyramid gives guidelines for ways to build fitness. Some activities build skill-related fitness. These help you improve your performance in a sport. Other activities promote health-related fitness. These help you improve your overall health and fitness. You can use the pyramid to plan physical activities based on the goals you want to achieve.

Sitting Still Watching TV; playing computer games **small amounts of time**

Strength and Flexibility Exercises Weight training, dancing, pullups **2–3 times a week**

Light Exercise Playtime; yardwork; softball **2–3 times a week**

Aerobic Exercises Biking; running; soccer; hiking **30 + minutes, 2–3 times a week**

Regular Activities Walking to school; taking the stairs; helping with housework **everyday**

If you are just beginning to exercise, you could do the following:

- Increase participation in everyday activities, like walking, whenever you can.
- Decrease the amount of time you spend watching television and playing video and computer games.

If you already exercise, you could use the activity pyramid to do the following:

- In the middle of the pyramid, find activities that you enjoy, and do them more often.
- Set up a plan to do your favorite activities more often.
- Explore new activities.

DRAW CONCLUSIONS Write down the activities you do in a typical day. At which level on the pyramid is most of your activity? What types of activities do you need to add to your routine?

Did You Know?

One video-arcade game is actually good for your health. Using background music as a guide, you follow lighted arrows with your feet. Young people report they really work up a sweat and it's fun, too!

Lesson 2 Summary and Review

❶ Summarize with Vocabulary

Use vocabulary from this lesson to complete the statements.

Exercise that makes the heart work hard builds _____. Exercise that increases the heartbeat rate is called _____. Exercise that works your muscles hard for a short time, such as sprinting, is called _____.

❷ Critical Thinking How can following the activity pyramid improve physical fitness?

❸ How does exercise benefit the respiratory system?

❹ (Focus Skill) MAIN IDEA AND DETAILS Draw and complete this graphic organizer to show ways that exercise helps your body.

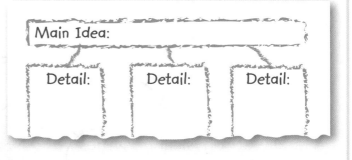

Main Idea:

Detail: Detail: Detail:

❺ Write to Inform—How-To

Write a description of how to use the activity pyramid to begin an exercise program.

Set Goals
About Family Fitness

To stay healthy and fit, you need to keep active. Because our lives are so busy, it's often hard to find time for physical activities. Using the steps for **Setting Goals** can help you build a successful exercise plan.

At the dinner table one evening, Marco's mother says she thinks the family doesn't get enough physical activity. She feels that if the family members do physical activities together, they'll be more physically fit. What should Marco's family do?

1 **Choose a goal.**

We should do things together!

Marco's mother suggests that the family do physical activities together. Marco decides to use goal setting to help his parents plan the activities.

2 **Plan steps to meet the goal, and determine whether you need help.**

Marco meets with his father to plan some activities. Marco knows that Mom likes biking and the whole family likes to cross-country ski in the winter.

3 Check your progress as you work toward the goal.

Marco writes the planned activities on a calendar. He checks them off as the family finishes each one.

4 Reflect on and evaluate your progress toward the goal.

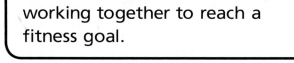

Marco is proud that his family is working together to reach a fitness goal.

 ## Problem Solving

A. Serena's goal is to be able to run a mile without stopping.
  • How can she use the steps for **Setting Goals** to help her reach this endurance goal?

B. Juan lives a block away from a park and wants to shoot 300 baskets each day during the summer.
  • How might Juan reach his goal while keeping up his responsibility to help with family chores?

Ways to Exercise

LESSON 3

Lesson Focus

Exercising in the right way helps you improve your physical fitness safely and enjoyably.

Why Learn This?

You can use what you learn to build your own fitness plan.

Vocabulary

muscular strength
flexibility
muscular endurance

Exercise Safely

Is exercise a part of your daily life? Exercising can include skill-related activities, such as basketball, tennis, or dancing. However, ordinary chores can provde health-related activity, too. These include walking the dog, raking the lawn, or vacuuming the carpet. To increase your level of physical fitness, try adding new activities to those you already do.

To help prevent injuries when you exercise, always begin with a *warm-up*. A warm-up is exercise that prepares your muscles—including your heart—to work hard. Always warm up your muscles gradually before harder exercise and before stretching.

Some stretching exercises help upper-body muscles.

Other stretching exercises help lower-body muscles. Always warm up before stretching.

126

One way to warm up is to do a slower version of your main activity. The warm-up might be easy pedaling if you are cycling, or jogging in place before running. Be sure to warm up for at least five minutes. After a warm-up, your body is prepared to stretch and exercise hard without harming muscles, joints, or your heart.

After exercising, do a *cool-down*. A cool-down includes doing your main exercise at a slower pace. That gives your heartbeat rate time to return to normal. Then stretch the muscles you used during your main exercise. Spend five to ten minutes cooling down.

Wearing the proper clothing for your activity and for the weather can help keep you safe. Wear loose, comfortable clothing that lets air move through. Choose cotton or other fabrics that allow sweat to evaporate. Use layers of clothing to keep warm in cold weather.

To prevent injury, wear shoes that provide support for your ankles and a cushion for your heels. The shoes must fit well and give you the traction you need. Also to prevent injury, always use the right safety gear. This may include a mouth guard, a helmet, shin guards, elbow pads, and kneepads.

MAIN IDEA AND DETAILS **To prevent injuries, what should you do before and after exercising?**

▲ Wear the proper safety gear for the sport you're playing. What safety equipment is used in baseball?

Quick Activity

Keeping Safe Talk with a parent about the physical activities he or she liked to do at your age. What safety equipment do people use now that was not used in the past for some of those activities?

▲ Chin-ups develop muscular strength.

Leg stretches increase your flexibility. ▼

Consumer Activity

To exercise and be fit, you don't need to belong to a gym. You can get lots of physical activity, at no cost, in your school playground, in a neighborhood park, or in your own home.

Kinds of Exercise

Aerobic exercises mostly strengthen your heart and lungs. They build cardiovascular fitness. Anaerobic exercises mostly strengthen your muscles. Many exercises help improve strength, flexibility, and endurance.

Strength: Exercises that build **muscular strength** make your muscles stronger. Several types of anaerobic exercises build strength. Walking up steps strengthens leg muscles. Crunches strengthen stomach muscles. Pull-ups and push-ups strengthen arm muscles.

Flexibility (flek·suh·BIL·uh·tee): Exercises that increase **flexibility** help your body bend and move comfortably. Stretching helps you become more flexible. Dancing is also good for flexibility.

128

Endurance: Exercises that build **muscular endurance** enable you to use your muscles for long periods without getting tired. Aerobic exercises build endurance. Hiking with the family, swimming, and biking are a few examples.

Include endurance exercises in your fitness plans. For these exercises, set both short-term and long-term goals. Suppose you want to be able to run a mile without stopping. Your short-term goal might be to run half a mile. When you can do that, add 100 yards several times until you reach your final goal.

SUMMARIZE **What kinds of exercises build strength, flexibility, and endurance?**

Did You Know?

A wearable heart monitor gives you immediate feedback about your heartbeat rate as you exercise. You can use a monitor to keep your heartbeat rate within a safe range. Some schools use monitors in physical education classes.

◄ Running builds muscular endurance and cardiovascular fitness.

Fitness Testing

You can measure your fitness by taking some simple tests. These tests will help you determine your fitness level and decide what you can do to improve. **Caution:** Don't take these tests if your doctor has limited your physical activity for any reason. To take the test for endurance, you need to have been doing aerobic exercises for at least eight weeks.

- Try doing at least 36 abdominal crunches in 2 minutes. This measures muscular strength.
- Try doing the sit-and-reach at 9 inches or farther. Using a box and a ruler, stretch as far as you can with your knees straight, toes up, and one hand over the other. This measures flexibility.
- Try jogging 1 mile on a measured track. If you are a girl, try to jog the mile in 12 minutes or less. If you are a boy, aim for 11 minutes or less. This measures muscular endurance and cardiovascular fitness.

DRAW CONCLUSIONS **After practicing, try all three of these fitness tests. What do the results tell you about your level of fitness?**

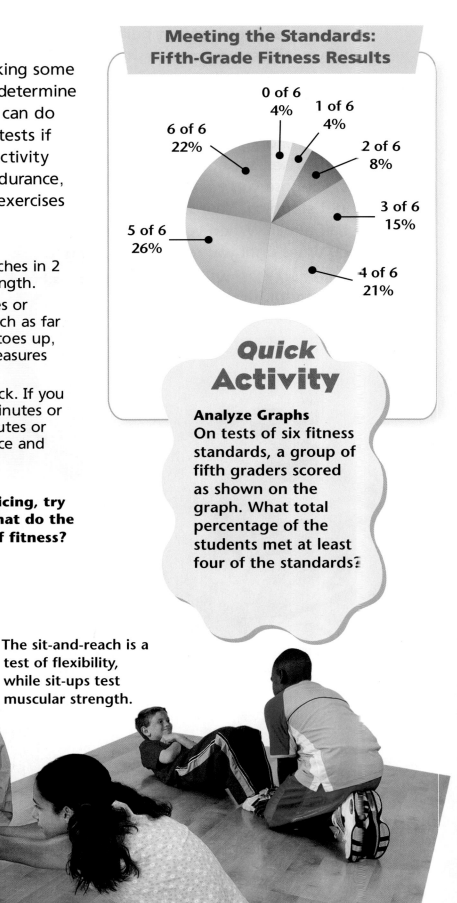

Meeting the Standards: Fifth-Grade Fitness Results

0 of 6 4%
1 of 6 4%
2 of 6 8%
3 of 6 15%
4 of 6 21%
5 of 6 26%
6 of 6 22%

Quick Activity

Analyze Graphs
On tests of six fitness standards, a group of fifth graders scored as shown on the graph. What total percentage of the students met at least four of the standards?

The sit-and-reach is a test of flexibility, while sit-ups test muscular strength.

Jumping rope is fun and a stress reliever. ▶

▲ Playing catch with a flying disk is fun. It also provides you with several different types of physical activity.

Fitness Is Fun

Many of the activities that improve your physical fitness are lots of fun. You can make up games with your friends, go on bike trips or hikes with your family, or swim at a local pool. Physical activities also help reduce stress. If you feel angry, sad, or just bored, exercising can lift your mood. Exercising can even give you a lift if you're feeling tired.

Try some physical activities with your family to enjoy different seasons of the year.

- Ice-skate, ski, or build snow sculptures in the winter.
- Fly kites, walk in the woods, or bicycle in the spring.
- Play beach volleyball, go canoeing, or go swimming in the summer.
- Take hikes, chop wood, or pick apples in the fall.

DRAW CONCLUSIONS Survey the members of your family about the activities they like to do. Then draw a conclusion about two activities your family would most enjoy doing together.

Playing ball is an activity that is easy and fun for people of all ages. ▶

Lesson 3 Summary and Review

1 Summarize with Vocabulary

Use vocabulary from this lesson to complete the following statements.

Jogging is an example of an activity that builds _____.

The sit-and-reach measures _____.

Weight lifting has become a popular activity because it builds _____.

2 How long should your cool-down last after you have been running for 15 minutes?

3 Critical Thinking When buying shoes, what are two important features to look for so you can exercise comfortably?

4 (Focus Skill) MAIN IDEA AND DETAILS

Complete this graphic organizer by starting with muscular strength as the main idea.

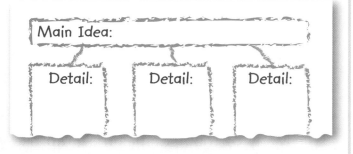

Main Idea:		
Detail:	Detail:	Detail:

5 Write to Inform—Narration

Write a story about the types of physical activities you like and the benefits you see in them. You might name your favorite activity and tell why you like it.

ACTIVITIES

Math

Add Up Activity Time Make a table of all the physical activities you do each week. Give yourself a point for each ten-minute period you spend doing each activity. Then make a bar graph that shows four weeks of each activity.

Science

Measure Time Differences Run the 100-meter dash on three trials, and find the differences in your times. First, measure a 100-meter distance, or use the markings on a track. Then run your three trials, with a 2-minute rest between runs. Your teacher or a partner can help you time them. Tell whether your times increased, decreased, or stayed the same. Find the size of each increase or decrease.

Technology Project

Based on the main ideas in this chapter, make a list of reasons to get SAFE—plenty of Sleep, Activity, and healthful Food choices, Every day. Make a computer slide show or a poster that shows examples of each of the four parts of SAFE.

For more activities, visit **The Learning Site.**
www.harcourtschool.com/health

Home & Community

Pro-Fitness Postage Stamp Make a postage stamp that promotes positive physical activity. The stamp should be labeled "Fitness Is Fun" and should show people doing fun activities or exercises.

Career Link

Physical Education Instructor
Suppose that you work as a physical education instructor at your school. Write out a lesson plan for one day. It should include aerobic and anaerobic activities. Make sure you indicate the length of time for each class and that you include warm-up and cool-down activities.

Reading Skill

IDENTIFY MAIN IDEA AND DETAILS

Draw and then use this graphic organizer to answer questions 1 and 2.

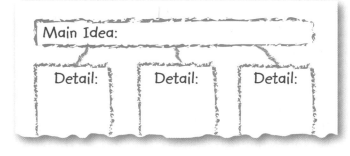

1 Using exercise as the main idea, write down details related to warm-ups.

2 Using physical fitness as the main idea, write down details that show how to measure muscular endurance.

Use Vocabulary

Match each term in Column B with its meaning in Column A.

Column A	Column B
3 What pull-ups can help build	A aerobic exercises
4 Should be done after hard exercise	B anaerobic exercises
5 Exercise that increases heartbeat rate	C activity pyramid
6 Should be done before exercise	D cool-down
7 Exercises that work your muscles hard for a short time	E muscular strength
8 Diagram that shows guidelines for activity	F warm-up

Check Understanding

Choose the letter of the correct answer.

9 The letter *S* in the acronym SAFE stands for _____. (p. 112)
   A Stretch   C Sleep
   B Stress   D Serving size

10 Sleep has been found to help _____ old cells. (p. 112)
   F destroy   H repair
   G feed   J change

11 Which of these behaviors is a poor health habit? (p. 114)
   A walking to school each day
   B playing video games for three hours
   C eating an apple each day
   D watching no more than one hour of TV

12 When you are starting a new physical activity, it's important to develop a _____ to help you reach your fitness goal. (pp. 122–123)
   F plan   H menu
   G label   J report

13 Being _____ helps you and others have fun and gain respect. (p. 117)
   A fair   C fast
   B strong   D first

14 Which of the following is the **BEST** example of anaerobic exercise? (p. 121)

F    G

H   J

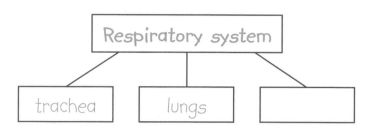

Respiratory system
- trachea
- lungs
-

15 Which detail is missing from the list of the parts of the respiratory system? (pp. 118–119)
A leg muscles   C heart
B liver   D alveoli

16 On the activity pyramid, the activities that build flexibility are located at the _____. (pp. 122–123)
F bottom   H center
G middle   J top

17 If you are following the activity pyramid to improve fitness, which section of the pyramid do you use least? (p. 122)
A bottom   C center
B middle   D top

18 Regular exercise reduces the amount of _____ in your blood. (p. 120)
F oxygen   H fat
G protein   J cells

19 Which of the following is the correct order for exercising safely? (pp. 126–127)
A cool down, warm up, exercise
B warm up, cool down, exercise
C warm up, exercise, cool down
D exercise, warm up, cool down

Think Critically

20 You are planning a long-distance hike and want to bring along the best beverage. What would you choose? Why?

21 Suppose you stayed up late studying for your math test and slept only six hours. How might this affect your ability to do well on the test?

22 You are telling others about the health benefits of the SAFE club. What are some of the benefits you would tell about?

Apply Skills

23 **BUILDING GOOD CHARACTER**
Fairness You are asked to fill in on a friend's soccer team. You notice that one of the rules is being broken. Apply what you know about fairness to help correct the problem.

24 **LIFE SKILLS**
Set Goals Your SAFE club is planning a game day for the school. Use what you know about setting goals to plan this activity.

Write About Health

25 **Write to Inform—Explanation** Explain how following a fitness plan can help you meet a goal.

Planning for Safety

SEQUENCE Sequence is the order in which events take place. It is also the order of the steps for carrying out a task. Use the Reading in Health Handbook on pages 372–383 and this graphic organizer to help you read the health facts in this chapter.

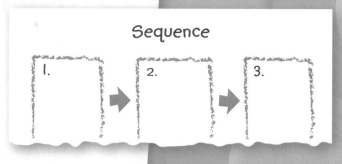

Sequence

| 1. | | 2. | | 3. |

Health Graph

INTERPRET DATA In the United States, an average of 98,000 people die as a result of unintentional, or accidental, injuries. What is the leading cause of death from unintentional injuries?

Leading Causes of Death from Unintentional Injuries

Number of Deaths (y-axis: 0 to 50,000)

Cause of Injury (x-axis: Motor vehicle crashes, Poisoning, Falls, Fires)

Daily Physical Activity

Staying safe is part of being healthy. So is getting some physical activity every day.

 Be Active!
Use the selection, Track 5, **Flexercise**, to practice safe warm-ups and exercises.

Preparing for the Unexpected

Common Hazards

Injuries often occur when people are tired or careless. Sometimes injuries happen when people don't realize that an action is unsafe.

Some injuries occur during everyday activities such as riding in a vehicle, riding a bike, swimming, and playing sports. Other injuries happen in the home. Whatever the setting or situation, you can avoid injuries by thinking through your actions before you act. The list below shows common causes of injuries among young people.

- drowning
- poisoning
- fires
- falls
- motor vehicle crashes
- bicycle crashes
- being shot by firearms

To reduce the risk of injury, always wear the right safety gear.

Common Hazards

At home
wet and slippery floors; broken glass; medicines and chemicals within reach of children; electrical appliances being used near water; broken and worn electrical cords; unattended lighted candles, fireplaces, stoves, and cigarettes

At school
people running in halls; people playing roughly, pushing, and fighting

In the neighborhood
speeding traffic; broken glass and trash on the ground; wet and slippery sidewalks

Quick Activity

Identify Hazards
Study the pictures of people doing everyday activities. Make a list of possible hazards in each activity. Tell how each hazard is being avoided.

The first step in preventing injuries is to be aware of hazards. A **hazard** is something in the environment or something about a person's actions that can cause harm or injury.

Sometimes people like to show off or take risks. They might play dangerously in a swimming pool or on the playground. They might give someone a ride on bicycle handlebars or play with matches. These actions are hazards because they place the person doing them and other people at risk. The table above lists common hazards at home, at school, and in the neighborhood.

 SEQUENCE **What is the first step in preventing injuries?**

ACTIVITY

Life Skills
Communicate
Yvonne is at her neighborhood swimming pool. She wants to use the diving board, but people are not taking turns. Instead, they are jumping off together. Act out how she can communicate to her friends that this behavior is unsafe.

Responding to a Serious Injury

When someone is seriously injured, it is an emergency. An **emergency** (ee•MER•juhn•see) is a situation that calls for quick action. If you come across an emergency, follow these three steps:

Step 1 Perform a ten-second survey. Quickly look over the scene. Try to answer the following questions. You will need this information when you call for help.

- What happened?
- How many people are injured?
- Is anyone at the scene in danger of further injury?

Step 2 Call 911 or your local emergency number. When you call for help, listen carefully to the emergency operator's questions and be prepared to

- give the location of the emergency, including the street address, landmarks, and the names of the nearest cross streets.
- give your name and, if asked by the operator, the phone number from which you are calling.

Quick Activity

Survey the Scene Take a ten-second survey of the emergency situation shown here. Answer the questions in Step 1 of the text at the right.

If you witness an accident, your body may react to the stress of the emergency. Remain calm and remember what you learned in this lesson. ▶

▲ Call 911 in emergencies such as drowning, severe bleeding, electrocution, choking, poisoning, severe burns, spinal cord injury, difficult or stopped breathing, and unconsciousness.

Enhanced 911 In the United States, nearly 100 percent of communities have Enhanced 911 (E911) service. With E911, emergency operators can automatically get callback numbers and street addresses for callers using traditional phones. However, operators can seldom locate callers who are using wireless phones.

- Tell what happened and how many people need help.
- Describe the conditions of the injured people and what help they are receiving.
- Remain on the phone until the operator instructs you to hang up.

Step 3 Care for the injured person. If it's safe for you to do so, give the person comfort. Inform the injured person in a calm voice that help is on the way. In cases of broken bones and possible head or spinal injuries, don't move or touch the injured person.

Sometimes it is safer to call for help instead of approaching an emergency scene or an injured person. For example, don't approach a wrecked car surrounded by moving traffic. That would be unsafe.

SUMMARIZE **Tell what information you should be ready to give an emergency operator.**

People trained to respond to emergencies include emergency medical technicians (EMTs), paramedics, and some firefighters and police officers. ▶

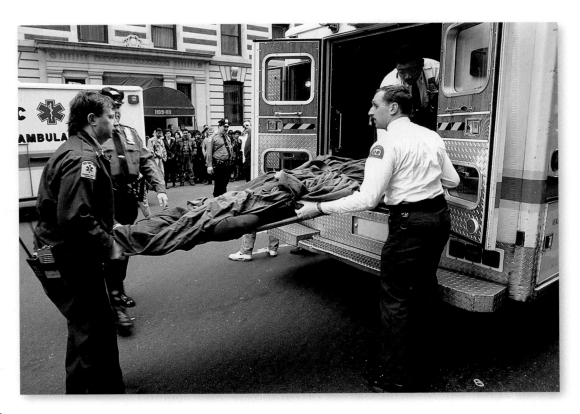

Treating Serious Injuries

Suppose you are out playing, and your friend falls and hurts himself badly. Would you know what to do? For the injuries described below, the first things anyone should do are to stay calm and call for help. When help arrives, a paramedic or EMT can give the injured person emergency treatment. Until help arrives, a person who knows first aid can provide help. **First aid** is immediate care given to an injured person.

First Aid for Serious Wounds The paramedic should be wearing disposable gloves. A *sterile bandage*, which is a bandage free of germs, should be placed over the wound. See also page 386.

- If there is bleeding from the wound, pressure should be applied. If gloves aren't available, the victim's hand should be used to apply pressure.
- If no bones seem broken, the wounded part of the body should be raised above the level of the heart. This slows the flow of blood to the wound.

142

First Aid for Burns Hot or burned clothing should be removed. However, clothing that is stuck to burned skin should not be removed. See also page 388.

- Less serious burns appear red or blistered and are painful. Cool the burned area by putting it under gently running cool water. Or, cover it with a sterile bandage that has been soaked in cool water. Then cover the burned area with a dry, sterile bandage.
- Severe burns appear whitish or black and are not felt by the victim. These should be treated by a doctor. In the meantime, protect burned areas with clean, dry cloth, like sheets.

Information Alert!

Latex Some people are allergic to latex. If the allergy is bad, it can even cause death. Latex-free gloves are worn by health-care workers in many places. Some states have even banned latex gloves for food-service workers.

For the most up-to-date information, visit The Learning Site. www.harcourtschool.com/health

First Aid for Concussions A concussion (kuhn•KUHSH•uhn) is a brain injury caused by a strong blow to the head. Signs of a concussion include vomiting, headache, unconsciousness, weakness, confusion, and blurred vision.

- If the scalp is bleeding, place a sterile bandage over the wound. The caregiver should wear disposable gloves or use the victim's hand to apply pressure to the wound.
- Remain with the injured person, monitoring breathing rate and heartbeat rate until help arrives.

A person who might have a concussion should be observed for at least twenty-four hours. ▼

DRAW CONCLUSIONS Why should a less serious burn be covered with a sterile bandage?

First Aid for Common Injuries

Everyone has gotten cuts, scrapes, muscle cramps, and bruises at one time or another. Most common injuries aren't serious. They hurt, but if you take care of them, they heal quickly.

A *cut* is a skin break, usually one that bleeds. Cuts are caused by sharp objects, such as broken glass, scissors, and knives. To treat a cut, first wash your hands with soap and water. Then do the following:

- Wash the cut with mild soap and running water.
- Control the bleeding. Place a sterile bandage or clean cloth directly over the cut, and apply pressure until the bleeding stops.
- Cover the cut with a sterile bandage.

A *scrape* is a wound in which skin has been rubbed or scraped away. It usually oozes blood. The scraped area may have dirt and germs in it. Begin by washing your hands with soap and water. Then do the following:

- Clean the scrape thoroughly, using mild soap and a washcloth under running water. Try to wash out any pieces of dirt and debris.
- Cover the scrape with a sterile bandage.

Cleaning a wound reduces the chance of infection. Signs of infection include redness, swelling, heat, and pus around the wound. ▶

144

A *muscle cramp* is a spasm, or an uncontrolled tightening of a muscle. To relieve a muscle cramp, gently and slowly stretch out the cramped muscle. Then relax the muscle by massaging it gently.

A *bruise* is an injury in which blood vessels break under the skin. Treat bruises with **R.I.C.E.**, which means **R**est, **I**ce, **C**ompress, and **E**levate.

1. Protect the bruised area from further injury by *resting* it.

2. Apply *ice* or cold packs to reduce swelling. Keep a cloth between ice and the skin.

3. If possible, *compress* the area, or apply pressure to it, by wrapping it to control swelling. Use an elastic bandage.

4. *Elevate*, or raise, the bruised area above the level of the heart. This helps limit swelling by slowing blood flow to the area.

(Focus Skill) **SEQUENCE What should a person do immediately after applying ice or a cold pack to a bruise?**

Muscle cramps occur when your muscles are tired, when your body needs water, or when you are overheated. ▶

Lesson 1 Summary and Review

❶ Summarize with Vocabulary

Use vocabulary from this lesson to complete the statements.

Something in the environment that can cause harm or injury is a(n) _____. If someone is seriously injured, it is a(n) _____. The immediate care given to an injured person is _____. An injury to the head may result in a(n) _____.

❷ Identify two common hazards in each of these places: at school, at home, and in the neighborhood.

❸ **Critical Thinking** Give an example of how a person's actions can be a hazard or cause an accident.

❹ (Focus Skill) SEQUENCE Draw and complete this graphic organizer to show the steps for handling an emergency.

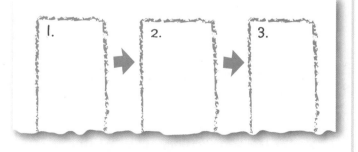

❺ Write to Inform—How-To

Write a short paragraph that describes how to treat a common injury, such as a cut or scrape.

Make Responsible Decisions

That Prevent Injury

Sometimes you need to make choices to protect your health and safety. You can use the steps for **Making Responsible Decisions** to help you make healthful choices.

Kelly is going to ride his bike to soccer practice after school. He can take several different routes. Which one should he choose for getting to practice safely?

1 Find out about the choices you could make.

Kelly looks at two possible routes—the main road and the park path.

2 Eliminate choices that are against your family rules.

The main road is shorter, but it has traffic. Kelly's parents have told him not to ride his bike where there is traffic.

3 Ask yourself: What is the possible result of each choice? Which choice would show responsibility?

4 Make what seems to be the best choice.

Kelly realizes that the path through the park is safer. Choosing the main road would not be a responsible decision.

Kelly takes the park path and gets to practice safely and on time. Riding a little farther helps him warm up, too. He is pleased with his decision.

Problem Solving

A. Jason is in a car pool with some of his basketball teammates. When he gets into the car, he notices that none of the other riders are wearing safety belts. Jason knows that he is supposed to wear a safety belt when he is in a vehicle.

  • Use the steps for **Making Responsible Decisions** to help Jason make the best decision.

B. Selena has an early-morning paper route. She rides her bicycle to deliver the papers. Today her bicycle headlight is not working. It is still dark outside.

  • How can Selena make a decision that shows responsibility for her safety in this situation?

Practicing Safety

You Can Prevent Injuries While Playing

One of the best ways to prevent injuries is to know and follow safety rules. Most safety rules are common sense. Here are some examples: Play in areas that are safe and familiar. Avoid places where people may carry weapons, such as guns and knives. Stay away from areas where you know crimes have taken place. Don't play in areas where there is traffic, such as in streets and parking lots. Never push, shove, or fight while playing with others. Always wait your turn.

Playground Safety

A playground is supposed to be a safe place to play. But every year in the United States, about 200,000 children are taken to emergency rooms because of playground injuries. It's important to be careful and to follow safety rules when using playgrounds.

◀ Always use playground equipment properly. For example, go down the slide feet first, and hold handrails or ropes tightly when climbing.

◀ Be careful when walking around swings. Never walk or play close to a moving swing.

Falls are common causes of injuries on playgrounds. Kids fall when climbing ladders, when running in slippery areas, and when climbing or standing on surfaces that slide or tip.

Some playground equipment is old or unsafe. It can have splinters, sharp corners, loose parts, or bolts and nails that stick out. Before you play, have an adult make sure the equipment is in good condition.

Another important part of playground safety is the surface on which the equipment is placed. Softer materials, such as sand, chipped or shredded bark, and shredded rubber, make good surfaces for playgrounds. These surfaces help break a fall. Hard surfaces, such as pavement and dirt, are not as safe to play on.

The clothes you wear can also help keep you from being injured. Always wear closed shoes when using playground equipment. Broken glass, splinters, and other sharp objects can be hidden in sand or wood chips and injure bare feet. Don't wear loose clothing or clothing with drawstrings. Keep your shoes tied. Remove necklaces or scarves at the playground. Loose fabric, drawstrings, shoelaces, and necklaces can get caught in playground equipment and lead to injury. Also remove bicycle or other helmets before playing.

SUMMARIZE List four things you can do to play safely on a playground.

Consumer Activity

Make Buying Decisions
Marla's neighborhood is getting a new playground. Marla's mom is a member of the neighborhood purchasing committee. Make a list of features the committee should consider as it chooses equipment for the new playground.

Adjust your safety belt so that it lies across your shoulder. The belt should not cross your neck or face. Adjust the lap part of the belt so that it fits snugly across your hips, not your stomach. Children shorter than 57 inches tall must use a booster so the safety belt fits correctly. ▶

Did You Know?

Although vehicle air bags help protect adults from injury during crashes, children age twelve and under should ride in the back seat of a vehicle to avoid being hurt by an air bag. Some vehicles have a switch that allows the driver to turn off the passenger-side air bag if there is no other place for a child to ride.

Safety Equipment Reduces the Risk of Injury

Helmets, mouth guards, kneepads, and safety belts are just some of the kinds of equipment that help prevent injuries. Using the right safety equipment is especially important when you are riding in motor vehicles, bicycling, skating, skateboarding, and playing any active sport.

Vehicle Safety

Following safety rules while riding in motor vehicles can save your life. The leading cause of accidental injury or death of children age five to fourteen is motor vehicle crashes. Wearing a safety belt is the most important thing you can do to prevent injury while riding in a car. In fact, many states have laws that require everyone in a vehicle to wear a safety belt. The best type of safety belt is one that crosses over your shoulder and lap. Never share a safety belt with another person.

Other ways to reduce the risk of injury while riding in a car include staying in your seat and not bothering the driver. Never lean out the car window. Be sure to keep your fingers and hands inside the vehicle.

Helmets

Some places require all children to wear helmets while bicycling, skateboarding, and riding scooters. Even if your area doesn't have this law, you should always wear a helmet.

For the best protection, a helmet should fit snugly but comfortably. It should be level on your head, not tipped forward or backward. People playing sports such as football, hockey, and baseball should wear helmets with face guards to protect the nose and eyes.

Mouth Guards and Goggles

Mouth guards help protect the mouth, teeth, and tongue from painful injuries during sports. Goggles help protect the eyes from impact with elbows, flying objects, and other hazards. Goggles are often worn when playing racquetball and while snowboarding.

Wrist Guards, Elbow Pads, and Kneepads

Skateboarders, skaters, and players of team sports can easily get wrist, elbow, and knee injuries. These injuries can range from minor scratches to broken bones. Wearing wrist guards, elbow pads, and kneepads when playing certain sports can help reduce the risk of injuries to these areas of the body.

DRAW CONCLUSIONS **Why should you know the correct safety gear to wear for a particular activity?**

Using safety gear that fits you properly is important. Gear that is too big or too small won't protect you as well as gear that fits correctly. ▶

Personal Health Plan ▶

Real-Life Situation
Wearing safety gear is an important part of preventing injuries while being active. Suppose you are going to add a sport to your health plan.
Real-Life Plan
Tell what sport you will choose. List the safety gear you will need.

How You Can Ride a Bike Safely

Besides always wearing a helmet, you should follow several other safety rules when you ride a bike. Always ride in the same direction as traffic. Wear reflective clothing or bright colors so that drivers can see you. Watch for doors of parked cars being opened and for hazards on the road. Keep your bike in good working condition. Never carry another person on a bike, and never ride by holding onto the back of a moving vehicle.

Riding your bike after dark is not a good idea. It's hard for you to see hazards and hard for drivers to see you. If you must ride your bike after dark, be sure to check with your parents. Make sure they know when you are leaving and what route you are taking. Your bike should have equipment for nighttime riding, such as reflectors on the front and rear, on the wheels, and on the pedals. Your bike should also have bright front and rear lights.

MAIN IDEA AND DETAILS **Give details to support this statement: *You can bicycle safely by following safety rules.***

▲ If you must ride your bike at dawn or dusk, be sure to wear a reflective vest. Also, be sure your helmet has reflective tape on it.

For Bike Riders

❶ Learn and practice riding straight, making turns, signaling, braking, stopping, and looking over your shoulder to change lanes.

❷ Obey all traffic signs, signals, and rules.

❸ Wear a bicycle helmet that fits correctly.

Helmet

Your bike should be the right size for you. Your feet should be able to reach the ground when you are sitting on the bike's seat.

Bell, horn, or whistle

Headlight

Red rear reflector

White front reflector

Pedal reflector

Wheel reflector

▲ If there is a pedestrian signal at an intersection, wait for a green light. Then walk your bike across the street.

ACTIVITY

Building Good Character

Citizenship An important part of being a good citizen is obeying the laws of your community. How can you show good citizenship while riding a bike? See page 273 for ideas.

Rules Make Bicycling Safer

When you ride a bike on a street, you are expected to know and obey traffic laws. Following the rules below also helps protect you and drivers from hazards and accidents.

- Ride in single file, close to the curb, and in the same direction as traffic. Ride in a straight line to the left of cars parked along the curb. Never ride between parked cars. Whenever possible, ride in bike lanes.
- Never wear headphones while riding your bike. You might not hear approaching traffic.
- Pass parked cars slowly, watching for people who might open doors into the street.
- Be careful around **pedestrians** (pih•DES•tree•uhnz), or people who are walking. If pedestrians are crossing a street, stop to let them cross in front of you.
- If you have to walk your bike in the street, walk facing traffic, on the left side of the street.
- Know and obey all traffic signs and signals.
- When entering the street from a driveway or starting to walk your bike across an intersection, STOP. LOOK left, right, and left again. LISTEN for traffic, and wait for it to pass. Again look left, right, and left. THINK, and decide whether it is safe to go.
- Use signals to alert other traffic before you make a stop or a turn.

In addition to these safety rules, here are a few other tips to help keep you safe on a bike: Think ahead ten seconds to avoid hazards. This means that you should check the road ahead one block at a time. Keep your eyes moving. Scan the areas around you. Watch for things that are about to happen, such as a car coming up behind you, a ball rolling into the street, or a car backing out of a driveway.

 SEQUENCE **Tell the steps you should follow when starting to cross an intersection with your bike.**

Quick Activity

Listing Steps Suppose you are riding a bike in traffic. You come to a busy intersection where you plan to turn left. List the steps you should take, including the hand signals you should use.

Using hand signals is an important part of bike safety. Study the hand signals, shown here from left to right, for a stop, a right turn, and a left turn. Then practice each one.

Traffic Signs and Signals

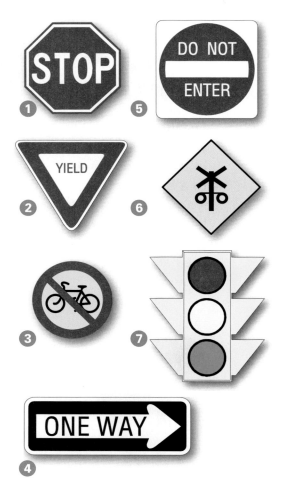

When riding a bike, you must obey the same traffic signs and signals that the driver of a vehicle does.

1 You must make a full stop before you enter or cross a street.

2 You must yield, or let other traffic pass, before you proceed. Slow down and be ready to stop.

3 You may not ride your bike on this road.

4 One-way traffic. Traffic may go only in the direction shown by the arrow.

5 Do not enter. If you did enter, you would be going against traffic.

6 Railroad tracks ahead. Before crossing, STOP, LOOK in both directions, and LISTEN.

7 Red means "stop." Yellow means "caution." Because the light will turn red soon, prepare to stop. Green means "go." Be sure traffic has stopped before you go ahead.

COMPARE AND CONTRAST **Compare and contrast the use of stop signs and yield signs.**

Lesson 2 Summary and Review

❶ **Summarize with Vocabulary**

Use vocabulary and other terms from this lesson to complete the statements.

When riding your bike, always wear a(n) _____ to protect yourself from a head injury. Watch for _____, or people who are walking. Using _____ tells drivers what you are planning to do next. When playing sports, wear a _____ to protect your teeth and _____ to protect your eyes.

❷ List six items necessary for riding a bike safely.

❸ **Critical Thinking** Suppose you are riding your bike and see a sewer grate in your path ahead. What should you do?

❹ (Focus Skill) **SEQUENCE** Draw and complete this graphic organizer to show the steps to take when entering the street from a driveway.

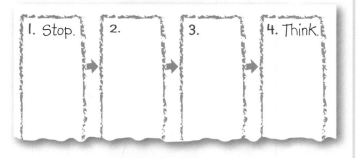

❺ **Write to Inform—Description**

Draw a map of a route you often take on your bike or when walking. List the safety rules to follow on this route.

Caring

Show Compassion for Others

When people have been injured, they need help—not just at the time of the injury, but during recovery as well. Here's what you can do to show that you care about a person who has been injured.

- **At an accident scene, stay with the person who has been injured. Call for help, if needed.**

- **Help the injured person stay calm by telling him or her that help is on the way.**

- **If a classmate has been injured and misses school, collect homework assignments for him or her. Help the classmate, if needed, with the work.**

- **Phone the injured person regularly to offer support. Ask what you can do for him or her.**

- **Visit the injured person. Take along games or funny videos to help cheer the person.**

Even when someone isn't injured, you can show you care by pointing out safety hazards. Offer to help reduce hazards at home, at school, or in your neighborhood.

Activity

Role-play with a partner situations in which someone is injured. Practice showing compassion by applying the tips on this page. Include other things you might do to help the person feel better.

Fire Safety

What You Can Do to Prevent Fires

Lesson Focus

You can do many things to prevent fires. You can take steps to safely escape a fire.

Why Learn This?

Knowing fire safety rules and how to escape a fire can save your life and the lives of others.

Vocabulary

flammable
natural disasters

Each year in the United States, almost 40,000 children under the age of fourteen are injured in fires. You can help prevent a fire in your home by acting responsibly with heat and flame, by eliminating fire hazards, and by practicing fire safety. The list on the next page tells how to prevent some fires.

Almost 25 percent of all fires are home fires. Having smoke alarms and knowing how to use a fire extinguisher can save lives. But the most important thing is to reduce the hazards that cause many home fires. Make a list of the fire hazards you find in this home. ▶

158

- Materials that will burn if they are exposed to enough heat are **flammable** (FLAM•uh•buhl). Things such as newspapers are flammable. Curtains and blankets may be flammable. They should be kept away from heat sources such as space heaters, lamps, and candles.

- Store flammable liquids, such as gasoline, outside your home in a well-ventilated area.

- Matches, lighters, and other sources of flame should be kept out of the reach of children.

- Electrical fires can start from overloaded electrical outlets. Avoid plugging several appliances, such as a microwave, a blender, and a toaster, into one outlet.

DRAW CONCLUSIONS Why should flammable liquids be stored outside the home?

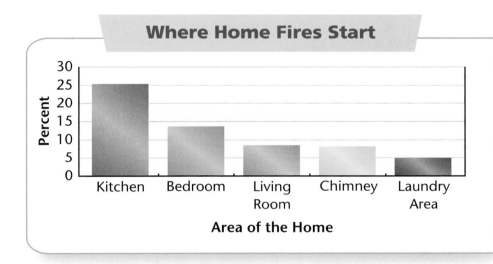

Where Home Fires Start

Percent / Area of the Home

(Kitchen, Bedroom, Living Room, Chimney, Laundry Area)

Quick Activity

Analyze Data Study the graph. In which of the areas shown do the most home fires start? Infer what the causes of fires in each area might be. How can each cause be eliminated?

Upstairs bedrooms should have an escape ladder next to each window. ▶

Escaping a Fire

When fires occur, people don't have time to plan. In less than one minute, a small flame can turn into a large, out-of-control fire. An important part of fire safety is to have a family escape plan. Include the steps below in your plan.

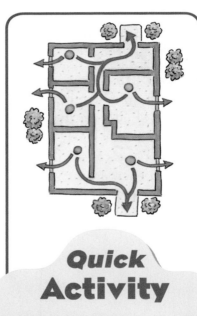

Quick Activity

Plan Your Escape
Make a floor plan of your own home, showing at least two ways to escape from each room. Then suggest some places the family could meet after a fire.

- Draw a floor plan, or a map of your home. Label all exits, the location of each smoke alarm, and an outside meeting place. Use arrows to show two ways to escape from each room.
- Make sure that everyone knows the escape routes and the sound of the smoke alarms. Be sure that all windows and doors open easily.
- Keep a whistle and a flashlight next to each bed. Make sure bedroom and hall doors are closed while you sleep. Closed doors slow the spread of a fire.
- Try out the whistles or other special signals to awaken and alert family members during a fire.

Practice the escape plan at least two times a year with your entire family. With your eyes closed, practice feeling your way out of your home. Practice crawling fast, and try to increase your crawling speed. Practice pounding on the walls, yelling, and using the whistles to alert family members during a fire.

▲ Make sure windows open easily. You should be able to remove screens or security bars quickly.

▲ Make sure all family members know how to use the escape ladders.

Suppose it's the middle of the night. You wake up to the sound of a smoke alarm! You smell smoke and realize your home is on fire. What do you do?

- Quickly roll out of bed and onto the floor. Smoke and other harmful gases from a fire rise toward the ceiling. The air is better near the floor.

- Crawl toward the door. If the smoke has made seeing difficult, reach out for a wall so you can feel your way. If possible, hold a damp cloth over your nose and mouth. Breathe through the cloth to screen out smoke.

- If you have a whistle, blow it loudly. Bang on the walls and yell "Fire" as loudly as you can.

- When you reach the door, feel it with the back of your hand. If it is cool, you may open it and crawl out as quickly as possible. If it is hot, do not open it. Use another exit, such as a window, to escape.

- Keep crawling until you are outside. Continue yelling to warn other family members.

CAUSE AND EFFECT **What is the cause if a closed door feels hot during a fire?**

Personal Health Plan ▶

Real-Life Situation
It is important to know the locations of fire-safety equipment, such as window ladders, fire extinguishers, and flashlights.

Real-Life Plan
Identify where fire-safety equipment is located in your home. Tell how to use it in case of a fire.

What to Do If You Are Trapped by a Fire

Suppose you can't escape from your home during a fire. The exits are completely blocked by fire and smoke. These pictures show several steps you can take to protect yourself.

DRAW CONCLUSIONS **Why should you close up cracks around a door and close vents?**

Step 1 Keep a closed door between you and the smoke. If the door is open, crawl quickly to it and close it to keep the smoke out. Breathe through your hand or a damp cloth.

Step 2 Stuff clothes or towels into the cracks under and around the door. Also close vents in the walls or floor.

Step 3 Open a window to let in fresh air. If smoke or flames come in, close the window.

Step 4 Stay by a window where you can be seen. Yell for help, and signal by waving your hand, a flashlight, or a sheet.

What to Do After You Escape a Fire

Having a plan for what to do after escaping a fire is important. Once you're outside, go right away to your family meeting place. This may be under a certain tree, at a certain street lamp, or at the end of a driveway. Having a specific location is important so no one gets hurt looking for someone who has already safely escaped the fire. If you wander around, others may not know that you have gotten out of the burning building.

Once you are out of the building, don't go back inside for any reason. Use a neighbor's phone or a cell phone to call 911, your local emergency number, or your local fire department. The emergency operator will need answers to the following questions:

- What is the location of the fire? Give the street address and the nearest cross streets.
- What type of fire is it? For example, is the fire in a house, in an apartment, in some trash, or in a car?
- Is anyone in danger? Is anyone still inside a burning building? Are pets inside?
- How big is the fire? Can you see flames or just smell smoke? How much of the building is burning?

Remember: When you are reporting an emergency, do not hang up until the operator tells you to do so. He or she may need more information. Allow firefighters and rescue workers to do their jobs. They have the equipment and training to deal with emergency situations.

CAUSE AND EFFECT **What is the effect of going directly to your family's meeting place after escaping a fire?**

Did You Know?

There are several different types of fire extinguishers. One type is used to put out wood and paper fires. Another type is used on fires of flammable liquids, such as gasoline, grease, and oil. A third type is used for electrical fires.

All family members should be able to quickly call for help, using a neighbor's home phone or a cell phone. ▼

163

Some natural disasters, such as hurricanes and winter storms, can be predicted. Other, such as tornadoes, earthquakes, and wildfires, can be very unexpected. See pages 402–403 for tips on safety during natural disasters.

Plan for Other Emergencies

By having a plan, your family can protect itself during other emergencies, such as natural disasters. **Natural disasters** are powerful events of nature that often result in the destruction of buildings and other structures. Earthquakes, tornadoes, hurricanes, floods, and volcanic eruptions are all examples of natural disasters.

To plan for these types of emergencies, your family must gather information and make some choices. All family members should understand and practice the parts of the plan.

Know What Could Happen

Learn about the kinds of natural disasters that can happen in your area. Emergency plans may differ, depending on the type of disaster. For example, the way you would protect yourself during an earthquake is different from what you would do during a tornado.

Have Two Meeting Places

Choose two places where you can meet in the event of an emergency. The first place should be where your family decided to meet in case of a house fire. The second location should be farther away.

Know Your Family Contact

Choose someone who lives far away to be a contact person. This person will help your family stay in touch. If a family member becomes lost during an emergency, he or she can call the contact person.

It's important that all family members are comfortable and familiar with the emergency plan. This helps reduce stress during an emergency situation.

Practice Evacuating

During a fire, you need to evacuate, or get out of, your home right away. Think of the natural disasters you identified for your area. Do you know what to do in the event of a tornado? An earthquake? In some cases, your entire community may have to be evacuated. The threat of hurricanes, floods, and wildfires may make it unsafe to remain in the area. Listen to the radio or television during an emergency to find out if your community is being evacuated. Be familiar with your community's evacuation procedures.

▲ Part of your emergency plan should include evacuation.

Learn How to Turn Off Utilities

Services that provide water, electricity, and gas are utilities. An emergency may damage utility pipes or wires and make them dangerous. They can damage or even destroy a home. With an adult's help, learn when and how to turn off utilities. CAUTION: If you turn off the gas, a professional must turn it back on.

SUMMARIZE **Name three things you can do to prepare for an emergency.**

Myth and Fact

Myth: Natural gas smells like rotten eggs.
Fact: Natural gas is colorless, odorless, and tasteless. For safety reasons the scent of sulfur, which smells like rotten eggs, is added to natural gas. Natural gas is highly flammable, so it's important to know if there is a leak.

◀ Leaking gas and live electrical wires can lead to fires. If tools are needed to turn off a utility, they should be stored close by.

Make an Emergency Supply Kit

After an emergency or natural disaster, you may not have access to everyday services. You may not have water, electricity, or gas service for several days or longer. You may not be able to get to the store. It's important to have an emergency supply kit for your family. The American Red Cross recommends that the following items be included in an emergency supply kit:

▲ Other items for an emergency supply kit include a blanket, soap, and books and games for entertainment.

- a three-day supply of drinking water (6 quarts per person), stored in plastic containers
- a three-day supply of canned food and a manual can opener
- a first-aid kit and extra prescription medications
- a fire extinguisher, tools, a flashlight with extra batteries, candles, matches, and a battery-operated radio
- money and important family papers

MAIN IDEA AND DETAILS Why is having an emergency supply kit important?

Lesson 3 Summary and Review

❶ Summarize with Vocabulary

Use vocabulary and other terms from this lesson to complete the statements.

Earthquakes and tornadoes are examples of _____. In the event of an emergency, it may be necessary to turn off _____, such as water and gas. You also may have to quickly _____ your home. Paper is _____, which means it will burn. Blankets, food, and water belong in a(n) _____ kit.

❷ Name four ways to reduce fire hazards at home.

❸ Critical Thinking A friend wants to keep a lighted candle in every window at holiday time. What should you tell her?

❹ (Focus Skill) SEQUENCE Draw and complete the graphic organizer to show the steps involved in escaping from a fire.

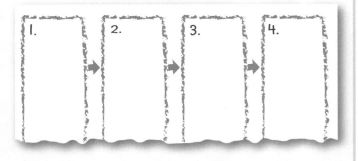

1.	2.	3.	4.

❺ Write to Inform—Description

Describe where your family could meet after escaping a fire. Include the steps you should follow once you have escaped.

ACTIVITIES

Physical Education

Walk for Safety Take a safety walk around your community. As you walk, make notes about hazards you find, such as holes in sidewalks and street signs hidden by trees. Then ask a parent to contact someone in authority about the unsafe conditions.

Science

Research Skin Why is the skin an important body organ? What are the functions of skin? How do burns affect skin? Find information about skin. Then make a poster that explains the functions of skin and how the three types of burns affect it. On your poster, include a labeled diagram of skin.

Technology Project

Make a Video Produce a video that shows how to make your home fire-safe. Include information about household fire hazards and how to prevent fires in the home. If a video camera is not available, use a software program to make a pamphlet with this information.

For more activities, visit The Learning Site.
www.harcourtschool.com/health

Home & Community

Communicating With a parent, look around your neighborhood for possible fire hazards. Then talk with your family about how to communicate with your neighbors about these hazards.

Career Link

Paramedic Paramedics provide first aid and medical treatment to injured people. They transport injured people to the hospital and work closely with fire and police departments. Suppose you are a paramedic. You arrive at the scene of a car accident. List the steps you would take to help the injured people.

Chapter Review and Test Preparation

Reading Skill

SEQUENCE

Draw and then use this graphic organizer to answer questions 1–3.

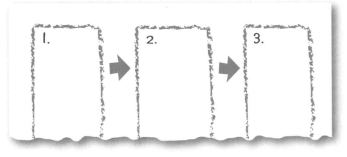

1 In the first box, write the first thing you would do to treat a cut.

2 In the second box, tell how to control the bleeding.

3 In the last box, tell what to do after the bleeding is stopped.

Use Vocabulary

Match each term in Column B with its meaning in Column A.

Column A	Column B
4 Something in the environment or some person's action that can cause harm	**A** flammable
	B hazard
	C concussion
	D emergency
5 Easily catching fire	**E** pedestrian
6 Situation that calls for quick action	
7 Brain injury caused by a blow to the head	
8 Person who is walking	

Check Understanding

Choose the letter of the correct answer.

9 Drowning, poisoning, and choking are examples of _____. (p. 140)
- **A** spinal injuries
- **B** unconsciousness
- **C** emergencies
- **D** first aid

10 The first thing to do when someone is seriously injured is to _____. (p. 142)
- **F** call for help
- **G** give oxygen
- **H** stop the bleeding
- **J** wait your turn

11 Which of the following shows the correct order of steps for treating a bruise? (p. 145)
- **A** C.I.R.E.
- **B** E.R.I.C.
- **C** I.R.E.C.
- **D** R.I.C.E.

12 A bandage free of germs is a _____. (p. 142)
- **F** dirty bandage
- **G** wet cloth
- **H** sterile bandage
- **J** dry cloth

13 Which hand signal would you use if you wanted to make a right turn while riding your bike? (pp. 154–155)

14 Each room in your home should have at least _____ escape route(s). (p. 160)

  F one   **H** three
  G two   **J** four

15 Which is the second step in the sequence of responding to an emergency? (p. 140)

  A Move the   **C** Give first aid.
     injured person.
  B Call 911.   **D** Call a friend.

16 What does this sign mean? (p. 156)

  F You may not ride your bike on this road.
  G Two-wheeled bikes are not allowed.
  H Only bikes can use the road.
  J No motorcycles.

17 All of the following are examples of fire hazards **EXCEPT** _____. (pp. 158–159)

  A an overloaded electrical outlet
  B a lighter left where a child can reach it
  C a newspaper left near a space heater
  D a working smoke alarm

18 The immediate care given to an injured person is _____. (p. 142)

  F a sterile bandage **H** first aid
  G an emergency   **J** stopping bleeding

19 Which is a playground safety rule? (pp. 148–149)

  A Run on wet surfaces.
  B Wait your turn.
  C Push and shove.
  D Go barefoot.

Think Critically

20 Why should an injured person not be moved unless it's necessary for safety reasons?

21 How can human behavior lead to accidents? Give examples of accidents caused by human actions. Explain how these accidents can be prevented.

22 Why is it important to talk to your parents or other trusted adults about unsafe behaviors you have observed?

Apply Skills

23 **BUILDING GOOD CHARACTER**
Caring Suppose you accidentally dropped a glass in your school cafeteria. The glass broke, and juice and pieces of glass are now on the floor. How can you show caring for your classmates by eliminating the hazards?

24 **LIFE SKILLS**
Make Responsible Decisions Your friends have found some firecrackers and want to play with them. You know that this is a hazard and that your parents do not allow you to play with firecrackers. Explain how you can make a responsible decision about playing with the firecrackers.

Write About Health

25 **Write to Inform—Explanation** Write a paragraph that compares the safety rules at your school with the safety rules you have at home. How are they similar? How are they different?

Preventing Violence

Reading Skill

IDENTIFY CAUSE AND EFFECT When you identify cause and effect, you tell what happens and why. An effect is what happens. A cause is the reason, or why, it happens. Use the Reading in Health Handbook on pages 372–383 and this graphic organizer to help you read the health facts in this chapter.

Health Graph

INTERPRET DATA Young people commit more crimes and acts of violence on school days than on nonschool days. At what time during school days are young people most likely to commit crimes?

Juvenile Offenses

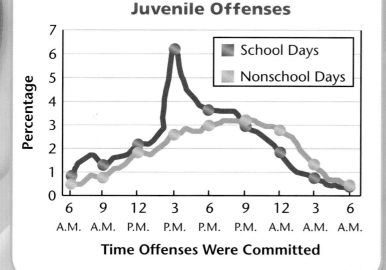

Daily Physical Activity

Staying away from potentially violent situations is one way to stay healthy. Being physically active every day is another way.

 Be Active!
Use the selection, Track 6, **Muscle Mambo**, to move your heart and other muscles toward good health.

Violence in Your World

LESSON 1

Lesson Focus
Identifying violent acts can help you reduce the risk of harm to yourself and others.

Why Learn This?
What you learn can help you protect yourself from harm and lead to a secure school environment.

Vocabulary
violence
terrorism

Violence and Terrorism

If you watch television, you might get the idea that bad things happen most of the time. Some TV shows are based on the lives of crime-fighting police officers. Other shows highlight violence. **Violence** is any act that harms or injures people. Acts of violence include fights, certain crimes, and threats. A person who threatens violence is acting violently. Although the average person is unlikely to experience violence, it can happen anywhere and any time. That's why it's important to understand what violence is and how it can affect you. It's also important to know how to prevent and avoid violence.

Many acts of violence begin with violent thoughts, feelings, or words. Violence never solves problems. It's dangerous and harmful to everyone involved.

Consumer Activity

Accessing Valid Health Information Violence costs everyone money—even those not directly involved. Many schools and communities now spend money on new safety procedures. Do research to find the cost of keeping schools safe. Summarize your findings.

A school resource officer helps make a school environment safe. How might this lead to a safe, healthy community? ▼

Sometimes, violent acts happen between individuals or small groups of people who know each other, such as classmates getting into fights. At other times the people involved in violence may not know each other. For example, you may remember the acts of terrorism that occurred on September 11, 2001. **Terrorism** is the use of force and violence against people or property for a political or social goal. Terrorism can happen in any country in the world.

Sometimes you can't avoid violence, such as during a terrorist attack. But you can do many things to reduce your chance of being harmed by violence. Learning safe ways to communicate is an important tool for preventing violence. Learning nonviolent ways to resolve conflicts, or disagreements, is another important tool. You also can help any organizations in your school and community that work to make these places safe and nonviolent.

 CAUSE AND EFFECT What is one effect of violence?

Cargo Security Devices
Many types of security devices are used to help protect people from violence and terrorism. One type of security device uses X rays to check cargo entering the country. X rays are high-energy waves that can be used to "see" what's inside trucks and containers. X-ray devices enable security officers to find weapons, bombs, and other dangerous items hidden among legal cargo.

173

Real-Life Situation
Violence can occur in any neighborhood. Suppose you walk home from school every day.

Real-Life Plan
Write three ways you could reduce the risk of violence as you walk home from school.

In the Know About Violence

The more you know about violence, the easier it is to avoid it. You can reduce your chance of being harmed by violence by avoiding gangs, staying away from weapons, and not using drugs or alcohol. Follow these tips to avoid violence:

- Be aware of what's going on around you.
- Avoid going places by yourself.
- Never try to break up a fight. If you see a violent act, tell a parent or another trusted adult.
- Walk away if someone threatens you.
- If you are walking and see people who look threatening, turn and walk in another direction.
- Tell your parents or another trusted adult if someone threatens you.

DRAW CONCLUSIONS How can paying attention to what is around you help you avoid violence?

Lesson 1 Summary and Review

❶ Summarize with Vocabulary

Use vocabulary and other terms from this lesson to complete the statements.

Any act that harms or injures someone is called _____. Acts of violence include fights, crimes, and _____. The use of violence for a political or social cause is _____. You can reduce your risk of harm from violence by not using drugs or _____.

❷ How do many acts of violence begin?

❸ Critical Thinking In a violent situation, why is it better to ask an adult for help instead of trying to solve the problem yourself?

❹ (Focus Skill) **CAUSE AND EFFECT** Draw and complete this graphic organizer to show how the tips for avoiding violence can help you stay safe.

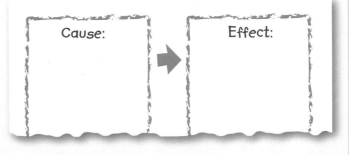

Cause:

Effect:

❺ Write to Express— Solution to a Problem

Write about an argument you heard. How could the conflict have been avoided?

Fairness

Listen to Others

Often, violence happens because people have conflicts, or disagreements. Good communication can help people work out a solution before a conflict turns violent. To be fair, each side must listen to the other. Fairness means giving both sides a chance to explain their points of view.

- **Give the other person time to share his or her feelings and thoughts.**
- **Don't interrupt. Wait until the person is finished before you speak.**
- **Use appropriate body language. Face the person, and make eye contact. Don't let your eyes wander. Keep your attention on the speaker.**
- **If you don't understand what the person is saying, ask questions or ask the person to say it again.**
- **Try to understand the other person's point of view. If you don't agree with it, don't say that the person is foolish or stupid. Respect the opinions of others, even if those opinions are different from yours.**

Activity

With a small group, think of a conflict that might occur between friends. Prepare and perform a skit in which the friends don't listen to each other. Then change the skit so that the friends do listen to each other.

Help Prevent Violence

Lesson Focus

You can take steps to reduce violence in your community and avoid being harmed yourself.

Why Learn This?

What you learn can reduce your risk of getting hurt if you are in a violent situation.

Vocabulary

weapon
bully
gang

What to Do If Someone Has a Weapon

Even if you try to avoid violent situations, you still may find yourself faced with one. For example, a classmate may bring a weapon to school. A **weapon** is anything that can be used to harm someone. Guns and knives are weapons. Anytime a weapon is present, you are in danger.

Suppose that you find a gun while at a friend's home. To stay safe, follow these steps:

- Stop. Don't touch the gun. If your friend wants to pick it up, try to talk him or her out of it.
- Leave the room or the area right away. If your friend doesn't go with you, leave anyway. Don't wait to see what happens.
- Tell an adult. Make sure the adult knows where you found the gun.

In schools, guns and knives are not allowed. Students can be suspended or expelled for taking weapons to school.

SEQUENCE List in order the steps you should follow if you find a gun.

◀ More than 20,000 people under the age of twenty are accidently killed or injured by gunshots each year in the United States. Guns should always be locked away, such as in a gun safe like the one shown here.

PERSONAL HEALTH PLAN ▶

Real-Life Situation
A bully at school begins calling you names and daring you to fight.
Real-Life Plan
·In advance, list things you could do to avoid getting into a fight with a bully.

What to Do If Someone Threatens You

A **bully** is someone who hurts or frightens others. Bullies usually pick on people who are alone or who seem different in some way. Staying with a group can help you avoid bullies. However, if a bully threatens you, you may be in physical danger. Here are some tips that can help you reduce your risk of harm:

- Calmly and confidently ask the person to stop.
- Ignore the bully. A bully will usually leave you alone if you don't seem angry or frightened.
- If someone tries to get you to fight, leave the area. A person who walks away from a violent situation is stronger and smarter than a person who doesn't.
- If the bully has a weapon, stay calm and get away as quickly as possible. You don't have to speak. Don't try to be brave.
- Tell a parent or a trusted adult that you were threatened. If the bully had a weapon, let the adult know.

SUMMARIZE Tell three things you can do to reduce your risk of harm from a bully.

ACTIVITY

Life Skills

Make Responsible Decisions Tiago is at Spencer's house. Spencer wants to show his parents' gun to Tiago. What should Tiago do to stay safe?

177

Making Schools and Communities Less Violent

It is important for people to feel safe in their communities or their schools. Yet violence affects many places across the nation. Some communities have gangs that make neighborhoods or schools unsafe. A **gang** is a group of people who have a close social relationship. Recently, the word *gang* has come to refer to a group that uses violence. Gang members typically commit crimes, use drugs, and carry weapons.

Most people need a sense of family and belonging. Being in a gang can seem to fill these needs. Some people join gangs because older family members belong to one. Others join because they think membership will give them power. Some join because they are bullied or threatened if they don't become a gang member.

People who join gangs often don't understand all the consequences of being a gang member. Gangs are dangerous, and being in one usually involves fighting, drugs, weapons, crime, and going to jail. Fights between rival gangs put the members, their families, and their neighbors in danger of injury or death.

You don't have to join a gang to belong to a group. You can find positive ways to spend your time. A few ideas are listed on the next page.

Being part of a group doesn't mean being part of a gang. ▶

◀ A parent, teacher, or other trusted adult can help you find ways to stay safe in your school and community.

Quick Activity

Evaluate a Leader
Think about a leader in your community or school. What makes him or her a good leader? Write a paragraph telling how you could be a leader and help improve your community.

- Get involved with a community group or start one of your own. Think about what you would like to change about your community to make it safer. Identify a person or a group that can help you.

- Join a school club or a sports team.

- Become a leader in your school's student government or become a member of your school's conflict resolution group.

- Volunteer for a good cause in your community. Encourage your classmates to join you.

COMPARE AND CONTRAST **How are gangs and community groups alike? How are they different?**

Lesson 2 Summary and Review

1 Summarize with Vocabulary

Use vocabulary and other terms from this lesson to complete the statements.

A _____ is something that can be used to harm someone. Someone who hurts or frightens others is a _____. Fighting, drugs, crime, and going to jail often are part of being a member of a _____. You can join a positive group in your school or _____ to gain a sense of belonging.

2 What happens to students who take weapons to school?

3 Critical Thinking Why might a bully stop calling you names if you ask him or her to stop?

4 **CAUSE AND EFFECT**
Draw and complete this graphic organizer to show some effects of being a gang member.

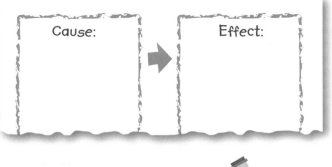

Cause: → Effect:

5 Write to Entertain—Poem

Write a poem telling how to prevent violence.

179

Resolve Conflicts
to Prevent Violence

It's normal for friends or classmates to disagree from time to time. However, if people don't resolve their disagreements, or conflicts, the result can be angry feelings and even fights. You can use the steps for **Resolving Conflicts** to prevent violence.

Sam is using a school computer to do research. Mark comes into the computer lab and wants to use the computer. When Sam doesn't leave the computer right away, Mark gets angry.

1 Use "I" messages to tell how you feel.

I need to finish my work. I'm almost done.

When Sam turns around, Mark looks angry. Sam speaks calmly and tells Mark how he feels.

2 Consider the other person's point of view.

I've missed a lot of school, and this is the *best* way for me to get caught up.

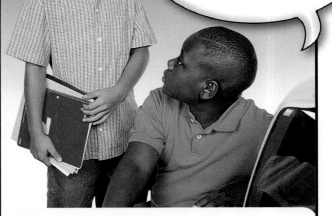

Sam and Mark talk about why they need to use the computer.

3 **Talk about a solution.**

If you can wait just a few minutes, I'll be finished with my assignments.

I need an hour to do my research.

Sam and Mark explain how much time they each need. The boys listen to one another without interrupting.

4 **Find a way for both sides to win.**

Thanks. I'm sorry I got angry.

Sam and Mark work out a plan that enables both of them to finish their assignments by sharing the computer.

Problem Solving

A. At school Matt bullies Jonah by calling him names. One day while Jonah is walking home from school, Matt walks up behind Jonah and shoves him.
- Use the steps for **Resolving Conflicts** to help Jonah prevent violence.

B. Laura and Anne used to be best friends. They got into an argument, and now they don't talk to each other. Last week Anne started to make angry phone calls to Laura at home. Laura knows she needs to do something about the problem before it gets worse.
- Explain a responsible decision that Laura could make to resolve the conflict with Anne.

Surviving Violence

Lesson Focus
You can take steps to protect yourself from violence.

Why Learn This?
What you learn can reduce your risk of being harmed by violent acts, including terrorism.

Vocabulary
zero-tolerance policy

Street Violence

Violence can sometimes take place in your own neighborhood. Street violence can involve gangs, drugs, theft, or *hate crimes*. Hate crimes are crimes based on race, religion, nationality, and other reasons.

The best way to protect yourself from street violence is to think ahead and follow these guidelines:

- Before you go out, ask permission. Tell a parent where you're going, how you'll get there, who you'll be with, and when you'll be home.
- Avoid places where violence occurs. Don't talk to strangers who come up to you. Yell for help if someone bothers you.
- Use the buddy system. Stay with other people when going places or just hanging out.

DRAW CONCLUSIONS **How does each guideline for protecting yourself help you stay safe?**

Quick Activity

Learn from Graphs
Study this circle graph. What is the biggest reason for hate crimes? What percent of hate crimes are committed because of nationality? How many more crimes are committed because of race than nationality?

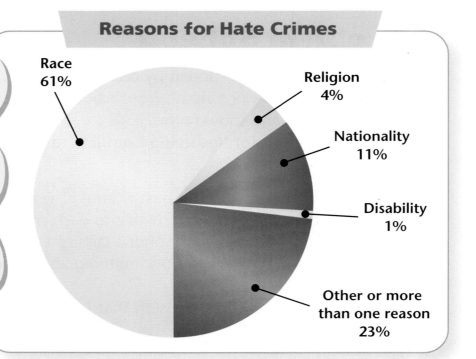

Reasons for Hate Crimes

Race 61%

Religion 4%

Nationality 11%

Disability 1%

Other or more than one reason 23%

Many schools expel students for having weapons, drugs, or alcohol; for fighting; or for making threats.

School Violence

Another place where you need to think about safety is at school. Almost half of all elementary schools report one or more violent situations each year. That's why many schools have zero-tolerance policies. A **zero-tolerance policy** means that no violence and no weapons of any kind are allowed in the school. It also promises punishments for students who don't follow the policy. These policies help keep students safe from weapons and threats. Students learn better when they aren't afraid.

Anger that gets out of control can lead to violence. Some schools have programs that help students learn how to manage anger and conflicts. You can learn more about dealing with anger and other emotions on pages 314–316.

Some schools take additional measures to reduce violence. Visitors must sign in before entering the school. School grounds and play areas may have fences around them. Some schools have security guards or resource officers.

MAIN IDEA AND DETAILS Give three details about how schools help keep students safe.

ACTIVITY

Building Good Character

Citizenship At school, José sees a knife sticking out of someone's coat. Explain how José can show good citizenship and help prevent school violence.

Terrorism

Another kind of violence that can affect people's safety is terrorism. If a terrorist attack occurs, you can reduce your risk of injury by doing the following:

- Stay calm. Panic can cause people to get hurt.
- Listen to the directions from the person in charge. At school, teachers and the principal will give instructions to help students stay safe. Outside of school, community leaders, police, and other officials will try to keep everyone free from harm.
- Have an emergency plan. An emergency plan for terrorism might include going to a secure place inside and staying away from doors and windows.

SUMMARIZE Tell what you should do if a terrorist situation happens.

Information Alert!

Department of Homeland Security After September 11, 2001, the United States government formed the Department of Homeland Security to protect the nation from attacks.

GO ONLINE For the most up-to-date information, visit The Learning Site. www.harcourtschool.com/health

---

Lesson 3 Summary and Review

1 Summarize with Vocabulary

Use vocabulary and other terms from this lesson to complete the statements.

Crimes based on race, religion, nationality, disability, and so on, are called _____. A school policy that does not allow any drugs or weapons is called a _____. Protecting yourself by hanging out with others is called the _____ system.

2 What is one thing you can do to protect yourself from street violence?

3 Critical Thinking What can individual students do to help reduce the risk of violence in their schools?

4 Focus Skill IDENTIFY CAUSE AND EFFECT

Draw and complete this graphic organizer to show causes and effects of a school zero-tolerance policy.

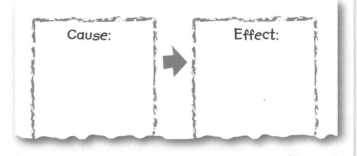

Cause:

Effect:

5 Write to Inform—Explanation

Suppose a friend's family invites you to go to the mall. What should you tell your parents when you ask permission to go?

ACTIVITIES

 Math

Keep a Record In a small notebook, make an entry each time you have a disagreement with someone. Then describe the problem or conflict. Think about whether you handled the situation well. If you didn't, write what you could have done differently. After one week, count the number of conflicts you have each day to see if they're increasing or decreasing. Share your notebook with a parent or other trusted adult.

 **Art**

Organize a Community Mural Project Organize or help to organize a community art project. Talk with a community leader to find a place for a mural, or large painting, on a wall or building. Post fliers to encourage people from your community to get involved with painting the mural.

 Technology Project

Research Community Youth Groups Identify local groups that are for kids your age. Use a computer to make a chart listing the groups and activities that young people can participate in. Which group would you like to join? Why? Explain how having young people active in local groups can help keep communities safe and healthy.

 GO ONLINE For more activities, visit The Learning Site. www.harcourtschool.com/health

 Home & Community

Discuss Conflicts on TV Keep a TV log with your family. As you watch each show, record any conflicts that you see. Later, discuss whether the conflicts could have been handled better. Record your observations in your log.

Career Link

Baggage Screener Baggage screeners check the bags that people carry onto airplanes. They also screen passengers' luggage that is carried onto the plane. Suppose that you're a baggage screener at an airport. Write a security report telling how you help keep people safe when they fly. Explain what you like about your job and why your job is important.

Reading Skill

CAUSE AND EFFECT

Draw and then use this graphic organizer to answer questions 1 and 2.

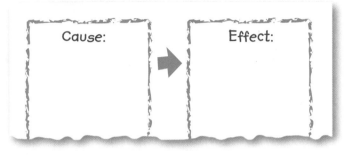

Cause: → Effect:

1 Write about an action you can take if a bully calls you names.
2 Write about a possible effect of your action on the bully's behavior.

Use Vocabulary

Match each term in Column A with its meaning in Column B.

Column A	Column B
3 Object used to harm someone is a _____.	A violence
4 Joining a _____ often leads to violence.	B terrorism C weapon
5 Any act that harms a person is _____.	D bully E gang
6 A crime based on race is a _____.	F hate crime
7 _____ is the use of violence for a political or social goal.	
8 A _____ is someone who hurts or frightens others.	

Check Understanding

Choose the letter of the correct answer.

9 A school's policy of not allowing any weapons is called a _____. (p. 183)
   A just-say-no policy
   B zero-tolerance policy
   C no-weapons policy
   D drug-free-zone policy

10 Which is **TRUE** about gun safety? (p. 176)
   F Toy guns are OK to bring to school.
   G Guns are not allowed in schools.
   H Guns should be stored loaded.
   J If a bully has a gun, take it away.

11 If a bully threatens you, _____. (p. 177)
   A kick the bully and get away
   B tell the bully he or she is stupid
   C get away as quickly as possible
   D laugh at the bully

12 Violence is **NOT** related to _____. (p. 172)
   F solving problems   H stealing
   G hate crimes   J fighting

13 Which of the following is the **BEST** way to prevent violence between the students in the picture? (p. 174)

   A Try to break up the argument.
   B Get them to talk about a solution.
   C Call the police.
   D Tell a teacher or principal.

14 Which of the following is **NOT** part of gang membership? (p. 178)
   F jail   H protection
   G crime   J sense of belonging

15 Which of the following is **NOT** a cause for being suspended or expelled if it's carried to school? (p. 183)

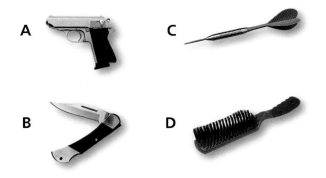

A

C

B

D

16 Which is **TRUE** of terrorism? (p. 184)
  F There is nothing you can do to stay safe during a terrorist attack.
  G Terrorism can happen anywhere in the world.
  H Terrorists use peaceful means to achieve social goals.
  J Terrorists always know their victims.

17 Which of the following is **NOT** a detail about staying safe? (p. 182)
  A Speak calmly to strangers.
  B Don't play alone.
  C Tell your parents where you will be.
  D Avoid places where violence occurs.

18 At which of the following places would you need to watch out for violence? (pp. 172)
  F school
  G your community
  H your neighborhood
  J all of these places

19 In the buddy system, you _____. (p. 182)
  A tell your parents where you're going
  B make friends with strangers
  C always stay with another person
  D call your friends on the telephone

Think Critically

20 Why do you need to know about violence?

21 Suppose you're walking down the street and see a group of people who look threatening. What should you do to protect yourself from harm?

22 How could joining a community group help keep other kids in your neighborhood from joining a gang?

Apply Skills

23 **BUILDING GOOD CHARACTER**
  Fairness A friend wants you to come home with her after school. When you tell her that you have other plans, she gets angry. How can you handle the problem fairly?

24 **LIFE SKILLS**
  Resolve Conflicts Your parents are away for the evening, and your older brother has been on the phone a long time. You're expecting a call from a friend. Your brother gives you an angry look when you signal that you need to use the phone. How could you resolve the conflict?

Write About Health

25 **Write to Inform—Explanation** Explain why preventing violence is an important part of staying healthy.

CHAPTER 7

Learning About Disease

SUMMARIZE When you summarize, you state the main idea and the most important details. Use the Reading in Health Handbook on pages 372–383 and this graphic organizer to help you read the health facts in this chapter.

Summarize

| Main Idea: | + | Details: | = | Summary: |

Health Graph

INTERPRET DATA Humans can get Lyme disease from the bites of infected deer ticks. Describe how the number of cases of Lyme disease changed over the time period shown on the graph.

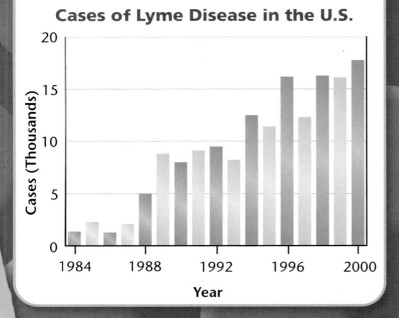

Cases of Lyme Disease in the U.S.

Cases (Thousands) vs. Year

Daily Physical Activity

Eating healthful foods, getting plenty of sleep, and being physically active are lifestyle choices that can help fight disease.

 Be Active! Use the selection, Track 7, **Moovin' and Groovin'**, to beef up your body's protection.

Causes of Disease

Lesson Focus

There are two main types of disease and many causes of disease.

Why Learn This?

Learning about disease will help you know how to avoid it.

Vocabulary

communicable disease
noncommunicable disease

Types of Disease

Terri's head aches, and her throat is sore. She feels weak. Although her illness isn't serious, there are things she should do to get better. She needs to rest, eat healthful foods, and drink lots of fluids. Terri is ill with influenza, or flu. Flu is a *disease*, a condition that damages or weakens part of the body.

There are two kinds of disease. One kind spreads from person to person. The other kind does not. A **communicable disease** (kuh•MYOO•nih•kuh•buhl dih•ZEEZ) is a disease that can be spread from person to person. Flu is a communicable disease because it spreads. Terri probably caught her flu from a classmate. Colds are also communicable diseases.

Other diseases do not spread from person to person. For example, Terri's best friend has diabetes. A disease that does not spread from one person to another is called a **noncommunicable disease**.

 SUMMARIZE How would you summarize the information you have just read about disease?

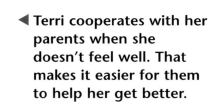

◀ Terri cooperates with her parents when she doesn't feel well. That makes it easier for them to help her get better.

◄ Children can inherit many things from their parents—hair color, eye color, and even some diseases.

Some Diseases Can Be Inherited

Noncommunicable diseases can be caused partly by things like smoking tobacco, breathing polluted air, and eating an unhealthful diet. Some noncommunicable diseases can even be inherited. *Heredity* is the passing of characteristics from parents to their children. For example, your hair might be the same color as your dad's, or your eye color might be the same as your mom's.

Sickle cell anemia is an inherited blood disease. It causes attacks of pain, often in the chest, abdomen, and bones. Over time it can damage many parts of the body. Children can inherit sickle cell anemia from parents who don't show any signs of the disease.

Other diseases, including heart disease and some kinds of cancer, can be partly caused by heredity. People who have close relatives with one of these diseases are more likely to get the disease than people who have no relatives with it.

MAIN IDEA AND DETAILS **What is an inherited disease? Give one example.**

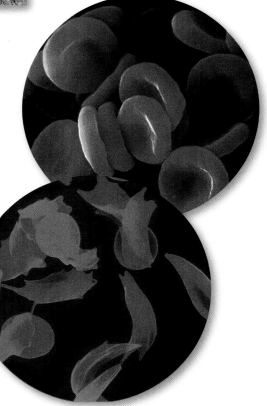

▲ The smooth, doughnut-shaped red blood cells in the top picture are normal red blood cells. The odd-shaped red blood cells in the bottom picture are from a person who has sickle cell anemia.

Healthful Choices Help Protect You from Disease

Personal Health Plan ▶

Real-Life Situation
You were ill five times during the past year, and you want to stay healthy this year.

Real-Life Plan
Plan things you might do this year to decrease your chances of becoming ill.

Terri's mother and grandmother both have heart disease. That means Terri has a greater chance than the average person of developing heart disease. However, Terri makes several healthful choices to lower her risk. She chooses foods that are low in fat, and she gets plenty of exercise. After school, instead of eating potato chips, Terri has an apple or some yogurt. Instead of getting a ride to school, she bicycles or walks.

Small daily choices such as these make up your *lifestyle*—the way you live your life. Your lifestyle and your health are closely related. People who make healthful lifestyle choices are less likely to become ill.

Choosing not to use tobacco is one of the most important lifestyle choices you can make. When you choose not to use tobacco, you lower your chances of getting lung cancer and heart disease.

CAUSE AND EFFECT Name two things that affect your risk for heart disease.

Members of the Rodriguez family are rarely ill. What lifestyle choices are they making to stay healthy? ▼

Respecting People with Illnesses and Disabilities

Thomas uses a wheelchair. Things that are simple for other people, such as riding a bus, taking a shower, and opening a door, are more complicated for Thomas to do. Thomas's disability also affects how others treat him and how he feels about himself.

You may feel awkward around people with disabilities or serious illnesses. However, a classmate who is ill with cancer or is disabled in some way may be just like you in every other way. You should always respect people who have serious illnesses or disabilities. Give them help when they need it, but otherwise treat them with respect, as you would anyone.

▲ People with disabilities can still be physically active.

 SUMMARIZE How should you treat classmates who have disabilities or serious illnesses?

Lesson 1 Summary and Review

1 Summarize with Vocabulary

Use vocabulary and other terms from this lesson to complete the statements.

There are two types of disease. A _____ disease can be passed from person to person. A _____ disease cannot. One factor that can increase your chances of getting a disease is _____, or the passing of characteristics from parents to their _____. Your _____ also affects your chances of getting certain diseases.

2 What determines whether you develop sickle cell anemia or not?

3 Critical Thinking Some people dislike sports. In what other ways can they be active to reduce their risks of becoming ill?

4 SUMMARIZE Draw and complete this graphic organizer to show key information about the risks of disease.

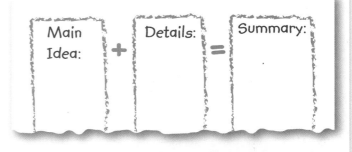

5 Write to Inform—Explanation

Two of the children next door have diabetes. Explain to your little brother why he can't catch diabetes and how his behavior might affect the children.

193

Pathogens and Communicable Diseases

Signs of Communicable Diseases

Julia had a cold but went to school anyway. In class she forgot to cover her mouth when she coughed. Rob sat at a desk near Julia and didn't notice her cough. Later that week Rob felt sick when he woke up. He had a cough and a sore throat, which are symptoms of a cold. **Symptoms** (SIMP•tuhmz) are the signs and feelings of an illness.

When you have a communicable disease, the symptoms of the disease usually identify it. One day you might wake up with a headache, a runny nose, and a cough. You might also be sneezing. These symptoms tell you that you probably have a cold. If you also have a fever and muscle aches, you probably have the flu.

A common symptom of many communicable diseases is fever. When you have a fever, your body temperature is a few degrees higher than normal.

COMPARE AND CONTRAST How are the symptoms of a cold and the flu alike and different?

◀ Fever is a symptom of many diseases, such as the flu.

Pathogens

Diseases that you can get from other people, such as colds and the flu, are spread by pathogens. **Pathogens** (PATH•uh•juhnz) are tiny organisms or viruses that cause diseases. Pathogens are all around you, but they are too small to see with your eyes. They can be seen only with a microscope. Their tiny size makes it difficult for people to tell when pathogens are being spread.

Pathogens can enter your body when you eat, drink, or just breathe. They can also enter your body through an open cut. Pathogens that get past your body's defenses and multiply can cause infection. **Infection** (in•FEK•shuhn) is the rapid growth of pathogens in the body.

Some pathogens kill body cells. Other pathogens produce substances that harm your body in other ways. Diseases caused by pathogens include athlete's foot, flu, food poisoning, chicken pox, and polio.

DRAW CONCLUSIONS Use what you read about pathogens to explain why Rob caught Julia's cold.

Information Alert!

New Diseases Emerging infectious diseases (EIDs) are diseases that have recently become common or are expected to in the future. Discuss any EIDs that you have heard about in the news.

For the most up-to-date information, visit The Learning Site. www.harcourtschool.com/health

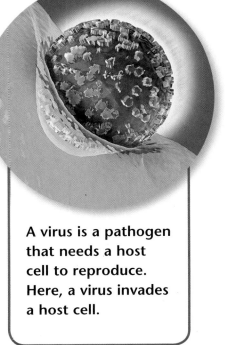

A virus is a pathogen that needs a host cell to reproduce. Here, a virus invades a host cell.

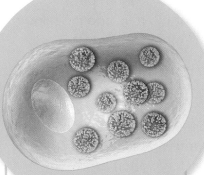

Once inside the cell, the virus takes over, forming new viruses.

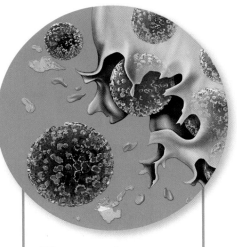

The new viruses burst out of the host cell, killing it. They move on to invade other cells.

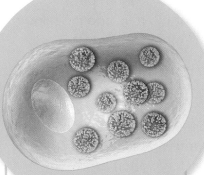

Kinds of Pathogens

Communicable diseases are caused by several kinds of pathogens. There are four main kinds of pathogens: *viruses* (VY•ruh•suhz), *bacteria* (bak•TIR•ee•uh), *fungi* (FUHN•jy), and *protozoa* (proh•tuh•ZOH•uh).

Diseases Caused by Pathogens

Pathogen	Characteristics	Diseases
Viruses	The smallest pathogens; the ones that cause most infectious diseases	Colds, chicken pox, AIDS, infectious hepatitis, influenza (flu), measles, mumps, polio, rabies, rubella (German measles)
Bacteria	One-celled living things that can—but do not always—cause disease; make people ill by producing harmful wastes	Strep throat, pertussis (whooping cough), some kinds of pneumonia, Salmonella food poisoning, tetanus, tuberculosis (TB), Lyme disease
Fungi	Small, simple living things like yeasts and molds; most often invade the skin or respiratory system	Ringworm, athlete's foot
Protozoa	One-celled organisms somewhat larger than bacteria; often cause serious diseases	Amebic dysentery, giardiasis

MAIN IDEA AND DETAILS **Name four kinds of pathogens, and tell what they do.**

▲ Mosquitoes spread a number of pathogens, including West Nile virus, shown at the right.

How Pathogens Spread

Different pathogens spread in different ways. Some spread through the air when people sneeze or cough. Other pathogens spread when infected animals or insects bite people. For example, a bite from an infected raccoon or skunk can spread the virus that causes rabies. Tick bites can spread Lyme disease and Rocky Mountain spotted fever.

Pathogens can spread when you touch things such as doorknobs, pens, and telephones. They can also spread in food and water.

Other pathogens spread in other ways. HIV, the virus that causes AIDS, can be spread by intimate contact or by sharing needles. Some types of hepatitis pathogens can also be spread by sharing needles, including those used to draw tattoos. The best way to prevent the spread of HIV and hepatitis is abstinence. **Abstinence** (AB•stuh•nuhns) is the avoidance of behaviors that put your health at risk.

CAUSE AND EFFECT **What could happen when a mosquito bites a bird infected with the West Nile virus?**

Myth and Fact

Myth: Only adults get HIV.

Fact: HIV can infect people of any age. Worldwide, there are more than 3 million people under the age of fifteen who have HIV. Children of mothers with HIV can even be born with the virus.

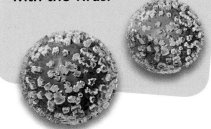

197

How Pathogens Enter the Body

Pathogens can enter your body in several ways. They can get in through your skin, your eyes, or the mucous membranes lining your nose and mouth. A cut or scrape on your skin can also let in pathogens.

Pathogens on your fingers or on a pen can enter your body if you put these things into your mouth. Pathogens can enter your eyes if you rub your eyes with your fingers.

The pathogens that cause food poisoning can enter your body through your digestive system when you eat spoiled or undercooked food. Pathogens can also enter if you drink water that has pathogens in it or you share a drink with someone who is sick. For example, protozoa called *Giardia* (jee•AR•dee•uh) can enter your digestive system if you drink untreated water from a

ACTIVITY

Life Skills

Refuse Beth buys veggie chips, and Lindsay buys fruit juice at a snack shop. Beth, who is sick with a cold, asks Lindsay for a sip of juice. Lindsay knows that this is not a good idea. Write a script to help her explain why she won't share her drink with Beth.

stream. These protozoa cause a disease whose symptoms include diarrhea, stomach cramps, and fever.

SEQUENCE **You come down with food poisoning after a picnic. What probably happened?**

Quick Activity

Stop Pathogens Look at the drawings on these pages. Use the drawings to help you write three ways to prevent the spread of pathogens.

Lesson 2 Summary and Review

1 Summarize with Vocabulary

Use vocabulary from this lesson to complete the statements.

Diseases are caused by four main types of pathogens: _____, _____, _____, and _____. If one of these multiplies in your body, you may get a(n) _____. If you are ill, you may notice certain signs or feelings, which are known as _____.

2 Critical Thinking Why is washing your hands regularly with soap a good way to stop the spread of disease?

3 When do people get fevers?

4 (Focus Skill) **SUMMARIZE** Draw and complete this graphic organizer to show details about pathogens entering the body.

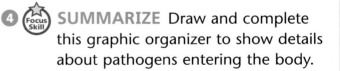

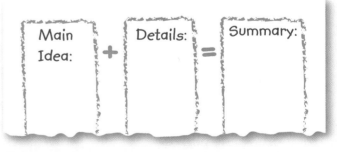

| Main Idea: | + | Details: | = | Summary: |

5 Write to Explain— Solution to a Problem

Your best friend asks you to play a game, but you have a cold. Write a story about the problem and what you decide to do.

Disease and the Immune System

First Line of Defense

There are millions of pathogens all around you. Fortunately, your body has ways to keep most pathogens out and to destroy most of the ones that do get in. Your body is a lot like a fort protected by many defenses. Even if pathogens get past one defense, they must overcome several others before they can cause an infection. Some defenses are physical barriers that block pathogens. Others are chemical defenses that kill or weaken pathogens.

Your skin is a thick barrier to pathogens. The outer layers are so tough that pathogens cannot pass through them unless the skin is broken in some way. Your skin also produces sweat, which contains chemicals that kill some pathogens.

Tiny hairs called *cilia* trap pathogens and keep them out of your lungs. ▶

▲ Your eyes are protected from pathogens by tears. Tears wash pathogens out of your eyes. Tears also contain chemicals that kill some pathogens.

Pathogens that enter through your nose must overcome mucus and cilia. *Mucus* (MYOO·kuhs) is a thick, sticky substance that traps pathogens. It covers the inside of your nose, throat, and trachea.

Tiny hairlike structures called *cilia* (SIL·ee·uh) line your breathing passages. Cilia move in waves. They push pathogens toward body openings, where your body gets rid of the pathogens. For example, the cilia in your throat push pathogens toward your mouth, where you get rid of them by coughing.

Saliva is a strong defense against pathogens that enter through your mouth. The chemicals in saliva kill many pathogens. If any survive, strong acid in the stomach usually kills them.

COMPARE AND CONTRAST As defenses, how are skin and tears alike? How are they different?

Quick Activity

Interpret Information Suppose pathogens are trying to enter your body through your respiratory system. List the main defenses your body has against these pathogens. You might want to refer back to page 7.

Your Body's Defenses

1 Tears kill and wash away pathogens that enter your eyes.

2 Earwax traps pathogens that enter your ears.

3 Chemicals in saliva kill pathogens that enter your mouth.

4 Mucus traps pathogens in your nose and keeps them from getting into your respiratory system.

5 Cilia along breathing passages keep pathogens out of your lungs.

6 The skin's outer layers block pathogens. Sweat kills some of them.

7 Stomach acid kills most pathogens in your digestive system.

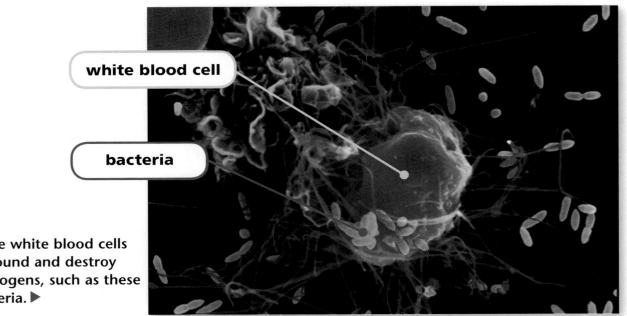

white blood cell

bacteria

Some white blood cells surround and destroy pathogens, such as these bacteria. ▶

How the Blood Fights Disease

If pathogens get past the first line of your body's defenses, they must face your blood. Blood contains white blood cells which circulate through your body and destroy pathogens. White blood cells are produced by the *immune system*, the body system that fights disease.

Antibodies (AN•tih•bahd•eez) are substances made by white blood cells to help fight pathogens. A different antibody is made for each kind of pathogen. When an antibody attaches itself to a pathogen, it can kill the pathogen, prevent it from entering body cells, or mark it to be killed by a white blood cell.

When a particular kind of pathogen enters your body for the first time, you show symptoms of disease while the pathogens multiply. After making antibodies, your body recovers and never "forgets" how to make them. The next time similar pathogens attack, antibodies can be made more quickly to keep the pathogens from multiplying. The body's ability to "remember" how to make antibodies quickly is called **immunity** (ih•MYOON•uh•tee).

DRAW CONCLUSIONS One winter you get the flu. A month later the same type of flu virus invades your body. Will you get sick again? Explain.

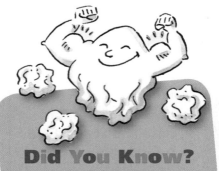

Did You Know?

A single drop of blood can contain 7,000 to 25,000 white blood cells. That number increases greatly when your body is fighting an infection. Lab workers count white blood cells in a small blood sample to determine whether a person has an infection.

How Vaccines and Antibiotics Fight Disease

People can also become immune to diseases through the use of vaccines. A **vaccine** (vak•SEEN) is a medicine that can give you immunity to a disease. In most cases, a vaccine is a killed or weakened version of the pathogen that causes the disease.

Most vaccines protect people from certain diseases caused by viruses. If you get a flu shot, the vaccine will cause your body to make antibodies against certain flu viruses. The next time you are exposed to those viruses, your body will "remember" how to make the antibodies to fight the viruses and keep you healthy.

Antibiotics also help your body fight diseases. An **antibiotic** (an•ty•by•AHT•ik) is a medicine that kills certain organisms, especially bacteria. Antibiotics can't kill viruses, so they can't fight diseases like colds and flu. However, scientists have developed a few medicines that destroy certain viruses.

CAUSE AND EFFECT **Nellie's sister has the flu. What do you need to know to decide whether Nellie is likely to catch the flu from her sister?**

Consumer Activity

Analyzing Advertising and Media Messages
Describe a medicine ad you have seen. What kind of information did the ad give you? What information did it leave out? What other information would your doctor need to decide whether this medicine is right for you?

▼ Scientists called *immunologists* study the immune system. They find ways to protect people from infection and to cure infections. Immunologists have developed many effective vaccines and antibiotics.

▲ In the 1880s, Louis Pasteur developed a vaccine against rabies, a disease that attacks the nervous system.

203

Helping Your Body Fight Disease

Practicing good hygiene is one way to keep pathogens out of your body. Always wash your hands before you eat and after you use the bathroom or handle a pet. Be sure to use plenty of soap and warm water. This will help remove pathogens from your skin.

To fight disease, you need to keep your resistance high. **Resistance** (rih•ZIS•tuhns) is your body's ability to fight pathogens on its own. The higher your resistance, the less often you will become ill and the sooner you will recover from an illness. You can boost your resistance by eating a variety of nutritious foods. Also, drink lots of water.

Other ways to build resistance are through regular exercise and plenty of sleep. Most young people need at least eight hours of sleep each night.

Jane and her dad get regular exercise by playing softball. Exercise helps them deal with stress and keep up their resistance to disease. ▼

Too much stress in your life can lower your resistance. Trying to do too many things or worrying about problems for too long can cause stress. You can manage stress by doing something relaxing. For example, you can talk with a parent or a friend, listen to music, play a game, read a book, or exercise.

Another way to manage stress is to get rid of things that cause stress. Instead of worrying about something, try to find a solution that will help you reduce your stress.

Focus Skill SUMMARIZE **How can you boost your resistance to disease?**

Keep clean to stay healthy. Use a fresh washcloth and warm—not hot—water. Using a towel to dry also gets rid of pathogens. ▶

Lesson 3 Summary and Review

❶ Summarize with Vocabulary

Use vocabulary and other terms from this lesson to complete the statements.

You have many defenses against disease. For example, your breathing passages are lined with a thick, sticky substance called _____, which traps pathogens. An entire system in your body, the _____ system, fights disease. You can get _____ to some diseases either on your own or with the help of a _____. Medicines called _____ may help you recover from bacterial infections.

❷ Where in the body are antibodies made?

❸ Critical Thinking In what way is getting a vaccine like having a disease?

❹ **Focus Skill** SUMMARIZE Draw and complete this graphic organizer to show how your body fights pathogens.

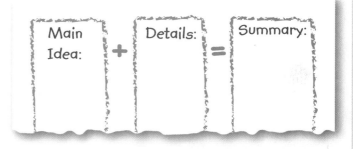

Main Idea: + Details: = Summary:

❺ Write to Inform—Explanation

Sara seems to catch every cold that her classmates get. She has no idea how to avoid disease-causing pathogens. Write a paragraph explaining how Sara can avoid pathogens and stay well.

When Someone Becomes Ill

Treating Disease

Jay had a bad headache, and his throat felt very scratchy. Jay's dad felt his head and said that it seemed hot. He took his temperature and found out that he had a fever. Jay's dad usually gives him medicine for minor illnesses, such as colds, but this time he thought Jay should see Dr. Phillips.

The doctor asked Jay to describe his symptoms. She then examined Jay, looking for signs of infection. She took his temperature and blood pressure. She listened to Jay's heart and lungs and examined his eyes, ears, and nose. She also looked at his throat and, using a swab, took a cell sample from it to test at the lab.

When Dr. Phillips finished her exam, she said Jay might have strep throat, a bacterial infection. She told Jay that he should drink plenty of fluids, like juice, and get extra rest. She asked Jay's dad to give him medicine

◀ It's important to let a parent know when you feel ill.

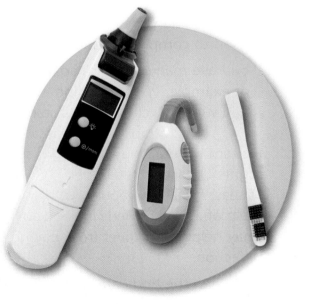

▲ All these thermometers measure body temperature. A fever may be a symptom of an infection.

206

During a visit to the doctor, he or she will record your symptoms and any other signs of disease.

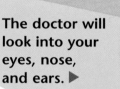

◀ The doctor will listen to your heart and lungs.

The doctor will look at your throat. ▶

The doctor will look into your eyes, nose, and ears. ▶

▲ Your blood pressure will be measured and recorded.

for his cough, fever, and headache. Dr. Phillips said she would prescribe an antibiotic if the lab results showed Jay had a bacterial infection.

As Dr. Phillips said goodbye to Jay and his dad, she gave Jay's medical record to Ms. Anders, a medical records technician. It is her job to keep patients' records. Jay's record contains information such as notes Dr. Phillips made during Jay's visits. The record also contains Jay's lab results and medical history.

 SUMMARIZE Why is it important to cooperate with a doctor both during an exam and after?

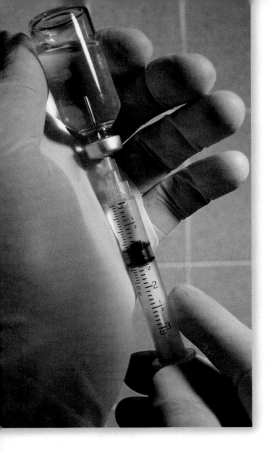

Preventing Disease

When the results from Jay's lab test came in, they showed no signs of a bacterial infection. Dr. Phillips concluded that a virus must be causing Jay's symptoms. Jay didn't need an antibiotic. He just needed to help his body fight the virus. After more rest and plenty of fluids, Jay felt much better.

To prevent some viruses from causing diseases, doctors use immunization. **Immunization** (im•yoo•nuh•ZAY•shuhn) is the giving of vaccines to people to prevent them from getting diseases. Immunization can prevent some diseases that spread easily. Before immunization was possible, most children got measles. When Jay's mom was young, measles spread through her class. However, no one in Jay's class

▲ The DTP vaccine protects against three diseases: diphtheria, tetanus, and pertussis (whooping cough). Before this vaccine was developed, many people died from diphtheria.

Immunization Schedule

Vaccine	When Needed
Hepatitis B Protects against hepatitis B virus	birth–2 months, 4 months, 6–18 months
DTP Protects against diphtheria, tetanus, and pertussis bacteria	2 months, 4 months, 6 months, 15–18 months, 4–6 years, 11–16 years (tetanus and diphtheria only); tetanus booster every 10 years
MMR Protects against measles, mumps, and rubella viruses	12–15 months, 4–6 years
HIB Protects against *Haemophilus influenza* bacteria	2 months, 4 months, (6 months), 12–15 months
IPV Protects against polio virus	2 months, 4 months, 6–18 months, 4–6 years
Pneumococcal conjugate Protects against pneumococcal bacteria	2 months, 4 months, 6 months, 12–15 months
Varicella Protects against chicken pox	12–18 months

has had measles. All the students were immunized against it. The vaccine they received is called MMR. It protects against measles, mumps, and rubella.

Jay will need a booster soon for diphtheria and tetanus. A *booster* is an extra dose of vaccine given to maintain immunity.

CAUSE AND EFFECT Throughout life, Jay will need tetanus boosters. How will they affect his immunity?

Quick Activity

Beating Polio Polio is caused by a virus that disabled and killed many children until a vaccine was developed in the 1950s. Find out how the number of people with polio has changed since the use of polio vaccines.

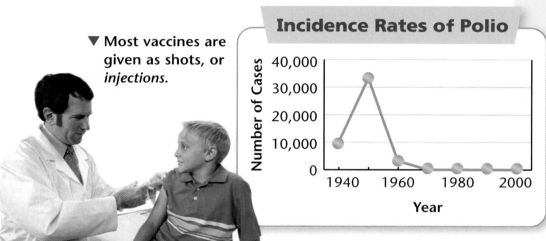

▼ Most vaccines are given as shots, or *injections*.

Incidence Rates of Polio

Number of Cases vs. Year

Lesson 4 Summary and Review

❶ Summarize with Vocabulary

Use vocabulary and other terms from this lesson to complete the statements.

Just after she was born, Serena's baby sister got a hepatitis B _____, which gave her immunity to that disease. In another few months, she will need a _____ to keep her immunity up. _____, which is the giving of vaccines, is an important part of disease prevention. Bacterial diseases can be treated with _____, but diseases caused by _____ cannot.

❷ Why does a doctor examine you even if you tell him or her your symptoms?

❸ Critical Thinking Why is it especially important to develop vaccines for diseases caused by viruses?

❹ (Focus Skill) SUMMARIZE Draw and complete this graphic organizer to show how communicable diseases can be treated or prevented.

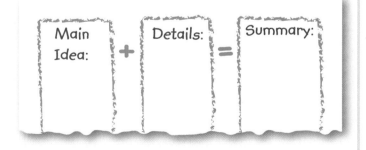

Main Idea: **+** Details: **=** Summary:

❺ Write to Inform—Description

Think about the last time you were ill. How could describing your symptoms help your doctor determine what is wrong?

209

Manage Stress
to Prevent Disease

Each of us feels stress in certain situations. Some stress can help us perform better. However, all stress feels uncomfortable, and people who feel stress over a long time are more likely to become ill. Using the steps for **Managing Stress** can help you get through a stressful situation.

On Monday, everyone in fifth grade will take a standardized reading test. On the Friday before the test, Michael starts to worry. He is nervous and upset, and he has a hard time sleeping. What should Michael do?

1 **Know what stress feels like.**

Michael's stomach hurts, and he feels jittery. He figures out that the feelings he has are due to stress.

2 **Try to determine the cause of the stress.**

Michael recognizes that he is feeling stress because he's afraid of doing badly on the test.

3 Do something that will help you relieve the feeling of stress. Talk to someone you trust about how you feel.

4 Think positively rather than negatively.

You're a good reader. You'll do fine on the test.

I'm really worried about that test on Monday.

Michael tells his mom that he's nervous about the test.

TEST 100%

Michael knows that he reads well. There's no reason to think that the test won't show that. "I can do it!" he thinks to himself. Now he can relax and sleep.

Problem Solving

A. Jocelyn has just learned that her grandfather is very ill. She is upset and worried about her grandfather.
   • Use the steps for **Managing Stress** to help Jocelyn manage her stress and deal with her grandfather's illness.

B. Rick is becoming friends with a popular group at school. He has noticed that many of those in the group smoke. He is feeling stress because he thinks they won't like him unless he smokes, too.
   • How can Rick manage his stress and show responsibility by not smoking?

Noncommunicable Diseases

Chronic and Acute Diseases

Darla has asthma. Her piano teacher has arthritis. These are two examples of noncommunicable diseases. Others include cancer, diabetes, heart disease, and epilepsy.

Many noncommunicable diseases are chronic. **Chronic** (KRAHN•ik) diseases are diseases that affect a person for a long time. But some noncommunicable and most communicable diseases are **acute**. Acute diseases don't last very long. For example, most colds are acute diseases. They usually affect a person for less than a week or two.

Doctors have discovered the causes of many noncommunicable diseases. They have learned that sometimes the causes are found in the environment. For example, too much exposure to sunlight can lead to skin cancer.

Darla's piano teacher has arthritis, which causes pain and stiffness in her joints. However, this doesn't stop her from teaching piano. ▶

WARNING: THE U. S. SURGEON GENERAL FINDS THAT SMOKING CAUSES LUNG CANCER

WARNING: The U.S. Surgeon General finds that **smoking causes lung cancer**

The sale of tobacco products to persons under age 18 is strictly prohibited by state law. If you are under 18, you could be penalized for purchasing a tobacco product; photo ID required.

▲ Why are there warning labels on tobacco vending machines?

Tobacco smoke can bring about lung cancer. Air pollution might have caused Darla's asthma.

Lifestyle choices can affect your chances of getting some noncommunicable diseases. Unhealthful habits such as using tobacco, drinking alcohol, and eating fatty foods increase your risk. So does having too much stress and getting too little exercise.

Using any form of tobacco puts you at greater risk for cancer and heart disease. Smokeless tobacco, for example, can give you cancer of the mouth. Drinking too much alcohol makes liver disease more likely.

People who overeat or eat a lot of junk food place themselves at risk for heart disease. People who get very little exercise also increase this risk.

Other factors, such as heredity, can affect your chances of getting a noncommunicable disease. Unlike lifestyle choices, you have little or no control over hereditary factors.

CAUSE AND EFFECT List three noncommunicable diseases and their possible causes.

ACTIVITY

Life Skills

Make Responsible Decisions One day a teenager offers Christa a cigarette. Use what you know about tobacco and noncommunicable diseases to help Christa decide what to say. Write a script for her to follow.

Cancer

Cancer is a noncommunicable disease that can take many forms. All forms of cancer occur when body cells that are not normal start to multiply in an uncontrolled way. In most cancers, cells clump together and form abnormal masses called tumors. However, not all cancers form tumors, and not all tumors are cancerous.

A cancerous tumor can kill normal cells around it and can damage healthy body tissues. Cancer can spread from one part of the body to another. The symptoms of cancer vary. Skin cancer can cause sores that don't heal. Lung cancer can cause a cough that doesn't go away.

The sooner a cancer is found, the greater the chances that it can be removed or treated. By learning the warning signs of cancer, you might be able to detect cancer in yourself or in someone else. (The disease occurs much more often in adults than in children.) Cancer can be detected earlier and treated more quickly through regular checkups by a doctor.

COMPARE AND CONTRAST
How are different forms of cancer alike and different?

Eight Warning Signs of Possible Childhood Cancer

❶ **C**ontinued, unexpected weight loss

❷ **H**eadaches with vomiting in the morning

❸ **I**ncreased swelling or persistent pain in bones or joints, sometimes accompanied by limping

❹ **L**ump or mass in abdomen, neck, or elsewhere

❺ **D**evelopment of a whitish appearance in the pupil of the eye or a sudden change in vision

❻ **R**ecurrent fevers not due to infections

❼ **E**xcessive bruising or bleeding (often sudden)

❽ **N**oticeable paleness or prolonged tiredness

From the Physician Oncology Education Program, Texas Medical Association

Many people with cancer lead active lives. Bill has leukemia (loo•KEE•mee•uh), a cancer of the white blood cells. ▶

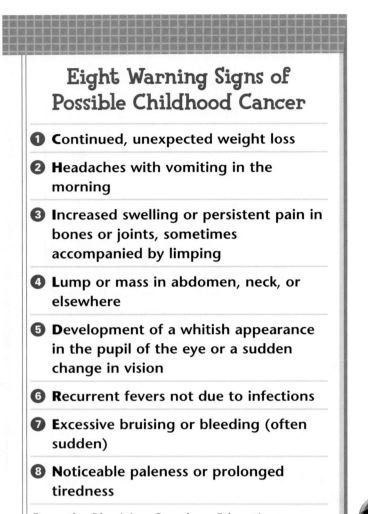

Diabetes

Diabetes is a disease in which body cells don't get the sugar they need for energy. There are two types of diabetes. In people with Type 1 diabetes, the body doesn't make enough **insulin** (IN•suh•lin), a hormone that helps body cells take sugar from the blood. In people with Type 2 diabetes, insulin does not work as it should. Over time, the body gradually loses the ability to use insulin.

When people have diabetes, their body cells get too little sugar. Body cells "starve." This causes the people to feel weak and tired. Because sugar cannot enter body cells, it stays in the blood. The high level of blood sugar can cause a number of health problems, such as blindness, poor blood circulation, and frequent infections.

With proper treatment, people can manage diabetes. They must follow a balanced diet, control their blood sugar levels, and get regular exercise. People with Type 1 diabetes must give themselves daily shots of insulin. Type 2 diabetes can often be controlled with diet, exercise, and medicines.

DRAW CONCLUSIONS
Why must some people with diabetes take insulin?

Marcus, who has diabetes, is checking his blood sugar level. ▶

Sugar Watches Today some people with diabetes can test their blood sugar levels without drawing blood. The monitor shown below, which looks like a wristwatch, painlessly collects fluid from under the skin. Sensor pads measure sugar levels in the fluid and show them on the dial.

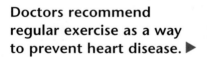
Heart Disease

Heart disease is a leading cause of death in the United States. One of the most common forms of heart disease is blocked arteries. People with this condition have fatty substances lining their arteries and blocking the flow of blood. If the flow to part of the heart muscle is completely cut off, a heart attack occurs.

Blocked arteries usually get worse over time. However, the advance of the condition can be slowed with medicine. Lifestyle choices, such as eating a low-fat diet and getting exercise, also help control the condition.

High blood pressure is another common disease of the circulatory system. If your blood pressure is too high, your heart must work harder to get blood to all your body tissues. Over time, this strains your heart and damages blood vessels. High blood pressure can usually be managed by weight control, medicine, a low-salt diet, and exercise.

 SUMMARIZE Identify and describe two forms of heart disease.

Doctors recommend regular exercise as a way to prevent heart disease. ▶

Normally, air moves freely through air passages.

During an asthma episode, muscles around air passages become tight, inflamed, and clogged with mucus. Air cannot move freely.

Asthma

Asthma is a noncommunicable disease of the respiratory system. Unlike many other chronic diseases, asthma is more common in children than in adults.

When a person with asthma coughs a lot and has trouble breathing, he or she is having an asthma episode. This is sometimes called an *asthma attack*. Some episodes are triggered by infections such as colds and bronchitis. Allergies, cold air, smoke, and air pollution can also cause asthma episodes.

The first step in treating asthma is to find out what things trigger the episodes. Those things might then be avoided. Medicines can also help. Some asthma medicines are swallowed, and some are given in shots. However, most asthma medicines are breathed in through devices called inhalers.

Students with asthma should cooperate with health-care professionals, such as the school nurse, to help manage their asthma.

CAUSE AND EFFECT **A girl in your class has an asthma episode. What could have caused it?**

Some people with chronic diseases wear medical ID bracelets or necklaces. These make it easier to get the right medical help if it is needed. ▼

Medical IDs

Epilepsy is a chronic disease of the brain. In people with epilepsy, signals between brain cells are sometimes out of control. The result is a **seizure** (SEE•zher), or sudden attack of unconsciousness or uncontrolled body movement.

People who have epilepsy can wear identification bracelets so that others can understand what is wrong during a seizure. People with certain other chronic diseases, such as asthma, diabetes, or serious allergies, may also wear medical IDs. If the people are unable to explain what might be wrong, the IDs can help explain their conditions.

DRAW CONCLUSIONS What might happen if someone with epilepsy had a seizure but was not wearing a medical ID?

This pen-shaped device contains medicine to treat severe allergic reactions. Many people with life-threatening allergies carry such devices. ▶

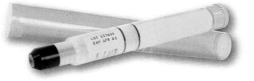

Lesson 5 Summary and Review

1 Summarize with Vocabulary

Use vocabulary and other terms from this lesson to complete the statements.

Many noncommunicable diseases are _____, which means that they cause health problems over a long time. In contrast, most communicable diseases are _____. Noncommunicable diseases include heart disease and _____. People with Type 1 diabetes inject _____ so that body cells can get sugar for energy. People with serious allergies sometimes wear _____.

2 Why is it important to find cancer early?

3 Critical Thinking Why do people with diabetes have to control what they eat?

4 (Focus Skill) SUMMARIZE Draw and complete this graphic organizer to show how noncommunicable diseases can be controlled or prevented.

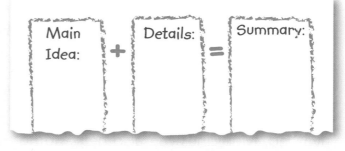

| Main Idea: | + | Details: | = | Summary: |

5 Write to Express—Letter

Write a letter to a friend with a chronic disease to show you understand the challenges of managing the disease.

Responsibility

Take Responsibility for Your Own Health

There are many ways to lower your chances of getting a disease. As you get older, it becomes more important for you to take responsibility for your wellness. Here are some tips to help you get started.

At play:

- **Warm up your muscles by stretching before you exercise. This helps get you ready for activity.**
- **Wear safety gear to keep you from getting hurt when you play sports.**
- **Make sure that the safety gear fits you properly and that you use it correctly.**

At home and at school:

- **Drink lots of water. Water is better for you than drinks containing caffeine or sugar. Most people drink too little plain water.**
- **Go to bed on time. Getting enough sleep is especially important while you're still growing. People your age need at least eight hours of sleep each night.**
- **Don't let others talk you into doing things that you believe are wrong or that can harm your health.**

Activity

Keep track of how much sleep you get each night and how many glasses of water or juice you drink during the day. Make a table that you can mark each day. At the end of the week, evaluate this table to see if you can improve your health by changing your habits.

Choosing a Healthful Lifestyle

Lesson Focus

The choices you make about food, activity, and tobacco have a major impact on your health.

Why Learn This?

By making healthful choices, you can reduce your risk of disease.

Healthful Eating and Exercise

You don't have any control over your heredity. You have only some control over your environment. But you can definitely control your lifestyle through smart and healthful choices. You can decide to eat right, exercise regularly, and not use tobacco. These choices will reduce your risk of getting many diseases.

Heart disease is more likely to affect people who eat a lot of foods that are high in fat. High-fat foods include ice cream, doughnuts, potato chips, French fries, and other foods at the top of the Food Guide Pyramid on pages 78–79. Which foods on the Food Guide Pyramid are low in fat?

Fats should be eaten only in small amounts. You don't have to completely cut them out of your diet in order to stay healthy. However, if you eat more foods from the Fats, Oils, and Sweets Group than from the Vegetable and Fruit Groups, you

◀ Have these two fifth graders made healthful food choices?

◀ Regular aerobic exercise can lower your chances of getting some diseases.

may be more likely to develop heart disease. It is important to eat the right amounts of bread, cereal, rice, and pasta, too. These foods should make up the largest part of your diet.

Regular aerobic exercise can reduce your risk of heart disease and also help you manage stress. Aerobic exercise is any activity that makes your heart pump faster, causing you to breathe deeply. Aerobic activities include swimming, cycling, jogging, and active team sports such as soccer. Aerobic exercise gives your heart muscle a workout, which makes it stronger. It also improves the flow of blood. People with high blood pressure can often lower their blood pressure through exercise and diet.

MAIN IDEA AND DETAILS **Give three reasons why you should eat a healthful diet and get regular aerobic exercise.**

Quick Activity

Analyze Foods Make a list of possible lunch foods. Then compare your list with the Food Guide Pyramid on pages 78–79. On your list, mark the foods that are lowest in fat. Draw a star next to foods that would be healthful choices.

Tobacco Use Harms Your Health

Using tobacco can cause a number of chronic diseases. It can cause lung, throat, and mouth cancer and heart disease. These diseases are the leading causes of death in the United States today. In spite of this, people still use tobacco. Why? Some use tobacco because they think it makes them look grown-up. Others want to fit in. Many people cannot stop—they have become addicted to tobacco.

It's easy to prevent tobacco from harming you. All you have to do is avoid tobacco and tobacco smoke. Refuse to use tobacco if it is offered to you. Using tobacco is a bad health habit and should be avoided.

CAUSE AND EFFECT What effects can smoking tobacco have on someone later in life?

Lesson 6 Summary and Review

1 Summarize with Vocabulary

Use terms from this lesson to complete the statements.

One factor that affects chances of getting a noncommunicable disease is _____, the passing of characteristics from parents to children. Your _____ plays a major role in whether you develop diseases. Eating low-_____ foods, getting regular _____ exercise, and not using _____ can decrease your risk of getting many chronic diseases.

2 What is aerobic exercise? Give examples.

3 Critical Thinking Explain why people who use tobacco are more likely to die at a younger age than people who don't.

4 SUMMARIZE Draw and complete this graphic organizer to show important parts of a healthful lifestyle.

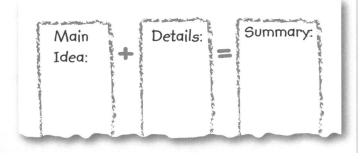

Main Idea: + Details: = Summary:

5 Write to Express—Idea

Suppose you have a friend who smokes cigarettes. Write an e-mail to your friend, warning about the dangers of using tobacco. Try to convince him or her that smoking is not cool. Use facts.

ACTIVITIES

Social Studies

Research Sanitation and Health
Florence Nightingale was a British nurse who lived in the nineteenth century. She is best known for her role in slowing the spread of communicable diseases by making hospitals more sanitary. Research Florence Nightingale's work during the Crimean War, which began in 1854. How did her work affect wounded soldiers?

Science

List Touched Objects You know that communicable diseases spread from person to person. This can happen by touching objects that were touched by a person with a communicable disease. Make a list of classroom objects you touched today that may have been touched by a classmate. What does this information tell you about how quickly diseases can be spread?

Technology Project

Use a computer to make a brochure that tells people how to keep their hearts healthy. Share your brochure with your family, and offer a copy to your school library. If a computer is not available, use construction paper and colored pencils or markers.

 For more activities, visit The Learning Site.
www.harcourtschool.com/health

Home & Community

Show Food Preparation Rules With a partner, make a poster about preparing food in a school cafeteria or at home. Show rules for preventing the spread of disease during food preparation. Decide where to display the poster in your home or community.

Career Link

Physician Assistant Physician assistants work closely with doctors. They help relieve the work of busy doctors by treating patients who have minor or chronic health problems. Suppose you are a physician assistant. One of your patients is a young boy with Type 1 diabetes. What should you ask his parents about his diet?

Reading Skill

SUMMARIZE

Draw and then use this graphic organizer to answer questions 1–3.

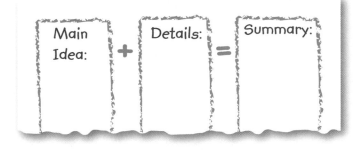

1 What causes communicable diseases?

2 What can cause a child to get a noncommunicable disease such as sickle cell anemia?

3 What kinds of choices help determine your risk for chronic diseases?

Use Vocabulary

Use a term from this chapter to complete each sentence.

4 The _____ is the body system that fights disease.

5 _____ are the pathogens that cause colds.

6 _____ is a hormone that helps body cells get sugar from the blood.

7 _____ are medicines that kill bacteria.

8 If pathogens have multiplied quickly in the body, _____ has occurred.

9 The condition in which antibodies protect a person from a disease is called _____.

10 Diseases that don't last long are _____.

11 The organisms that cause diseases such as amebic dysentery are _____.

Check Understanding

Choose the letter of the correct answer.

12 This boy and his mom look very much alike because of _____. (p. 191)
A resemblance **C** heredity
B lifestyle **D** transmission

13 Which disease occurs when body cells multiply out of control? (p. 214)
F asthma **H** heart disease
G diabetes **J** cancer

14 Your body's natural ability to fight off disease on its own is called _____. (p. 204)
A antibiotic **C** defense
B resistance **D** immunity

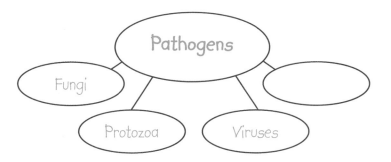

15 Which kind of pathogen is missing from the graphic organizer? (p. 196)
F bacteria
G vaccines
H *Giardia*
J antibodies

16 Which are the tiny hairlike structures that push trapped pathogens toward a body opening? (p. 201)

A antibodies   C cilia

B white blood cells   D saliva

17 An extra dose, or a _____ , of a vaccine is given to maintain immunity. (p. 209)

F shot

G injection

H booster

J antibiotic

18 Which of these body defenses is a thick, sticky substance that traps pathogens? (pp. 200–201)

A mucus

B sweat

C tears

D urine

19 If you are trying to eat a healthful diet, which of these foods will you eat **LEAST** often? (pp. 220–221)

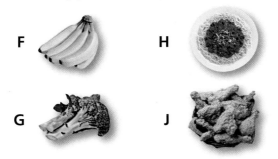

F   H

G   J

20 The special care you get when you are ill is called medical _____. (pp. 206–207)

A vaccination

B stress

C treatment

D heredity

21 Ana's younger brothers often share licks from their ice-cream cones. What can Ana tell her brothers to make them understand that each boy should eat his own ice cream?

22 Juan wonders if he is more likely than the average person to get diabetes. What is one thing he could find out to help him answer his question?

23 **LIFE SKILLS**
Manage Stress Tests make Dante feel jittery, so he puts off studying until the last minute. What would be a better way for Dante to manage the stress of tests?

24 **BUILDING GOOD CHARACTER**
Responsibility You have just switched doctors, and your new doctor doesn't have your medical records. You think you might be due for a tetanus booster shot, but your new doctor hasn't mentioned it. What should you do?

25 **Write to Entertain—Poem** Write a funny and informative poem to explain to a younger student how the body fights pathogens.

Legal and Illegal Drugs

Focus Skill Reading Skill

IDENTIFY CAUSE AND EFFECT An effect is what happens. A cause is the reason, or why, it happens. Use the Reading in Health Handbook on pages 372–383 and this graphic organizer to help you read the health facts in this chapter.

Identify Cause and Effect

Cause:		Effect:

Health Graph

INTERPRET DATA Anabolic steroids are prescription medicines, but some people abuse them—that is, they use them for a purpose other than what was intended. About what percentage of high school students have used anabolic steroids?

Illegal Drug Use by High School Students

Percent of Students Who Have Used Drug

35
30
25
20
15
10
5
0

Marijuana   Cocaine   Inhalants   Anabolic Steroids

Illegal Drugs

Daily Physical Activity

Staying away from illegal drugs is a good way to stay healthy. So is getting some physical activity every day.

Be Active!
Use the selection, Track 8, **Jumping and Pumping**, to make your body feel better.

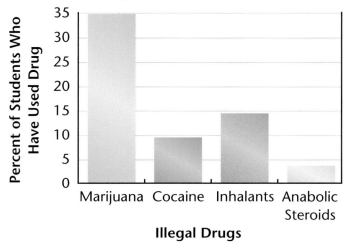

How Medicines Help the Body

Drugs and Medicines

Everyone becomes ill or gets hurt. Harmful bacteria in food can give you an upset stomach. An allergy can make you sneeze, and a scraped knee can be painful. Sometimes a medicine, which is a kind of drug, can help you feel better or heal you more quickly, but only if it is used the right way.

A **drug** is a substance, other than food, that affects the way your body or mind works. A **medicine** is a drug used to prevent, treat, or cure an illness. Illegal drugs, such as cocaine and marijuana, also cause changes in the body. But unlike medicines, illegal drugs cause changes that do not improve your health. Illegal drugs are harmful to use and can even be deadly.

Many medicines come from plants like these that live in rain forests. ▶

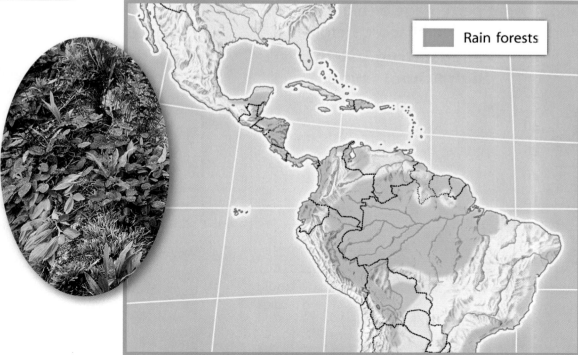

Rain forests

228

▲ Some rainforest plants have been used to treat illnesses for many years.

▼ Today, many medicines are made in laboratories.

Different medicines improve health in different ways. Vaccines help prevent diseases such as polio, measles, and chicken pox. Antibiotics kill organisms that cause infections, such as strep throat. Pain relievers help reduce aches and pains. Some people take medicines to control health problems such as allergies, asthma, diabetes, and high blood pressure.

Scientists working for drug companies are always developing new, more effective medicines. They make many new medicines in laboratories by using chemicals. They also find new medicines in plants, animals, and minerals. Before a new medicine can be sold, however, the government must approve it. Scientists who work for the government test every new medicine to make sure it is safe and effective. It often takes years of testing before a new medicine can be sold.

Focus Skill **CAUSE AND EFFECT** **What effect does an antibiotic have on an infection, like strep throat?**

Health & Technology

Laboratory Drugs

When scientists find useful new drugs in plants, they then usually try to make the drugs in a lab. It's often easier to do that than to grow large numbers of the plants that the drugs came from. Laboratory-made drugs are also safer than natural drugs. For example, different soils and weather conditions can change the chemicals in plants. Drugs made in labs are always the same.

Prescription Medicines

Suppose you go to the doctor about a sore throat. The doctor examines you, decides what's wrong, and prescribes a medicine. Following the doctor's orders, a pharmacy prepares a prescription medicine for you.

Prescription medicines are medicines that can be bought only with a doctor's order. They are strong and can be harmful if not used correctly. That's why you should always have a parent or other trusted adult give you any prescription medicine.

A doctor considers many things before writing a prescription. These include the patient's symptoms, age, weight, other medicines being taken, and any allergies.

Your doctor writes your prescription for you only. It's dangerous to take a medicine prescribed for someone else, even if both of you have the same health problem.

SUMMARIZE Why is it important to take medicines prescribed for you only?

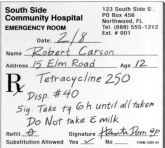

South Side
Community Hospital
EMERGENCY ROOM

123 South Side St.
PO Box 456
Northwood, FL
Tel. (888) 555-1212
Ext. # 001

Date: 2/8
Name Robert Carson
Address 15 Elm Road   Age 12
℞ Tetracycline 250
    Disp. #40
    Sig. Take tq 6h until all taken
    Do Not take c̄ milk
Refill 0   Signature Harold Dom QP
Substitution Allowed   Yes ✓   No ____   FORM 2083-84

A prescription medicine has a label that may also have special directions, such as "Take with food" or "Do not take with other medicines." ▼

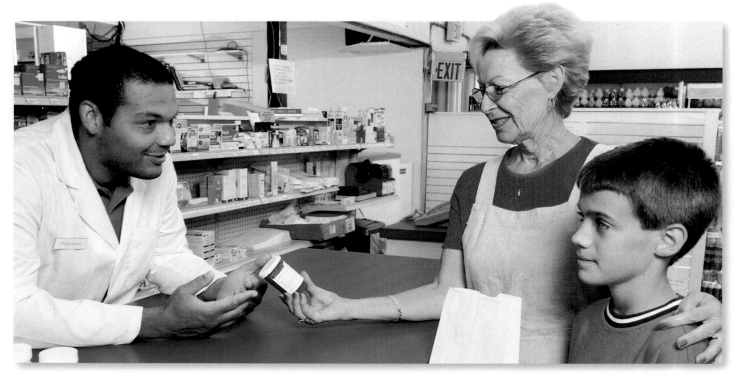

Pharmacies and supermarkets sell many OTC medicines, such as pain relievers, nasal sprays, eye drops, cough syrups, and acne creams.

Over-the-Counter Medicines

If you have a slight headache, you probably don't need to see a doctor. Instead, your parent can give you an over-the-counter pain reliever. **Over-the-counter (OTC) medicines** are medicines that can be bought without prescriptions. OTC medicines usually treat minor health problems. They are for short-term use. Some cough medicines, nasal sprays, and pain relievers are OTC medicines.

Like prescription medicines, OTC medicines can be harmful if not used correctly. That's why it's important to always have a parent or other trusted adult help you with an OTC medicine.

The label on an OTC medicine tells what the medicine treats and how it should be taken. The label also tells the length of time to take the medicine. In addition, it lists warnings for people who should not take the medicine. For example, an aspirin label might say, "Children and teens should not use this medicine for flu symptoms."

COMPARE AND CONTRAST What are the similarities and differences between prescription medicines and OTC medicines?

Did You Know?

Hundreds of OTC medicines were once prescription medicines. After a prescription medicine has been used safely for many years, the government may reclassify it as an OTC medicine.

Myth and Fact

Myth: All medicines made with "natural" ingredients are safe.

Fact: "Natural" does not always mean "safe." Always consult a doctor before using natural medicines. For example, ephedra, or ma huang, is a dangerous herbal drug that can cause heart attacks and strokes.

How Medicines Affect the Body

Medicines come in many forms. Some are creams rubbed on the skin. Others are drops placed in the eyes, ears, or nose. Most medicines are pills or liquids that are swallowed. From the small intestine, a medicine enters the bloodstream and is carried to all parts of the body.

Different medicines have different side effects. **Side effects** are unwanted effects of a medicine. For example, an allergy medicine might make you sleepy. Most side effects are not serious. But if you ever feel strange after taking a medicine, tell a parent or other trusted adult right away.

You should also avoid taking two or more different medicines at the same time without your doctor's directions. This can cause side effects that are different from those listed on either medicine's label. These effects can be very dangerous. That's why it's important for your parent to ask your doctor or pharmacist before giving you more than one medicine at a time.

SEQUENCE After you swallow a pill, how does the medicine reach different parts of your body?

232

Drug Facts

Active ingredients
(in each 5 mL teaspoonful)   Purpose

Acetaminophen,
USP 160 mg ....Pain reliever/fever reducer
Dextromethorphan HBr,
USP 7.5 mg...............Cough suppressant
Pseudoephedrine HCl,
USP 15 mg.............Nasal decongestant

Uses temporarily relieves:
■ nasal congestion
■ cough
                    ■ sore throat   ■ fever
                    ■ minor aches and pains

Warnings
Alcohol warning: If you consume 3 or more
alcoholic drinks every day, ask your doctor
whether you should take acetaminophen or
other pain relievers/fever reducers.
Acetaminophen may cause liver damage.
Do not use
■ if you are now taking a prescription monoamine
oxidase inhibitor (MAOI) (certain drugs for
depression, psychiatric or emotional conditions,
or Parkinson's disease), or for 2 weeks after
stopping the MAOI drug. If you do not know if
your prescription drug contains an MAOI, ask a
doctor or pharmacist before taking this product.
Ask a doctor before use if you have
■ heart disease   ■ diabetes
■ been placed on a sodium-restricted diet
■ high blood pressure   ■ thyroid disease
■ trouble urinating due to an enlarged prostate gland
■ cough that occurs with too much phlegm (mucus)
■ chronic cough that lasts such as occurs with
smoking, asthma or emphysema
**When using this product do not use more
than directed.**
Stop use and ask a doctor if
■ new symptoms occur
■ nervous, dizzy or sleepless
■ you get nervous, dizzy or sleepless
■ fever gets worse or lasts more than 3 days
■ pain gets worse or lasts more than 7 days
■ symptoms do not get better within 7 days,
cough lasts more than 7 days, comes back, or
■ cough with rash or headache that lasts. A persistent
cough may be a sign of a serious condition.
2 days, sore throat is severe, lasts for more than
headache, rash, nausea or followed by fever,

Quick Activity

Read Labels The OTC medicine shown here has important information printed on the side of its box. It's important to read this information before taking the medicine. Use the information on this box to write a dialogue between a pharmacist and a patient who has questions about this medicine.

Lesson 1 Summary and Review

❶ Summarize with Vocabulary

Use vocabulary from this lesson to complete these statements.

A _____ is a _____ that is used to treat an illness. Some medicines are _____ medicines, and others are _____, both of which can cause _____, such as sleepiness.

❷ What is the difference between over-the-counter medicines and prescription medicines?

❸ Critical Thinking How do medicines benefit people, and how can they harm people?

❹ **CAUSE AND EFFECT** Draw and complete this graphic organizer to show the effects of antibiotics on the body.

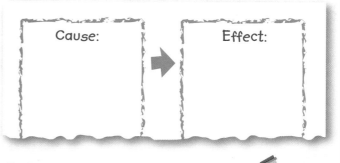

Cause: Effect:

❺ Write to Inform—Description

Write a paragraph describing some effects of helpful drugs and harmful drugs.

Medicine Use, Misuse, and Abuse

Use Medicines Safely

It's important to remember that medicines can have strong effects on your body. Always make sure you talk with a parent or other trusted adult before taking any medicine. Medicines will help you only if you use them correctly. If you take medicines incorrectly, they can harm you. To use a medicine safely, always read the directions on the label. It tells you when and how to take the medicine and when not to take it. Never use a medicine that is not labeled. You might take the wrong medicine or take it incorrectly.

It is also important to store medicines as directed. If you store them incorrectly, they might not work the way they should or they could make you ill.

Most medicines should be kept in a cool, dark place, away from moisture. Some medicines must be kept in the refrigerator. Check medicine labels for storage directions.

Never take any medicine without the direction of a parent or other trusted adult. ▶

① Patient's name
A doctor writes a prescription for one patient. The doctor considers the symptoms, age, weight, and allergies of the patient. Never take someone else's medicine or give your medicine to someone else.

② Directions
Follow the directions that come with your medicine. Be sure to take it at the right time and in the right dosage. The **dosage** is the amount of medicine to take.

③ Warnings
Pay attention to the warnings and cautions printed on the label. This can help you avoid some side effects of a medicine. It also helps ensure that the medicine is stored and given correctly.

④ Refills
This tells you if you can get more of the medicine without getting a new prescription.

⑤ Date
This is the date the prescription was filled. The label might include an **expiration date**, the last date the medicine should be used.

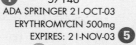

TOWN DRUG
49 HARDING RD. PHONE 555-8531 SPRINGFIELD, OH 46203
Federal law prohibits transfer of this drug to any person other than patient for whom prescribed.
① 57146 Dr. Greg Hardy
ADA SPRINGER 21-OCT-03 **③** Q: 20 ORG: 21-OCY-30
ERYTHROMYCIN 500mg **⑤** **MAY CAUSE DROWSINESS**
EXPIRES: 21-NOV-03
② DIRECTIONS: Take 1 tablet a day orally four times daily. Finish all medication
④ REFILL: NONE

To use prescription medicines safely, always read the information on the label.

You must also be careful about the foods you eat when taking some medicines. Some foods stop medicines from working. For example, some antibiotics shouldn't be taken with fruit juice. The acid in the juice reduces the ability of the antibiotics to kill bacteria.

Using medicines safely requires a great deal of care and caution. That's why it's important never to make decisions on your own about medicines. A parent or other trusted adult should always help you use medicines.

MAIN IDEA AND DETAILS **Make a list of rules you can follow to always use medicines safely.**

ACTIVITY

Life Skills
Communicate
Christina has a prescription for a new medicine. Her mother isn't sure how often Christina should take it or what side effects to expect. What could Christina's mother do to learn more about the medicine?

Medicine Misuse and Abuse

Jason's head hurts and he feels warm. He finds some aspirin in the medicine cabinet. The label says, "Relieves pain and fever." What should he do?

Jason should NOT take the aspirin. Doing so would be self-medication. **Self-medication** is deciding on your own what medicine to take. Children and teens should never take asprin unless a doctor orders it.

If Jason took the aspirin, he would also be misusing a medicine. **Medicine misuse** is taking a medicine without following the directions. The directions warn that children and teens should never take aspirin unless a doctor says it's all right. Aspirin can cause Reye's syndrome, a serious condition that can lead to brain damage and even death. Using leftover prescription medicines or taking too much of a medicine are also examples of medicine misuse.

Some people abuse medicines. **Medicine abuse** is taking medicine for some reason other than treating an illness. The medicines people abuse most are those that cause changes in the brain and nervous system. People who abuse medicines can even develop an addiction. An **addiction** is the constant need for and use of a drug, even though it is not medically necessary. People addicted to drugs sometimes feel they need the drugs, much as other people need food and sleep. Addiction is dangerous. It can lead to serious illness or death.

◀ Sometimes you don't really need medicine. Sarah has a stomachache from eating too many snacks. She thinks she needs some medicine to feel better. However, her mother has her lie down with a warm water bottle, and soon she is feeling well again. ▶

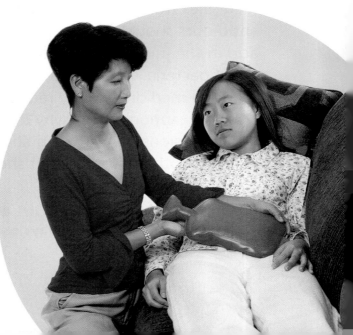

Some OTC medicines can be abused. Prescription medicines, especially those for pain, can also be abused. **Anabolic steroids** are prescription medicines that are used to treat certain health problems. But they are also abused by some people. Anabolic steroids have unpleasant and dangerous side effects. These include hair loss, irritability, depression, fatigue, severe acne, and violent behavior. Longtime use of anabolic steroids can cause liver and heart disease and kidney failure.

DRAW CONCLUSIONS Why are anabolic steroids dangerous?

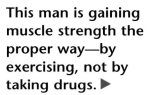

Personal Health Plan ▶

Real-Life Situation
Exercise can help you in several ways. Suppose you want to be stronger.
Real-Life Plan
Make a list of exercises you enjoy that can increase your strength.

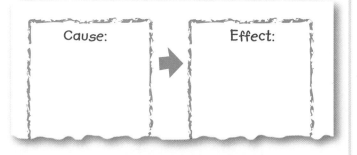

This man is gaining muscle strength the proper way—by exercising, not by taking drugs. ▶

Lesson 2 Summary and Review

1 Summarize with Vocabulary

Use vocabulary and other terms from this lesson to complete the statements.

Children and teenagers should never _____ because they can easily _____ medicine by taking the wrong _____. When a person starts using medicines for a reason other than treating an illness, he or she is _____ medicine. This can lead to _____. One commonly abused medicine is _____.

2 What are three things you can do to make sure you use medicine safely?

3 Critical Thinking What is the difference between medicine misuse and medicine abuse?

4 IDENTIFY CAUSE AND EFFECT
Draw and complete this graphic organizer to show the effects of medicine abuse and addiction.

Cause:		Effect:
	→	

5 Write to Entertain—Short Story

Write a story describing a person who has started abusing medicines. Include in your description the consequences of the abuse.

237

Illegal Drugs

Illegal Drugs Harm the Body

Lesson Focus
Illegal drugs used in any amount can harm the body.

Why Learn This?
Learning about illegal drugs and their harmful effects can help you avoid them.

Vocabulary
illegal drugs
overdose
withdrawal
inhalants

Medicines are legal drugs if they are used correctly. But some drugs should never be used. They are **illegal drugs**—drugs that are not medicines and that are against the law to sell, buy, have, or use.

People who break the law by using or selling illegal drugs may be sent to prison. But even more serious than going to prison are the harmful effects that illegal drugs have on the body. Some illegal drugs can damage the body or even kill a person. Some illegal drugs can make the heart beat so fast that the user can have a heart attack and die. They can also make blood vessels burst in the brain and cause a stroke.

Illegal drugs also have long-term effects. For example, smoking one illegal drug can lead to memory loss, asthma, and lung cancer. Sniffing another illegal drug can damage the nose, causing sores to form

One of the jobs of the United States Coast Guard is to stop illegal drugs from coming into the country. Each year, the coast guard seizes billions of dollars' worth of illegal drugs. ▼

inside. It can even break down the septum, the wall that separates the nostrils.

Long-term illegal drug users often do not eat as they should. They may become thin and weak. They are also ill more often than people who don't use drugs. Using an illegal drug during pregnancy can cause birth defects or cause the baby to be born addicted to drugs.

Using some illegal drugs can lead to *tolerance*—the need to use more and more of a drug. A user's body gets used to a drug, and the user needs more of the drug to feel the same effect as before. As tolerance increases, so does the risk of an overdose. An **overdose** is a dangerously large dose of a drug. It can cause severe illness or even death.

The use of illegal drugs has serious effects on a person's life. Users of illegal drugs often become drug addicts. Drug addicts' lives are ruled by drugs. Addicts may no longer care about school or work, family, or friends. They care only about getting more drugs. They can't stop taking drugs because their bodies need the drugs. If the drugs are taken away, the users experience withdrawal. **Withdrawal** is the painful reaction that occurs when someone suddenly stops using a drug. Symptoms can include vomiting, shaking, seeing and hearing things that aren't there, seizures, and even death. Drug addicts usually need medical help to get through withdrawal.

 CAUSE AND EFFECT What are the causes and effects of withdrawal?

Drug use and the Effect on Grades

Grades

Drug use

■ = Grades   ■ = Drug use

When a young person uses illegal drugs, his or her grades usually fall. He or she also may start to lose friends. ▶

Cocaine and Crack

Cocaine is an illegal drug made from the leaves of the coca plant. It's usually sold as a white powder and sniffed through the nose. Sometimes it's injected into a vein. *Crack* is a rocklike form of cocaine that users smoke. The term *crack* refers to the crackling sound the drug makes when someone smokes it. All forms of cocaine are extremely harmful to the body.

Cocaine affects the user just minutes after it is sniffed. It increases blood pressure and speeds up breathing and heartbeat rates, making the user think he or she is more alert or has more energy. Cocaine is so addictive that it can make the user violent. Cocaine addicts have become violent enough to hurt or even kill people to get money to buy more cocaine.

▲ Coca plants, which grow in South America, are used to make cocaine and crack.

Quick Activity

Analyze Graphs Study the graph showing the number of emergency room visits related to illegal drug use. How many more emergency room visits were caused by using cocaine than by using the other three drugs?

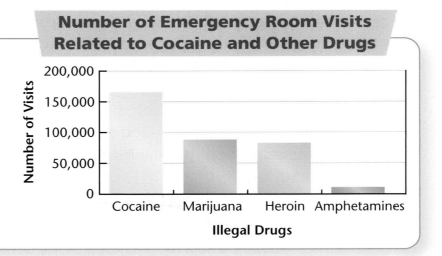

Number of Emergency Room Visits Related to Cocaine and Other Drugs

Number of Visits (y-axis): 0, 50,000, 100,000, 150,000, 200,000

Illegal Drugs (x-axis): Cocaine, Marijuana, Heroin, Amphetamines

1 People who use cocaine sometimes hear and see things that are not there. Long-term cocaine use can lead to brain damage.

2 Sniffing cocaine over a long period can destroy the inside of the nose.

3 Cocaine and crack raise blood pressure, increase heartbeat rate, and can cause a heart attack.

4 When a person takes in cocaine or crack, he or she starts to breathe more rapidly.

The body absorbs crack even faster than powdered cocaine. The user gets a sudden, intense effect in seconds. Some users report feelings of restlessness, anger, and fear. The drug's effects wear off very quickly. The user then becomes very depressed and wants more crack.

Some crack users become addicted after trying it only once. It is considered one of the most addictive illegal drugs. It is also one of the most dangerous. Even a first-time user of crack can die suddenly from a heart attack or a seizure. And it is impossible to predict who might die from a first-time use of crack.

SUMMARIZE List three reasons why using cocaine is dangerous.

241

Marijuana

Marijuana (mair·uh·WAH·nuh) is an illegal drug that comes from a tall, leafy plant with small white and yellow flowers. Marijuana is made from the crushed, dried leaves and flowering tops of the plant. Marijuana is usually smoked. Some users put it into foods and eat it. Marijuana is sometimes called grass, pot, or weed. The plant's thick, sticky resin, called *hashish* (HASH·eesh), is a powerful drug that is smoked or eaten.

Marijuana contains more than 400 substances that affect the body. Some of the chemicals affects the brain, changing the way a user sees, hears, and feels things.

Marijuana affects different people in different ways. It can even affect one person differently at different times. In general, people who smoke marijuana feel relaxed at first. They may also have a fast heartbeat and a dry mouth and feel hungry. Marijuana affects the mind in strange ways. Time may seem to move more slowly than usual or everything may seem funny for no reason. Marijuana users often do things that embarrass themselves. Sometimes marijuana causes sudden feelings of panic.

Marijuana users often find it hard to concentrate and to remember things. Marijuana disrupts nerve cells in the part of the brain that forms memories. This makes it difficult to learn and do schoolwork. Young people who smoke marijuana tend to lose interest in school and get poor grades.

Heavy marijuana use affects coordination. This makes it hard to do physical things, like playing sports and exercising.

Growing marijuana is illegal in the United States. Each year, law enforcement officers find and destroy tons of marijuana plants. People who grow the plants can be fined or jailed.

A person who has smoked marijuana has slower reflexes, making it dangerous for him or her to drive a car or even ride a bike.

Marijuana use can also damage the lungs. Marijuana smoke contains many of the same harmful chemicals found in tobacco smoke, but in larger amounts. People who use a lot of marijuana face many of the same health problems as people who smoke cigarettes. These problems include asthma, heart disease, and lung cancer. Marijuana use may also lower the body's defenses against other diseases. So, marijuana smokers tend to be ill more often than nonsmokers.

DRAW CONCLUSIONS How can smoking marijuana lead to getting hurt in an accident?

Quick Activity

Research Use the Internet to research the effects of marijuana smoke on the body. Then make a diagram of the body to show all of the effects you learned about.

Inhalants

If you look around most homes, you will find chemicals that give off fumes. In many cases, the fumes are poisonous. In fact, some chemical products have warnings that say breathing the fumes can be very harmful. Those products should be used only in places with a lot of fresh air.

As dangerous as these chemical products are, some people breathe the fumes on purpose. Chemicals that people breathe on purpose are called inhalants. **Inhalants** are common products that some people abuse by breathing their fumes. Inhalants are very addictive. Effects of breathing inhalants include nosebleeds, headaches, confusion, memory loss, nausea, and changes in heartbeat and breathing rates. Long-term use of inhalants can damage the brain, kidneys, liver, and lungs and can even cause death.

▲ Many chemicals give off fumes that are dangerous to breathe.

MAIN IDEA AND DETAILS What are some ways to avoid breathing dangerous fumes?

Lesson 3 Summary and Review

❶ Summarize with Vocabulary

Use vocabulary and other terms from this lesson to complete the statements.

_____ are chemicals whose fumes are breathed. They are particularly dangerous when used for a period of time, because people become _____ to them. When someone has a ____ for drugs, it is easier to _____ on the drugs. If drug users suddenly stop taking the drugs they are addicted to, they go through ____.

❷ Critical Thinking Analyze the short-term and long-term effects of two different illegal drugs.

❸ What are the differences between legal and illegal drugs?

❹ (Focus Skill) IDENTIFY CAUSE AND EFFECT

Draw and complete this graphic organizer to show the physical and social effects of taking illegal drugs.

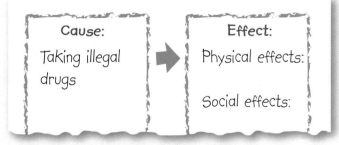

Cause: Taking illegal drugs → Effect: Physical effects: Social effects:

❺ Write to Inform—Explanation

Write an article explaining why people might try illegal drugs, and the consequences of illegal drug use.

Trustworthiness

Be Trustworthy About Not Using Drugs

People who are trustworthy are honest, tell the truth, and keep promises—and other people can trust them. Not using drugs shows your parents that you are trustworthy. Here are some tips on how to be trustworthy about not using drugs:

- **Talk with your parents about illegal drugs.**
- **Don't become friends with people who abuse medicines or who use illegal drugs.**
- **Make friends with people who respect your decision not to use illegal drugs.**
- **Play sports or develop other healthful hobbies.**
- **Avoid events that might involve using illegal drugs.**
- **Practice different ways of refusing to abuse medicines and choosing not to use illegal drugs.**
- **Tell your parents, a teacher, or other trusted adult if someone ever offers you illegal drugs.**

Activity

With a friend, role-play a conversation between a parent and a child about using illegal drugs. Plan a conversation opener. For example, as the "child," you could start by asking your friend—the "parent"—if he or she has ever known somebody who used illegal drugs. After role-playing, try a similar conversation with your mom, dad, or other trusted adult.

Staying Away from Drugs

Lesson Focus
You can avoid drugs by knowing about them and by having a plan for how to refuse them.

Why Learn This?
Knowing how to refuse drugs is an important part of staying healthy and drug-free.

Vocabulary
refuse

You Should Refuse Illegal Drugs

To **refuse** something is to say *no* to it. There are many reasons you should refuse to use illegal drugs. If you buy, sell, or use drugs or you simply have an illegal drug in your possession, you are breaking the law.

Using drugs can prevent you from doing well in school and sports. They can stop you from caring about anything except getting more drugs. Drugs can ruin your health, too. They can lead to addiction and overdose. Drugs can even kill you.

Drugs hurt not only the users but also everybody around them. Drug users often stop making positive contributions to their families, friendships, and communities. The use of illegal drugs often leads to

Some kids use drugs to "fit in." What they don't realize is that most kids never use illegal drugs. To really fit in, say *no* to drugs.

Having fun doesn't need to include using drugs.

violence and crimes. Many innocent people become victims of crimes committed by drug users.

People have many good reasons for refusing drugs. They want to stay out of jail. They want to stay in control and healthy. They want to do well in school or in sports. They don't want to disappoint or embarrass their parents or teachers. They have plans for the future, such as sports or college, and they know that drug use can ruin those plans.

Drugs can interfere with your ability to enjoy most activities. How well can you play basketball, ride a bike, read a book, enjoy an amusement park, or take photographs when your mind and body are out of control?

DRAW CONCLUSIONS **Describe how family, friends, and school influence a person's choice to refuse illegal drugs.**

Consumer Activity

Analyze Media Messages Many TV ads encourage young people to decide what is more important to them than taking drugs. Research current anti-drug campaigns on TV and other places. How effective do you think the campaigns are in helping people refuse drugs?

247

You Can Say *No*

You have the right and a responsibility to refuse drugs. Remember that drug users are the ones who are not cool. Get advice from a parent about how to avoid drugs. Make friends with other drug-free students. Plan ahead for how you will respond if someone asks you to take a drug. You don't have to give excuses, and you don't have to argue with people who want you to use illegal drugs.

Learn from a parent about the harmful effects of drugs. Remember that using drugs is illegal. Think about how drugs can ruin your relationships with your family and friends. Drugs can take over your whole life. They can make you ill and can kill you.

MAIN IDEA AND DETAILS Where can you get good information about the harmful effects of illegal drugs?

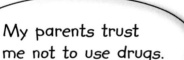

Personal Health Plan ▶

Real-Life Situation
There are a lot of different reasons to refuse to use illegal drugs.
Real-Life Plan
Make a list of reasons you would use to refuse illegal drugs.

My parents trust me not to use drugs.

It's against the law to use drugs!

Using drugs is stupid!

Drugs can make you sick.

Quick
Activity

Reasons for Saying *No*
Make a poster that shows at least one reason to avoid illegal drugs. Include an alternative to drug use, such as learning to play a musical instrument. After you make your poster, make of list of other ways you can communicate information about drugs.

What reason do you have for not using drugs?

Lesson 4 Summary and Review

1 **Summarize with Vocabulary**

Use vocabulary and other terms from this lesson to complete the statements.

"I'm going to _____ drugs because I want to stay _____ and live a long life. If I take _____, I might go to prison. I have too many plans for that. I want to go to college."

2 **Critical Thinking** List two social effects and one legal effect that might result from using drugs.

3 What are three things you can do to avoid using drugs?

4 Focus Skill **CAUSE AND EFFECT**

Draw and complete this graphic organizer to show some effects of Josh's decision about illegal drugs.

Cause:
Josh has decided not to use illegal drugs.

Effect:

5 **Write to Inform—Explanation**

Suppose you are a parent. Write a letter to your children, explaining how peer pressure can influence their views about illegal drugs.

Refuse
Illegal Drugs

At some time you may be asked if you want to use illegal drugs. You need to have your decision made and your answers ready ahead of that time. Learning several different ways to **Refuse**, such as the ones shown here, will help you stay drug-free.

George is walking home from school when he sees Ned, another student in his class. Ned waves George over and asks if he wants to smoke some marijuana. George has many different options for how to refuse Ned. Which one of the following four options would you choose?

1 **Say *no* and tell why not.**

2 **Suggest something else to do.**

When Ned offers George the marijuana, George says, "No way! My mom trusts me not to use drugs."

George says, "No thanks. Why don't we go play basketball instead?"

3 Reverse the peer pressure.

4 Just turn and walk away. You can create an opportunity for the other person to join you.

Hey! Wait up!

After Ned suggests they smoke marijuana, George shakes his head and says, "Not on your life! Only losers use drugs."

George rolls his eyes and starts to walk away. He says over his shoulder as he is leaving, "Ned, I'm going home to shoot some hoops. You can come if you want to, but you've got to get rid of those drugs first."

Problem Solving

A. Sophia's older brother uses marijuana. One day Sophia walks into the backyard and finds her brother smoking some marijuana. He offers to share it with her. Sophia does not want to use drugs.

  • Tell how Sophia can use ways to **Refuse** in this situation.

B. Craig and Bob are cleaning up Craig's father's workshop. Craig tells Bob that he often sniffs fumes from some of the chemicals in the workshop. He offers to show Bob how to do it. Bob knows that his parents trust him not to sniff chemicals.

  • Explain the most trustworthy decision for Bob to make to show that he won't disappoint his parents.

How Drug Users Can Get Help

LESSON 5

Lesson Focus

Drug users and their families can get help from sources at home, at school, and in the community.

Why Learn This?

If you or someone you know needs help to refuse drugs or to stop using drugs, it is important to know where to get help.

When Someone Needs Help

You might know someone who needs help in refusing drugs. Or you might know someone who actually may be abusing medicines or using illegal drugs. How can you help the person? To help someone who is abusing drugs, you must first know what the signs of drug abuse are. One of the signs is changes in behavior. If you know anyone who shows some of the signs listed below, he or she might have a drug problem.

COMPARE AND CONTRAST Compare and contrast normal behaviors with the signs that a person might be using drugs.

Some of the warning signs of medicine abuse or illegal drug use are listed on the notepad. If you know someone who shows some of these warning signs, you can help by telling a parent or other trusted adult. ▶

Drug Abuse Warnings

A person who displays some of the following signs may be abusing drugs.

❶ Neglects personal health.

❷ Becomes secretive.

❸ Suddenly loses weight without trying.

❹ Frequently misses school or work.

❺ Is anxious and nervous.

❻ Has trouble being responsible.

❼ Explodes in anger without reason.

❽ Often asks to borrow money.

Getting Help

There are many people who can help someone who has a problem with drugs. The drug user can talk to a parent, teacher, school nurse, or school counselor. If you are worried about a family member who may have a drug problem, talk to another adult in your family. Don't worry about getting someone in trouble. You could actually be helping a person with a drug problem.

Many communities have programs to help people who are abusing medicines or using illegal drugs. Drug users can call local drug prevention and treatment centers or community drug hotlines. The people who work there can provide information or counseling to help drug users stop abusing drugs.

Many county and state governments also have drug treatment programs. You could check with the media specialist at your school or the librarian at your local library for the names, phone numbers, and addresses of these programs.

Talk to a parent, grandparent, older brother or sister, teacher, counselor, or other trusted adult if you or someone you know has a drug problem. ▼

ACTIVITY

Building Good Character

Caring Rebecca has noticed that her friend Jennie has been showing signs of illegal drug use. She asks Jennie if she is using illegal drugs. Jennie admits that she is, and she begs Rebecca not to tell anyone. How can Rebecca act in a caring way toward Jennie?

There are several national groups that can provide information to help drug users stop abusing drugs. They include the National Clearinghouse for Alcohol and Drug Information, the National Council on Alcoholism and Drug Dependence, and Narcotics Anonymous. Your parents or another trusted adult can help you contact one of these groups for information.

DRAW CONCLUSIONS How can you help a friend or family member who is using illegal drugs to take responsibility for his or her health?

Help Line

If you or someone you know has a problem with drugs, help can be just a phone call away.

Lesson 5 Summary and Review

1 Summarize with Vocabulary

Use terms from this lesson to complete the statements.

If you are worried that a friend is using drugs, watch for _____, such as weight loss and often asking to borrow _____. You can help your friend handle the problem if you talk to a _____.

2 List three warning signs of drug use.

3 Critical Thinking Suppose you tell a parent about a family member who shows some signs of drug use. Explain how you are really helping the family member.

4 (Focus Skill) **CAUSE AND EFFECT** Draw and complete this graphic organizer to show the effects of choosing to get help for a drug problem or choosing not to get help.

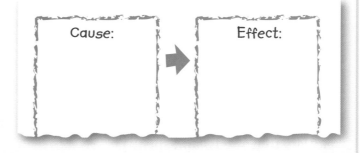

Cause: → Effect:

5 Write to Express—Business Letter

Write a letter to an organization that deals with drug problems. Request information for a friend who might be abusing drugs.

ACTIVITIES

Language Arts

To Tell or Not to Tell Work in a team of five to eight students. Write a skit about a situation in which someone you know has a drug problem. Perform the skit for your classmates.

Science

Reaction Time With a partner, explore how reaction time might be affected by drug use. Have your partner hold the top of a yardstick so that the zero mark is hanging between your open thumb and forefinger. Your partner should drop the yardstick without warning. You should try to catch it. Record the number of inches that dropped before you caught the stick. Repeat this exercise several times. What do you think might happen to a person's reactions if he or she were using drugs?

Technology Project

Use a computer to make a database containing drug information, such as the effects of drugs on the body. Present your information to your family or classmates.

For more activities, visit The Learning Site.
www.harcourtschool.com/health

Home & Community

Promote Health Ask a parent for permission to survey your family's medicine cabinet. List the names of the medicines, their uses, whether they are prescription or OTC medicines, and their side effects.

Career Link

School Resource Officer Imagine you are a school resource officer. A school resource officer is a police officer who provides information to people at schools. Make a pamphlet that can teach the students at your school about illegal drug use. Include information about how and where people can get help if they have drug problems or if they know others who do.

255

Reading Skill

IDENTIFY CAUSE AND EFFECT

Draw and then use this graphic organizer to answer questions 1 and 2.

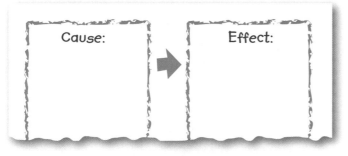

Cause: → Effect:

1 Write three effects of drug use.
2 Write three causes of addiction.

Use Vocabulary

Match each term in Column B with its meaning in Column A.

Column A	Column B
3 Chemical that changes the way the body or mind works	A drug
	B medicine abuse
4 Taking a medicine without following the directions	C medicine misuse
	D overdose
	E side effect
	F withdrawal
5 Unwanted reaction to a medicine	
6 Taking a medicine for a reason other than an illness	
7 Dangerously large dose of a drug	
8 Reaction that occurs when someone suddenly stops using a drug	

Check Understanding

Choose the letter of the correct answer.

9 Medicines you can buy without a doctor's prescription are called _____. (p. 231)
  A illegal drugs   **C** anabolic steroids
  B drugs   **D** OTC medicines

10 Illegal drugs include _____. (pp. 240–243)
  F crack
  G marijuana
  H cocaine
  J all of these

11 Which of the following gives off dangerous fumes? (p. 244)
  A paper paste   **C** soda
  B gasoline   **D** watercolor paints

12 Which information should be on a prescription medicine label? (p. 235)
  F how much of the medicine to take
  G the name of the patient
  H the number of refills left
  J all of these

13 Deciding what medicine to take without asking a doctor is _____. (p. 236)
  A self-medication
  B medicine misuse
  C medicine abuse
  D overdosing

14 Which of the following is **NOT** a warning sign of drug abuse? (p. 252)
  F missing a lot of school
  G borrowing money often
  H getting angry for no reason
  J doing well in school

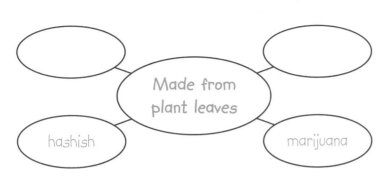

Made from plant leaves

hashish

marijuana

15 Which illegal drugs are missing in the graphic organizer? (p. 240)
  A cocaine
  B crack
  C neither A nor B
  D both A and B

16 Which drug is related to hashish? (p. 242)
  F marijuana
  G crack
  H anabolic steroids
  J cocaine

17 Which warning on a label relates to a side effect of a medicine? (p. 235)
  A Take with food.
  B May cause drowsiness.
  C Shake well.
  D No refills.

18 When do drug users begin suffering from withdrawal? (p. 239)
  F when they take too much of a drug
  G when they stop using drugs they are addicted to
  H when they have a high tolerance to a drug
  J when they start using drugs

19 Most medicines should be stored in a _____. (p. 234)
  A warm, bright place
  B place that children can get to easily
  C cool, dark place
  D bottle without a label

Think Critically

20 Why is it important to know the warning signs of drug use?

21 Why is it difficult for drug users to quit using drugs?

22 Look at this prescription label. Tell what each piece of information means and why it is on the label.

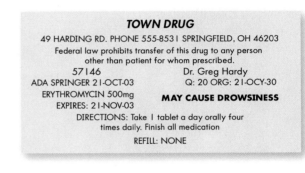

TOWN DRUG
49 HARDING RD. PHONE 555-8531 SPRINGFIELD, OH 46203
Federal law prohibits transfer of this drug to any person other than patient for whom prescribed.
57146   Dr. Greg Hardy
ADA SPRINGER 21-OCT-03   Q: 20 ORG: 21-OCY-30
ERYTHROMYCIN 500mg
EXPIRES: 21-NOV-03   **MAY CAUSE DROWSINESS**
DIRECTIONS: Take 1 tablet a day orally four times daily. Finish all medication
REFILL: NONE

Apply Skills

23 **BUILDING GOOD CHARACTER**
Trustworthiness Suppose you have a stomachache. Your parents are not at home, but you know where they keep the medicine that they take for stomach problems. Should you take the medicine? Explain what you should do to show that you are trustworthy.

24 **LIFE SKILLS**
Refuse A friend has started to use drugs. She wants you to try them, too. She says that if you're a good friend, you'll join her. Describe two ways you could say *no* to her.

Write About Health

25 **Write to Inform—Explanation** Why do people use drugs, and what are some reasons not to do so?

About Tobacco and Alcohol

Reading Skill

DRAW CONCLUSIONS Sometimes authors don't directly tell you all the information in what you read. You have to use information from a passage plus what you already know to draw a conclusion. Use the Reading in Health Handbook on pages 372–383 and this graphic organizer to help you read the health facts in this chapter.

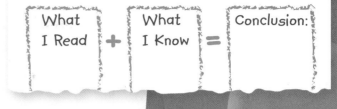

Draw Conclusions

| What I Read | + | What I Know | = | Conclusion: |

Health Graph

INTERPRET DATA The costs of smoking go far beyond the price of cigarettes. Look at the graph below. How much per year are the combined medical and social costs of smoking?

Costs of Smoking

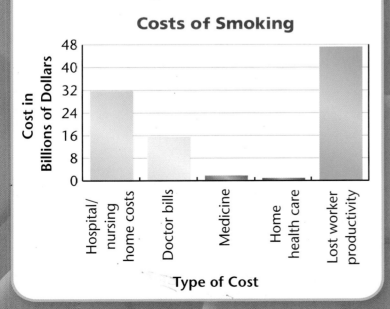

Cost in Billions of Dollars

48
40
32
24
16
8
0

Hospital/ nursing home costs | Doctor bills | Medicine | Home health care | Lost worker productivity

Type of Cost

Daily Physical Activity

You should keep alcohol and tobacco out of your life. They can harm your growing body. However, physical activity should be part of your life every day.

 Be Active!
Use the selection, Track 9, **Hop To It**, to practice some healthful activity choices.

Tobacco Affects Body Systems

Short-Term Effects of Using Tobacco

In the last fifty years, people have learned more and more about the harm tobacco does to the human body. Many people believe that tobacco will harm them only if they use it for a long time. This just isn't true. There are also many short-term effects of tobacco use.

One of the first effects of smoking tobacco is a bad smell. A smoker's hair and clothes often smell of stale cigarette smoke. A smoker's breath usually smells bad, too. Tobacco smoke makes the eyes and nose burn. People who chew tobacco have bad breath, also, and chewing tobacco turns teeth yellow or brown.

Smoking makes it hard to breathe. People who have trouble breathing have a hard time playing sports and doing other activities. There is another danger that can result from smoking. Ashes from a smoker's cigarette can fall on clothing, carpets, and furniture. Sometimes these ashes burn little holes or even start fires.

 DRAW CONCLUSIONS How can using tobacco affect a person's relationships with others?

Smoking makes people smell bad—and look bad, too. ▶

◀ This is a machine used to test the effects of smoking on various body organs.

What Tobacco Smoke Contains

Tobacco smoke contains more than 4,000 substances. More than 50 of these are linked to cancer. Substances that cause cancer are called **carcinogens** (kar•SIN•uh•juhnz).

One substance tobacco contains is nicotine. **Nicotine** (NIK•uh•teen) is a poison. In fact, in the past it was used to kill insects. Nicotine speeds up the nervous system. It also makes the blood vessels smaller. As a result, the heart must work harder to move blood through the body.

Tobacco smoke contains a poisonous gas called **carbon monoxide** (KAR•buhn muh•NAHK•syd). This gas takes the place of oxygen in the blood. A little carbon monoxide makes you tired. Too much can kill you.

Tobacco smoke also contains tar, a dark, sticky paste. When people smoke, tar coats the air passages in their lungs. The tar builds up and makes breathing difficult. In time, some smokers are not able to get enough oxygen to keep their bodies working. They may even get lung cancer, because tar is a carcinogen.

SUMMARIZE **Identify three harmful substances in tobacco smoke, and describe their effects on the body.**

▲ These lungs are black because of the tar in cigarettes. Tar causes cancer.

Information Alert!

Chemicals in Tobacco Researchers keep finding new chemicals in tobacco smoke that harm the body.

For the most up-to-date information, visit The Learning Site. www.harcourtschool.com/health

261

Long-Term Effects of Using Tobacco

The respiratory system is the body system that is harmed the most by smoking tobacco. Breathing in tobacco smoke over and over again irritates the nose, throat, trachea, and lungs. Eventually, these irritations cause smokers to cough a lot.

Smokers are much more likely to die of *chronic bronchitis* and *emphysema* than nonsmokers. Chronic bronchitis starts with a buildup of tar in the respiratory system. The buildup causes the breathing tubes leading to the lungs to produce excess mucus and to swell. This makes it hard for the person to breathe.

Emphysema destroys the tiny air sacs in the lungs. When these air sacs are destroyed, it takes longer for the lungs to do their job. People with emphysema have a hard time breathing. Often they can't

1 **Brain** Nicotine reaches the brain 10 seconds after being inhaled. Taking in nicotine leads to addiction.

3 **Esophagus** Smokers get about 80 percent of all cases of cancer of the esophagus.

5 **Circulatory System** Chemicals in tobacco smoke decrease the amount of oxygen in the blood and narrow the blood vessels. This makes the heart work harder, leading to heart diseases.

2 **Mouth** Tobacco juice damages gums, exposing the roots of the teeth. It also affects the sense of taste. Smokeless, or "spit," tobacco causes mouth, tongue, and lip cancer.

4 **Throat** Tobacco smoke irritates the throat and may cause throat cancer.

6 **Lungs** Tar collects inside the lungs, causing coughing and shortness of breath. Long-term smoking is the leading cause of cancer and other lung diseases.

This woman has to breathe through a hole in her neck because smoking caused a cancer in her throat.

▲ Using smokeless tobacco causes sores to form in the mouth. These sores often turn into cancer.

get enough oxygen to exercise or even walk short distances.

Lung cancer is the disease most people relate to smoking. Cancer destroys healthy tissues and organs. The longer a person smokes cigarettes, the more likely he or she is to get lung cancer. Smokers are also at risk of getting cancer of the mouth, esophagus, larynx, throat, and digestive system.

Heart diseases caused by smoking kill people every year. Chemicals in cigarette smoke make the heart work faster and harder. Smokers are four times more likely to die of heart disease than are nonsmokers.

Tobacco smoke also harms nonsmokers. People who are around smokers breathe **environmental tobacco smoke (ETS)**—tobacco smoke in the air. ETS has the same harmful poisons that smokers inhale. People who breathe ETS all the time can end up with lung diseases, cancer, and heart disease. They also have more allergies, asthma, and respiratory infections than people who stay in smoke-free places.

CAUSE AND EFFECT **List four possible long-term effects of using tobacco.**

Myth and Fact

Myth: **Smokeless tobacco is harmless.**

Fact: **People who use smokeless tobacco are fifty times more likely to get oral cancer than people who don't. Oral cancer is cancer of the mouth, lips, gums, tongue, or inside of the cheeks.**

Stop—Or Don't Start

Most people who use tobacco continue to do so because they can't stop. So why do people start? Some young people start using tobacco because they wonder what it's like. Others start because their friends urge them to start.

Many young people think using tobacco makes them look grown-up and cool. But the facts are that most grown-ups don't use tobacco and that cigarettes make people sick! Also, in most states a person under the age of eighteen who is caught buying tobacco can be arrested or fined.

Don't think you can smoke a cigarette once in a while or quit whenever you want. Nicotine is an addictive drug. When you smoke a cigarette, you will soon want another. People who are addicted to nicotine become nervous, depressed, and irritable if they don't use tobacco often. The best way to avoid this is to never use tobacco in the first place!

Most adults who smoke want to quit. As soon as a smoker quits, his or her body begins to heal. The chances of developing cancer, lung diseases, and heart diseases go down.

Nicotine Withdrawal and Recovery

After 12 Hours	After a Few Days	After a Few Weeks
Carbon monoxide and nicotine levels decline	Senses of smell and taste return	Heart and lungs begin to repair themselves
Person feels hungry, tired, edgy, short-tempered	Person often eats more and experiences temporary weight gain	Risk of death from disease, stroke, cancer, emphysema is reduced
Coughing increases	Mouth and tongue are dry	More healthy, productive days
	Most nicotine is gone from the body	Chances for a longer life improve

Many people need help to quit smoking. Hospitals, support groups, and health organizations are sources that offer help. Also, doctors can suggest special medicines to help smokers get over their addiction.

 DRAW CONCLUSIONS Why does taking responsibility for your own health mean not smoking?

◀ You can be cool and have fun with friends without smoking!

Lesson 1 Summary and Review

① Summarize with Vocabulary

Use vocabulary from this lesson to complete the statements.

Tobacco smoke contains cancer-causing substances, or _____, such as the sticky substance known as _____. Tobacco smoke also contains the addictive drug _____ and the poisonous gas _____. Even nonsmokers can be hurt by tobacco by way of _____.

② Describe two ways in which nicotine affects the body.

③ Critical Thinking Once a person has started using tobacco, why should he or she stop?

④ DRAW CONCLUSIONS Draw and complete this graphic organizer to show how you might arrive at the following conclusion.

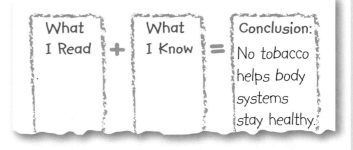

| What I Read | + | What I Know | = | Conclusion: No tobacco helps body systems stay healthy. |

⑤ Write to Inform—Description

Write a paragraph describing how to avoid tobacco products and ETS. Also describe how avoiding tobacco helps reduce health problems.

Alcohol Affects Body Systems

LESSON 2

Lesson Focus
Alcohol is a drug that can cause immediate and long-term effects.

Why Learn This?
Knowing the effects of alcohol will help you make good decisions about its use.

Vocabulary
blood alcohol level (BAL)
intoxicated
alcoholism

Short-Term Effects of Using Alcohol

You may see alcohol being served at family gatherings, in restaurants, or even in church. When used by adults in small amounts, alcohol can even have positive effects on the circulatory system. However, drinking too much alcohol can be dangerous or even deadly. Even small amounts of alcohol can harm a young person.

Alcohol is a drug. It is found in beer, wine, and liquor. Alcohol changes the way a person feels, acts, and thinks. It also changes the way the body works. How much a person is affected by alcohol depends on the person's blood alcohol level. **Blood alcohol level (BAL)** is a measure of the amount of alcohol in a person's blood. The more alcohol a person drinks, the higher the person's BAL. The higher the BAL, the more the person is affected by alcohol.

Each of these drinks contains about $\frac{1}{2}$ ounce of alcohol.

It is dangerous for someone who has been drinking a lot to drive a car! It is also illegal. An intoxicated person who drives could have his or her license taken away or even be put in jail.

Alcohol affects the parts of the brain that control speech, balance, and coordination. People who drink a lot of alcohol sometimes have trouble speaking and even standing.

Alcohol also affects the parts of the brain that control judgment, attention, and memory. Drinking a lot of alcohol causes people to make bad decisions. They may do things they would otherwise never do. They may also forget what they have done.

As alcohol builds up in a person's body, the person becomes drunk, or intoxicated. Being **intoxicated** (in•TAHK•sih•kay•tuhd) means being strongly affected by a drug. This happens to different people at different rates. A small or young person will become intoxicated faster than a large adult. Some people become loud, angry, or violent when intoxicated. Some become sleepy, sad, or silly. Others may vomit.

Alcohol slows down a person's breathing. If a person's BAL is high enough, he or she may fall asleep or become unconscious. Alcohol is a poison. Too much alcohol can kill a person.

SEQUENCE What are some of the short-term effects a person experiences as his or her BAL increases?

Did You Know?

Every year in the United States, more than 17,000 people die in car crashes linked to drinking alcohol. That's about two people killed every hour.

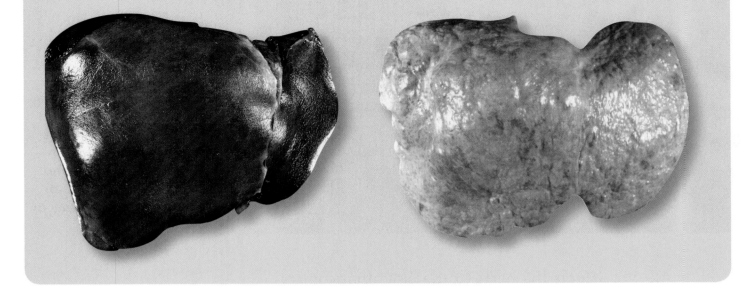

The liver cleans the blood. A healthy liver (left) is a network of smooth tissue. Over time, abusing alcohol can cause scar tissue to form in the liver (right).

Long-Term Effects of Using Alcohol

Drinking alcohol causes changes in a person's brain and body. These changes can cause the person to become addicted to alcohol.

People who start drinking alcohol at a young age become addicted more quickly than people who begin as adults. In fact, a young person can become addicted after drinking alcohol for only a few months. That's one reason why it's against the law for people under the age of twenty-one to buy alcohol.

Drinking a lot of alcohol over a long time can cause many health problems. Alcohol can damage nerve cells in the brain and other parts of the nervous system. This can make it hard for people to remember things or to think clearly.

Drinking alcohol for a long time can also cause damage to the liver, an important organ that cleans the blood of certain wastes. Liver damage due to alcohol or other drugs is called *cirrhosis*.

Myth and Fact

Myth: Alcohol hurts only the people who drink it.
Fact: Each year thousands of nondrinkers are killed in alcohol-related violence or car crashes.

Alcohol keeps some people from feeling hungry. So a person who drinks a lot of alcohol may not eat enough. As a result, the body may not get the nutrients it needs. This makes the body less fit and less able to protect itself from disease.

MAIN IDEA AND DETAILS Describe how alcohol affects the body.

1 **Brain** Alcohol slows nerve activity that controls speech, motor skills, judgment, thinking, and memory. Alcohol makes the blood vessels in the brain expand, causing headaches. Long-term alcohol use can cause permanent brain damage.

2 **Mouth** Alcohol numbs and irritates a drinker's mouth and esophagus. Long-term use of alcohol can cause cancer of the mouth.

3 **Heart** Alcohol makes the heart beat faster. It also causes blood pressure to rise. Heavy drinking can cause lasting high blood pressure.

4 **Stomach** Alcohol causes the stomach to secrete juices for digestion. If there is no food in the stomach, these juices irritate the stomach, causing small sores, called *ulcers,* to form.

5 **Liver** The poisons in alcohol collect in the liver and form blisters. Over time these blisters form scar tissue that keeps the liver from cleaning the blood. Eventually the liver stops working.

269

▲ Alcohol use causes more car-crash deaths than any other factor.

Other Problems Caused by Alcohol

Health effects are not the only risks connected to alcohol use. Remember that alcohol affects the brain in many ways. Intoxicated people may say hurtful things, take foolish risks, and damage property. They may also injure or kill themselves and others. Thousands are killed in car crashes each year because of people who think they can drive safely after drinking.

People who can't stop drinking have a disease called alcoholism. **Alcoholism** (AL•kuh•hawl•iz•uhm) is an addiction to alcohol. People who suffer from alcoholism are *alcoholics*

Quick Activity

Analyze Data Look at the bar graph at the right. What percent of car-crash deaths are related to alcohol use?

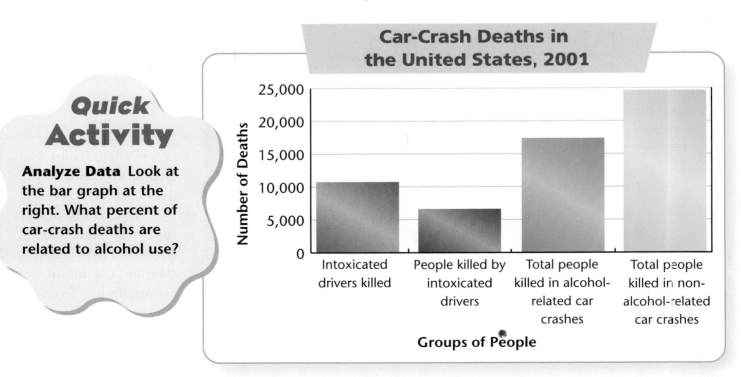

Car-Crash Deaths in the United States, 2001

Number of Deaths (y-axis): 0, 5,000, 10,000, 15,000, 20,000, 25,000

Groups of People (x-axis):
- Intoxicated drivers killed
- People killed by intoxicated drivers
- Total people killed in alcohol-related car crashes
- Total people killed in non-alcohol-related car crashes

270

(al•kuh•HAWL•iks). Alcoholism can affect people of any age, any race, and either gender.

Many alcoholics want to stop drinking. When they try to stop, though, they go through withdrawal. Recall from Chapter 8 that withdrawal is the physical and emotional changes addicts go through when they stop using an addictive drug.

Withdrawal is different for different people. Some sweat a lot or become very confused. Some see or hear things that aren't there. Some get severe headaches or feel sick to the stomach. Others get nervous and are unable to sleep. Nearly all alcoholics in withdrawal want to drink to feel better.

Trained health-care workers at hospitals and treatment centers can help alcoholics going through withdrawal. The workers can offer counseling and medicine to lessen the effects of withdrawal.

Going through withdrawal is not the end for an alcoholic. He or she may still need help for months or years to keep away from alcohol. Most alcoholics can't stop drinking by themselves. They need help from doctors or from organizations that understand alcoholism and know how to treat it.

COMPARE AND CONTRAST **Compare and contrast the health risks of an alcohol user with the health risks of a non-user.**

ACTIVITY

Building Good Character

Trustworthiness You trust people not to use alcohol or other drugs while they are working. For example, a school-bus driver should never drink alcohol before going to work. Name other jobs that require workers to be trustworthy about not using alcohol while they are working.

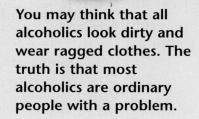

You may think that all alcoholics look dirty and wear ragged clothes. The truth is that most alcoholics are ordinary people with a problem.

Alcohol Affects Others, Too

Alcoholism doesn't affect just the alcoholic. It causes problems for the alcoholic's family and friends, too. Alcoholics may not always notice others. Their moods may go up and down a great deal, depending on how much they have been drinking. They buy alcohol with money that should be used for family needs. Family members get used to being treated badly. They adjust their lives around the alcoholic's behavior. They lose their sense of worth. Al-Anon is an organization that sponsors support groups for people close to an alcoholic. Alateen support groups are for teens and younger children who have an alcoholic friend or relative.

SUMMARIZE List two programs of support groups for family members of alcoholics.

◄ Alateen offers support groups in most communities. Find out where Alateen groups meet in your community.

Lesson 2 Summary and Review

❶ Summarize with Vocabulary

Use vocabulary and other terms from this lesson to complete the statements.

When a person drinks a lot of _____, he or she can become _____ and have a high _____. A person who continues to drink too much alcohol can become a(n) _____.

❷ Critical Thinking How is a person's blood alcohol level (BAL) affected by the number of drinks he or she has had?

❸ Make a table showing times or places in which you might be offered alcohol. For each situation, list a reason not to drink.

❹ (Focus Skill) DRAW CONCLUSIONS Draw and complete this graphic organizer to show how you might arrive at the following conclusion.

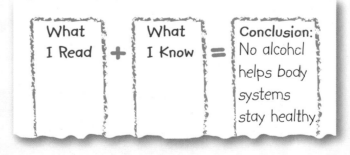

What I Read + What I Know = Conclusion: No alcohol helps body systems stay healthy.

❺ Write to Inform—How-To

Write a short how-to guide that teaches young people how to reduce health risks related to alcohol use.

Citizenship

Showing Respect for Authority

Being a good citizen means helping to keep your community safe, clean, and a good place to live. There are many ways that you can be a good citizen. One way is to show respect for people who have authority, including parents, teachers, police officers, firefighters, bus drivers, store security guards, and crossing guards. Here are some ways to show respect:

- **Always follow instructions given to you by people in authority.**
- **If you see others not following instructions given by a person in authority, tell the person about it.**
- **When you're outside and you see a person in authority, pay attention in case he or she needs to signal you to stop or come over.**
- **If you see people breaking the law, such as a young person using alcohol or tobacco, tell a parent or report it to someone in authority.**

Activity

Working with a partner, make a list of people in authority, who need respect in order to do their jobs. Then role-play some of these people as they try to enforce rules. Decide how both the authorities and the people they direct should act. Make sure everyone involved shows respect.

273

Refusing Alcohol and Tobacco

Some People Choose Not to Use Alcohol and Tobacco

Sometimes it might seem as if you have to use alcohol and tobacco to have fun. You see adults smoking and drinking in movies, videos, magazines, and TV shows. The media make the people using these drugs look glamorous, healthy, and full of energy. However, this image is *not true*. Adults who use tobacco and too much alcohol are harming their bodies. That is why most adults have chosen to avoid tobacco and large amounts of alcohol.

There are many reasons not to use alcohol. Some people find that alcohol makes them feel tense, sad, or worried. Other people are allergic to chemicals in some alcoholic drinks. People may also avoid alcohol because they regret how they act when they drink.

Young people may choose not to use alcohol because it's illegal or because of family rules. They may

Follow your family rules! This will keep you healthy and show your parents that you are trustworthy. ▶

FAMILY RULES

1. Don't Smoke
2. Don't Drink
3. Do Your Chores
4. Call if you will be late.

also want to do well in school. They know that alcohol affects their ability to think and remember. They know about the health risks linked to alcohol use, too.

Most people also choose not to use tobacco. For them it's more important to avoid the health risks, like cancer, heart disease, and respiratory diseases. They also know that using tobacco would make it harder for them to enjoy sports and other activities.

The cost of tobacco is also a concern to many people. Smokers may buy a pack or two of cigarettes a day. Users of smokeless tobacco may buy a pouch or tin every day or two. That's a lot of money to spend on things that make people ill!

Many young people don't want to get hooked on a behavior that not only costs a lot of money but also is dangerous. Young people may decide not to use tobacco because it's against the law for them. Bad breath, smelly clothes, and stained teeth may also keep them from smoking or chewing tobacco. Even friends don't want to be around people who smoke or chew.

DRAW CONCLUSIONS **How do family, school, and peers influence your choice not to use alcohol and tobacco?**

PERSONAL HEALTH PLAN ▶

Real-Life Situation
You're hanging out with your best friends, and all of you are bored. One of your friends suggests you go to her house to drink a few beers.
Real-Life Plan
Make a list of fun activities you and your friend could do that don't involve alcohol.

These students are proud of their good grades. How might using alcohol and tobacco keep them from doing well in school? ▶

275

Ways to Say *No*

1. Politely say *no*, and walk away.

2. Explain that you would rather do something else.

3. Explain that you choose not to use alcohol or tobacco because of the risks.

4. Change the subject.

5. Make a joke.

6. Express surprise that your friend would be so foolish.

7. Express disappointment that your friend would want to do something so unpleasant.

Under 18 No Tobacco

We Card

You Can Refuse Alcohol and Tobacco

At some time most young people must decide whether to use or refuse alcohol and tobacco. People your age might try to pressure you to use these products. This is called *peer pressure*. Choosing to say *no* to alcohol and tobacco is one of the most important decisions you can make. Preparing for peer pressure can help you stick to your decision to refuse.

It's important to practice ways of saying *no*. There are many ways to do it. You can simply say "No thanks" and walk away. You can explain that you would rather do something else. You can explain that you don't want to use these drugs because of their health and safety risks. You can also simply change the subject. Any way you can think of to say *no* will be better than using tobacco and alcohol!

Knowing the serious health risks of tobacco and alcohol can help you refuse them. But there are serious safety risks, too. Cigarettes are the main cause of fires

Young people who want to stay healthy say *no* to cigarettes. How can friends help each other say *no*?

in homes, hospitals, and hotels. Alcohol is a leading cause of car crashes.

One of the most important reasons to refuse alcohol and tobacco is to feel good about yourself. When you feel good about yourself, you won't want to follow the bad habits of others. You won't need alcohol or tobacco to feel grown-up.

You can also avoid places where you know there will be drinking or smoking. Parties where there are no responsible adults are often places where young people feel they can get away with drinking or smoking. You can also protect yourself by making friends with young people who don't drink or smoke.

MAIN IDEA AND DETAILS **Identify ways to resist peer pressure to use alcohol and tobacco.**

ACTIVITY

Life Skills

Communicate

Colette is watching television with her older brother Jim when a beer commercial comes on. Jim says, "Hey, we have some of that in the refrigerator! Want one?" What are some ways Colette can say *no*?

Analyze Advertising Messages

Companies that make and sell tobacco and alcohol products spend a lot of money on advertising. Their ads suggest that people who use their products are rich, cool, and always have fun. They want you to think that using alcohol or tobacco products will make you popular and fun to be with.

People who see these ads should remember the harmful effects of alcohol and tobacco. These ads never show how hard it is to quit using the products. They never tell how much money the products cost. You would never know by looking at the ads that people become ill and die from using alcohol and tobacco.

Consumer Activity

Analyze Advertisements and Media Messages
Watch a TV commercial for an alcoholic beverage. Write down the ways the commercial tries to make drinking alcohol seem fun or cool. Then work with a partner to make a commercial that tells the truth about alcohol.

The style may have changed over the years, but the messages in cigarette ads are still the same—even now that we know how dangerous smoking is. ▶

DISTINCTIVE_

FATIMO
CIGARETTES

with a truly different flavor and aroma _ extra-mild FATIMO continues to grow in favor among King-Size cigarette smokers everywhere.

THE D'

YO   oothing smoke
              n of

ALITY

Ads for alcohol and tobacco often show young adults using these products. Alcohol and tobacco companies know that young people want to be like adults. These companies also know that people who start drinking and smoking have a hard time stopping.

Beer companies often show their commercials during sporting events. The commercials are designed to make people think that drinking beer is as exciting as playing sports. Cigarette companies are no longer allowed to advertise on TV. But they still get the names of their products on TV by sponsoring sporting and cultural events. When you see the names of alcohol and tobacco products or ads for them, be sure to think about what's not being shown.

SUMMARIZE List ways the media influence a person's view of alcohol and tobacco.

Health & Technology

New Forms of Media
Alcohol and tobacco companies are always finding new ways to advertise. Pop-up ads on the Internet enable these companies to reach a wide audience. These companies also sponsor major sporting events, such as baseball and football games and car races, to get their names on the uniforms, scoreboards, and cars.

Lesson 3 Summary and Review

❶ Summarize with Vocabulary

Use terms from this lesson to complete the statements.

TV, magazines, and other _____ often encourage young people to use alcohol and _____. They don't show how _____ these products are. An honest media message would encourage people to _____ rather than use alcohol and tobacco.

❷ Why do you think it's illegal for young people to buy or use tobacco and alcohol?

❸ Critical Thinking Why is it a good idea to think of reasons for refusing alcohol and tobacco before you are offered these drugs?

❹ (Focus Skill) DRAW CONCLUSIONS Draw and complete this graphic organizer to show a conclusion you might make about using alcohol and tobacco.

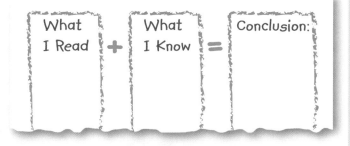

What I Read	+	What I Know	=	Conclusion:

❺ Write to Inform—How-To

Write a how-to manual that teaches young people the attitudes and skills for making responsible decisions about tobacco and alcohol.

LIFE SKILLS

Refuse
Alcohol

There will be times when you need to make decisions for yourself about alcohol and tobacco use. Learning ways to **Refuse** will help you stay healthy.

Cory and Nicki had been playing tennis together. When the game was over, they headed to Nicki's house. Nicki's parents weren't home at the time. Nicki said, "Hey, my dad bought a six-pack of beer last night. Do you want to try one?" Cory may want to drink alcohol but knows she shouldn't. Here are some ways she can say *no*.

1 **Say *no*, and tell why not.**

2 **Use humor to make your point.**

Cory can say *no* and explain why they shouldn't be drinking alcohol.

Cory can make a joke, hoping Nicki will forget about drinking.

280

3 Suggest something else to do.

Nah, let's go see that new spy movie.

Cory can suggest something else for them to do instead of drinking alcohol.

4 Just ignore what the person has said.

Did you *see* that TV show last night?

Cory can just not respond to Nicki's suggestion and can change the subject.

Problem Solving

A. Anna and Kay are looking at a magazine. They see a picture of a beautiful woman advertising cigarettes. Kay suggests that they smoke some cigarettes so they can look like the model. Anna does not want to smoke.

  • Choose and explain one way to **Refuse** in Anna's situation.

B. Dave and his older friend Chuck are camping out. As Chuck is unpacking the food, Dave notices a six-pack of beer. Dave doesn't want to drink alcohol, and he doesn't want to be around if Chuck is going to drink.

  • What are some ways Dave can get out of this situation? How can Dave show respect for his family's rules about not using alcohol?

Where Users Can Find Help

When Someone Needs Help

"I want to do it myself!" You've probably heard small children say this. Maybe you've said it, too. It expresses a natural feeling. You feel proud when you do something without any help. But everyone needs help sometimes. Asking for help when it's needed is a sign of being responsible.

Overcoming a problem with alcohol or tobacco is difficult. Most people need help with it. Fortunately, there are many kinds of help for overcoming alcohol or tobacco addiction.

How much alcohol use is too much? You may be worried about the drinking habits of someone you know. Maybe you've noticed someone drinking more alcohol now than he or she used to. Maybe you've seen someone drinking alone. In both cases, the person might need help.

Warning Signs of Problem Drinking

1 Drinking more now than in the past

2 Hiding alcohol or sneaking drinks

3 Forgetting things as a result of drinking

4 Missing school or work as a result of drinking

5 Lying about drinking

6 Needing a drink to have fun or to relax

7 Drinking alone

8 Thinking and talking about alcohol a lot

Drinking more and more alcohol can mean that the person has become an alcoholic. A person who drinks alone may be using alcohol to deal with feelings such as anger, sadness, or grief. To the person who is drinking, alcohol seems to make these feelings go away. In fact, however, alcohol will only make the feelings worse. With the right help, a person can learn to deal with his or her feelings in healthful ways.

If someone's drinking worries you, chances are that the person needs help. To know for sure, check the warning signs listed on page 282. These signs can help you know whether someone needs help.

Anyone who uses tobacco should also get help. Most people who use tobacco want to quit. They know how dangerous and expensive the habit is. But quitting is hard, especially for someone who tries to do it alone. Medicine is available now to help people quit smoking. Encouragement from family and friends helps, too.

CAUSE AND EFFECT **Describe a situation that might lead a person to drink too much alcohol.**

Quick Activity

Be a Friend The attitudes of friends can make a big difference to people who are trying to quit using tobacco. Make a list of ways you could help a person close to you who wants to stop smoking.

If somebody is trying to quit using tobacco or alcohol, you should support that person by encouraging his or her efforts. ▶

If you know somebody who has a problem with alcohol or tobacco, one of the best people to go to is a parent. ▼

Getting Help

If someone close to you has a problem with alcohol or tobacco, talk about the problem with a parent or another adult you trust. You might worry that telling someone will get the person who needs help in trouble. The truth is that people who have an alcohol or tobacco problem need help before they do more harm to themselves. Telling someone about a person's problem will let the person know that you care about him or her. It will also give you the chance to share your concerns with someone else.

Talking with someone can also help the person with the problem find other kinds of support. For example, your community may have clinics, hospitals, or community organizations that help people deal with alcohol and tobacco problems.

SUMMARIZE Describe a plan for getting help for a person who has an alcohol or tobacco problem.

Lesson 4 Summary and Review

❶ Summarize with Vocabulary

Use terms from this lesson to complete the statements.

To recognize when a person has a problem with drinking, know the _____. Some people drink because they think it will get rid of unwanted _____. They need _____ to stop drinking. If you know a problem drinker, you should talk with a (an) _____.

❷ Suppose you are looking for help for a person with an alcohol or tobacco problem. Name some people and groups in your community that you might call.

❸ Critical Thinking Why do you think some people drink when they are feeling stress?

❹ DRAW CONCLUSIONS Draw and complete this graphic organizer to show what you can conclude from the following facts.

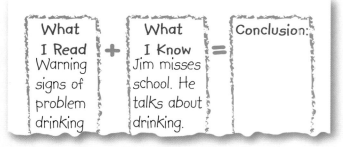

What I Read		What I Know		Conclusion:
Warning signs of problem drinking	+	Jim misses school. He talks about drinking.	=	

❺ Write to Inform—Description

Describe the importance of seeking advice from parents, teachers, or school counselors about unsafe behaviors such as using alcohol and tobacco.

ACTIVITIES

 Language Arts

Smoking Skit Write a humorous skit about why some people don't smoke cigarettes. Include several scenes so you can show the many different reasons people have for not smoking. Perform the skit for your class.

 **Science**

Effects of Alcohol Take two leaves from a living plant. Cover one leaf with water. Have your teacher or a parent cover the other leaf with clear alcohol. Keep a log of your observations of what happens to the two leaves over the next three days. At the end of the three days, try to explain some of the changes you observed.

WATER   ALCOHOL

 Technology Project

Identify at least ten local athletes who do not use tobacco. Ask them to give their top two reasons for not using tobacco. Use a spreadsheet on a computer to record your results. If you don't have a computer, use a paper spreadsheet.

 For more activities, visit **The Learning Site.** www.harcourtschool.com/health

 Home & Community

Analyze Ads Find three or more magazine ads that feature alcohol or tobacco products. Analyze them by listing the negative results of smoking or drinking that the ads don't show and by describing why the ads are misleading. Then discuss your findings with a parent.

Career Link

Magazine Editor Imagine you are the chief editor for a top-rated teen magazine. You'd like your next issue to include a two-page feature article that gives readers positive and effective tools for refusing tobacco and alcohol. The article should offer readers things they can do and things they can say. As the editor of the magazine, what other guidelines will you give the writer of this article?

Reading Skill

DRAW CONCLUSIONS

Draw and then use this graphic organizer to answer questions 1 and 2.

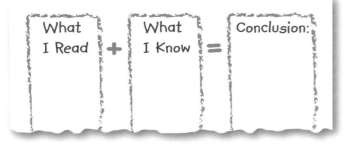

What I Read + What I Know = Conclusion:

1 Write three facts that lead to the conclusion that tobacco can be dangerous.

2 Write three facts that lead to the conclusion that alcohol can be dangerous.

Use Vocabulary

Match each term in Column B with its meaning Column A.

Column A	Column B
3 Poison that speeds up the nervous system	**A** tar
4 Sticky, dark paste in tobacco smoke	**B** environmental tobacco smoke (ETS)
5 Poisonous gas from burning tobacco	**C** intoxicated
	D carcinogens
6 Affected by alcohol	**E** carbon monoxide
7 Causes of cancer	**F** blood alcohol level (BAL)
8 A person who is addicted to alcohol	**G** nicotine
9 Amount of alcohol in the bloodstream	**H** alcoholic
10 Tobacco smoke in air	

Check Understanding

Choose the letter of the correct answer.

11 All forms of tobacco contain a poison called _____. (p. 261)

A tar
B a tumor
C carbon dioxide
D nicotine

12 The only disease below that is **NOT** a serious risk for smokers is _____. (pp. 262–263)

F cirrhosis **H** emphysema
G cancer **J** heart disease

13 Alcohol is found in all of the following products **EXCEPT** _____. (p. 266)

14 Who probably does **NOT** have a problem with alcohol? (p. 282)

F a person who hides his or her drinking
G a person who drinks only at religious celebrations
H a person who thinks about alcohol often
J a person who drinks alone

15 People who don't smoke can suffer from respiratory problems and other diseases if they breathe a lot of _____. (p. 263)

A smokeless tobacco
B environmental tobacco smoke (ETS)
C carbon dioxide
D unfiltered air

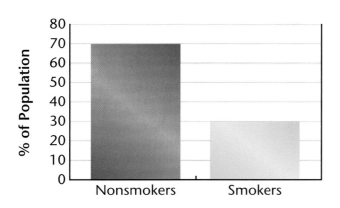

16 Look at the graph above. Which of the following statements is **TRUE** according to the data in the graph? (p. 274)

   F Most adults smoke.

   G Almost half of all adults are smokers.

   H Most adults do not smoke.

   J Most adults who smoke are able to quit.

17 Cigarette smoke contains many _____, or substances that cause cancer. (p. 261)

   A poisons

   B carcinogens

   C depressants

   D fibers

18 Carbon monoxide makes the heart work harder because it takes the place of _____ in the blood. (p. 261)

   F tars   **H** nicotine

   G air sacs   **J** oxygen

19 The _____ system is the body system **MOST** damaged by smoking tobacco. (p. 262)

   A digestive   **C** respiratory

   B circulatory   **D** nervous

20 Alcohol affects a person's _____. (pp. 267–269)

   F judgment

   G personality

   H memory

   J all of these

Think Critically

21 You overhear two adults talking. One of them says, "Alcohol is not a problem for me. I drink only a few beers each night." Review the warning signs of problem drinking. Then tell whether you agree with this person or not. Explain your answer.

22 Someone you know quit smoking two days ago. "Wow," he says, "I thought my cough was caused by smoking. But I'm coughing worse than ever now that I've quit." What would you tell him?

Apply Skills

23 **BUILDING GOOD CHARACTER**
Citizenship You arrive at a party where an adult was supposed to be in charge. However, only young people are there, and many of them have been drinking. Some of them are intoxicated and talking about going swimming. What should you do to be a good citizen?

24 **LIFE SKILLS**
Refuse You've been working hard all season because you want your team to make it to the state finals. One day a teammate takes out a pouch of chewing tobacco and offers you some. What would you do or say?

Write About Health

25 **Write to Explain—How-To** Explain what you should do if you know someone who has a problem with drinking.

Focus Skill Reading Skill

COMPARE AND CONTRAST When you compare things, you tell how they are alike. When you contrast things, you tell how they are different. Use the Reading in Health Handbook on pages 372–383 and this graphic organizer to help you read the health facts in this chapter.

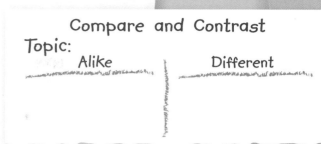

Compare and Contrast
Topic:
Alike   Different

Health Graph

INTERPRET DATA Not everyone has the same feelings in the same situation. Students in one class wrote on slips of paper how they feel about going to school. Then the students made a graph of their feelings. How many of the students have positive feelings about going to school?

Feelings About Going to School

Number of Students

12

8

4

0

Excited   Happy   Unsure   Nervous

Feeling

Daily Physical Activity

Knowing when and how to relieve stress can help keep you healthy. Getting some physical activity every day can help with stress, too.

 Be Active!
Use the selection, **Super Stess Buster**, to relax you and give your mood a boost.

LESSON 1

Your Self-Concept

Lesson Focus
Your attitude toward yourself plays a big part in how you act every day.

Why Learn This?
A healthy self-concept—a positive attitude toward yourself—helps you enjoy life and do your best.

Vocabulary

attitude
habit
self-concept

Think Positively

You probably know people who always seem to be in a good mood. These people enjoy life. They have a good **attitude**, or feeling, toward themselves and toward life in general. In this lesson you will learn ways to strengthen or develop a good attitude.

First, remember that you are in charge of your thoughts. You are a powerful person. You can use this power to make healthful choices about how you think.

Each person tends to develop a habit of thinking positively or negatively about things. A **habit** is something you do again and again without thinking about it. If you have a habit of thinking positively about yourself, you will probably have a good self-concept. If you think negatively about yourself, you may have a poor self-concept. Your **self-concept** is how you see yourself *most* of the time.

I've become a good bike rider!

290

I know how to play the saxophone.

Quick Activity

Make a List Draw yourself doing something you are good at and like to do. Then make a list that includes six positive qualities of yourself. Relate these qualities to things you do a lot.

I have a good sense of humor.

As you begin to think about yourself positively, you might find ways to help your family and friends. You might want to do your best on your homework and to get higher grades on tests!

As your self-concept becomes more positive, you might decide to try something new. Maybe you will try out for a team, for the school band, or for a school play. Maybe you will learn a new skill or take up a new hobby. You might develop the courage to make some important changes in your life. Maybe you will get more exercise or eat more healthful meals.

As you make such changes, your self-concept gets even better. You become proud of yourself. You also enjoy life and the people around you. And they, in turn, enjoy being around you.

Focus Skill **COMPARE AND CONTRAST How are a positive self-concept and a negative self-concept alike? How are they different?**

Maintain a Positive Attitude

Cars need tuneups to keep them running smoothly. A regular "tuneup" can also help you keep a positive attitude toward yourself. As part of your tuneup, ask yourself these questions:

- Am I treating my friends better than I treat myself? Do I forgive them more easily than I forgive myself? Do I stand by them but give up on myself?

Don't be your own enemy! Forgive yourself for mistakes and stand by yourself, no matter what.

- Do I remember that no one is perfect? Making mistakes does not make me a failure. If I am trying new things and learning new skills, I will make mistakes.

Don't worry about your mistakes. Mistakes are part of living. Laugh at them!

- Am I sharing my thoughts and feelings with people who care about me? These people could include my parents, other relatives, a teacher, or close friends.

Treat yourself as well as you treat your friends. ▼

You can also share your thoughts by talking to yourself. When you say out loud what is bothering you, it might be easier to identify the real problem.

- Do I remember that each person is unique, or different from others? If I am quieter or more outgoing than my friends, do I think, "This is me! I am the way I am."

When you have a positive self-concept and treat yourself well, it's easy to be unique.

CAUSE AND EFFECT What might be one effect of giving your self-concept a tuneup?

Being willing to try new things is one of the outcomes of a positive self-concept. ▶

Lesson 1 Summary and Review

1 Summarize with Vocabulary

Use vocabulary from this lesson to complete the statements.

Your _____ toward life influences how you think about yourself. A person's way of looking at life is an example of a _____. If you look at yourself in a positive way, you will develop a positive _____.

2 What shapes your self-concept?

3 Critical Thinking How can laughing at yourself help you maintain a positive self-concept?

4 (Focus Skill) **COMPARE AND CONTRAST** Draw and complete this graphic organizer to show how a student with a positive attitude and a student with a negative attitude prepare for a test.

Topic:

Alike | Different

5 Write to Express—Business Letter

Write a business letter to the owners of a company, asking them to use "real" people instead of "perfect" people in ads.

Setting Goals

Needs and Wants

We all have the same physical *needs*: shelter, food, water, air. To stay alive, we must meet these needs. We also have emotional needs, including love, security, and a place to belong and to be accepted.

For most people, physical and emotional needs are met within the family. When our physical and emotional needs are met, we feel good. We have **wellness**, a state of good health.

In addition to needs, we have *wants.* These are the things we would like to have but do not need to stay alive. For example, we *need* food, but we might *want* pizza with all the toppings.

We sometimes confuse wants with needs. We think we need something, but we really only want it. It's not wrong to want things. If our wants are important to us, we can set goals and work toward reaching them.

SUMMARIZE **How can you tell the difference between a need and a want?**

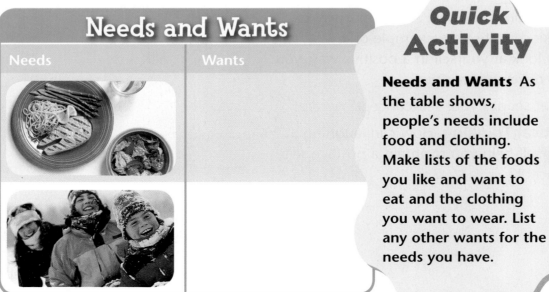

Needs and Wants

Needs	Wants

Quick Activity

Needs and Wants As the table shows, people's needs include food and clothing. Make lists of the foods you like and want to eat and the clothing you want to wear. List any other wants for the needs you have.

Set Goals

When you were younger, you probably wished for the things you wanted, such as a special present for your birthday. Now that you are older, you are more responsible for what happens in your life. You can still wish for things, but now you can set goals and try to make those wishes come true. **Goal setting** is the process of choosing goals and working toward them.

You can set goals to make many kinds of positive changes in your life, but you should choose your goals carefully. If you set a goal that is unrealistic, you may not be able to reach it. Then you might decide that setting goals is a waste of time. Your goals should be:

- realistic and within your abilities.
- important to you—things you really want to do.
- things you can do yourself, not things that depend on someone else's actions. You can ask for help, but you should be the one working toward your goals.

DRAW CONCLUSIONS **What is likely to happen if you choose a goal that's not very important to you?**

ACTIVITY

Life Skills

Set Goals Set a goal you would like to reach within one week. Make sure it's realistic, important to you, and something you can achieve by yourself. After one week, decide whether you have reached your goal.

◄ Kaley has a goal of being a member of her school's jazz group.

▲ One step toward Kaley's goal is practicing every day.

Reaching a Goal

When you say, "I'm going to finish my book report by Friday," you are setting a *short-term* goal. When you say, "I plan to be a teacher," you are setting a *long-term goal*. You don't have to set goals by yourself. You can ask parents, other family members, teachers, religious leaders, and counselors to help you.

After setting a goal, think about what you need to do to reach it. You might break down a long-term goal into several short-term goals. Write down the short-term goals you decide on, and list them in the order you will tackle them. Then set a deadline for each one. This will serve as a guide to help you reach your final goal. As you work toward your goal, check your progress. Do you need to change a short-term goal or even your final goal?

Another step toward Kaley's goal is taking trumpet lessons.

Did You Know?

Animal horns and conch shells were the world's first trumpets. The ancient Egyptians made silver and bronze trumpets with long, straight tubes. In today's American elementary and middle schools, more students are involved in music than any other activity except sports.

After you reach your goal, feel proud of yourself! Then review your experience. Did this goal turn out to be a good one for you? Will you do anything differently next time? Use what you have learned when you set your next goal.

SEQUENCE **What are the steps in goal setting?**

PersoNaL HeaLth PLaN ▶

Real-Life Situation
Getting in physical shape is a good goal to set. Suppose you want to play soccer this year.

Real-Life Plan
Choose a physical fitness goal that you think you can reach within one month. Then plan steps for meeting that goal.

◀ Kaley has reached her goal! For her it was worth all the hard work.

Lesson 2 Summary and Review

❶ Summarize with Vocabulary

Use vocabulary and other terms from this lesson to complete the statements.

You must meet your basic _____ in order to have good health, or _____. Your _____ are things you would like to have. _____ is a way to get the things you would like to have. Learning how to shoot baskets is a _____ goal. Becoming a professional athlete is a _____ goal.

❷ How can reaching short-term goals help you reach a long-term goal?

❸ Critical Thinking Why should you choose a goal that depends on your own actions and not on the actions of others?

❹ (Focus Skill) COMPARE AND CONTRAST Draw and complete this graphic organizer to show how these two goals are alike and different.

Goal 1: Win a gold medal in swimming.

Goal 2: Take 5 seconds off my best time.

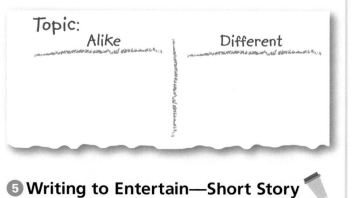

Topic:
| Alike | Different |

❺ Writing to Entertain—Short Story

Write a short story about someone who set a goal and how he or she reached it.

Friends and Feelings

Your Actions Affect Others

When you were very young, you may have learned that to have a friend, you need to be a friend. No matter how old we are, this advice still works.

We all try to treat our friends well, but sometimes we hurt their feelings. Suppose you want to walk home with a new student in class instead of your old friends. How can you avoid hurting your friends' feelings? Think about how you would feel if your friends did something without you. You might feel hurt and left out, the same way your friends might feel. By thinking ahead, you can make sure your actions and words strengthen your friendships.

Lesson Focus

To be a good friend, you must pay attention to how you affect your friends and how they affect you.

Why Learn This?

As you learn more about yourself, you will be better able to make and keep friends.

Vocabulary

aggressive
peer pressure
clique

Quick Activity

Write a Letter During class one of your friends talks out loud— trying to be the center of attention. Write a note to this friend, explaining why his or her method for getting attention is not acceptable.

Being a friend means being aware of others' feelings. ▼

Friends' actions affect us in many ways. Friends make us laugh, listen to our thoughts and feelings, and help us feel accepted. Sometimes our friends tease us or do things that make us feel angry or hurt.

When you're angry, you might feel like saying mean things or even hitting another person. Feeling this way is normal. Acting on these feelings is not. Acting in ways that can hurt other people on purpose is being **aggressive**. Aggressive words and actions can end friendships. Later in this chapter you will learn to deal with anger and other uncomfortable feelings.

Think about what you want in a friend. Do you want someone who talks a lot or someone who is a good listener? Maybe you'd like to have both kinds of friends. You certainly want friends who care about you. Knowing what makes a good friend can help you be a good friend to others.

ACTIVITY

Life Skills

Responsibility

David has lost a CD he borrowed from his friend Chandra. Role-play how he can be responsible and save this friendship.

MAIN IDEA AND DETAILS Explain the most important thing about making and keeping friends. Then describe two ways to keep friendships strong.

Friends can help each other learn new skills. ▶

▲ Peer pressure is good when friends encourage each other to do helpful things, such as washing cars.

Friends Help You

Friends are always important, but friends will become especially important as you enter your teen years. Teenagers want to be accepted by their friends and want to be part of a group. To belong to a group, teenagers may feel they must dress, act, and think like others in the group. However, if you have a strong, positive self-concept, you will make different choices when you don't agree with the rest of the group.

Teenagers who do not have a strong self-concept let friends make decisions for them. They go along with the group even when they know certain actions are wrong or harmful. They're afraid they'll be left out if they make their own decisions. These teenagers are giving in to peer pressure. **Peer pressure** is the influence a group has over the actions or decisions of group members.

Active Listening Techniques

Technique	Example
Encourage	"Good for you! What did you do next?"
Clarify	"Was your brother there, too?"
Restate	"So Jeff said he would meet you, but he didn't show up?"
Reflect	"That must have been scary."

Often, teenagers who are not sure of themselves do something because "everyone is doing it." They are afraid to disagree. They are afraid to say *no.*

On the other hand, good friends respect one another's right to have different opinions. They talk things over and listen carefully to each other.

Practice using active listening techniques to show your friends and family members that you are listening. Soon, good listening will be a habit for you. If you learn to listen respectfully, your friends and family members will be ready to listen to you!

Focus Skill **COMPARE AND CONTRAST How are expressing a different opinion and arguing alike? How are they different?**

Work is fun when you do it with a friend. ▶

Did You Know?

Friends never give up on each other—even animal friends. A family from Ohio lost its dog while vacationing in Oregon. Months later the dog arrived back in Ohio. It had traveled hundreds of miles to find its home.

Healthy and Unhealthy Relationships

▲ Being in a clique is unhealthy, because someone is always left out.

In a *healthy* relationship, friends have fun together, respect each other, help each other solve problems, and learn new things. Some relationships, like those in cliques, are *unhealthy*. A **clique** is a group that leaves other people out. People in cliques rarely make new friends.

Being *in* a clique can be just as harmful as being *left out* of a clique. For example, one clique member might pressure another member to tease a new student. If you find yourself in an unhealthy relationship, remember your positive self-concept. Say *no*!

CAUSE AND EFFECT What might cause someone to join a clique?

Lesson 3 Summary and Review

1 Summarize with Vocabulary

Use vocabulary and other terms from this lesson to complete the statements.

A friendship in which two people help each other is _____. However, a _____, which leaves others out, is _____. Some young people use _____ to get others to dress and act in certain ways. A(an) _____ person might threaten to hurt anyone who disagrees.

2 What can you say or do if you or your friends are teased by members of a clique?

3 Critical Thinking How can having a strong self-concept help you make choices that are different from those of your friends?

4 (Focus Skill) **COMPARE AND CONTRAST** Draw and complete this graphic organizer to show how a healthy relationship and an unhealthy relationship are alike and how they are different.

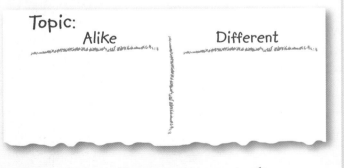

Topic:
Alike   Different

5 Writing to Entertain—Poem

Write a poem about friendship. You might write about an ideal friend, about someone who wants a new friend, or about someone who has had the same good friend for a long time.

Respect

Accept Individual Differences

Friends recognize and respect ways that they are different from each other. No two people on Earth are exactly the same. People are tall or short, pale or dark. They wear different kinds of clothes, and they eat different foods.

Different people also speak different languages, and some speak English with an accent. Some people have difficulty speaking because of a hearing loss or other reasons.

If you have difficulty understanding someone, you might repeat what you think you heard. For example, you might ask, "Did you say you forgot your homework?" If you can't understand a certain word, think of other words, related to the topic you are discussing. Then you might use those words to make sure you understand what your friend is saying.

Don't miss out on having good friends just because other people are different from you. Remember: You are also different from them! You wouldn't want them to pass you by because you are different, would you?

Activity

Some people who have a hearing loss communicate with sign language instead of spoken words. They use their hands to express their ideas. Work with a small group to learn some words and phrases in American Sign Language. Practice your signs until you can use them to communicate with other group members. Then describe some other ways to adapt class activities for people with hearing losses.

Actions, Reactions, and Stress

Your Feelings Show

Did you ever believe that if you didn't cry, no one would know you were sad? Have you ever thought that if you didn't say anything, no one would know you were scared—or angry? The truth is, your feelings show, no matter how quiet you are.

Your feelings show in your actions, which can range from smiling to shaking your head to stomping out of a room. Your feelings show in your words, too. They show in both what you say and how you say it. You might explain what is bothering you, or you might try to hide your feelings. You might speak by whispering or by shouting.

You might not realize that your feelings also show in your body language. **Body language** is the way your body expresses your feelings. Body language includes your posture and facial expressions, the clothes you choose to wear, the way you take care of yourself, and much more. Are you surprised that your body gives away your feelings?

◄ What does the body language of these three people tell you? Which person is angry, and which person is excited? Which one is not even listening?

When you fold your arms across your chest, your body language may be saying, "I won't do it, and you can't make me do it." When the teacher asks for volunteers and you stare at the floor, your body language says, "Please don't call on me!"

Sometimes our words say one thing but our body language says another. For example, did you ever tell a friend you were not angry anymore, but you stared at the wall instead of looking at him or her? Your body language was showing that you *were* still angry. You were sending your friend a "mixed message."

We communicate clearly when our words, actions, and body language all express the same thing. When we show our feelings clearly, others understand them. And people are more likely to respond in the way we want them to.

We must also express our feelings calmly and remember that others have feelings, too. If we shout in anger, people will move away from us. If we calmly explain what is wrong, without blaming or insulting anyone, others will be more willing to listen and understand.

DRAW CONCLUSIONS **Why are "mixed messages" confusing and unfair?**

Quick Activity

Show Your Feelings
Work with a partner to act out feelings. Take turns using body language to show a positive or negative feeling. See if your partner can guess which feeling you are showing.

You don't have to tell someone when you're listening. Your body language shows it. ▶

305

Manage Stress

You probably know what stress feels like. **Stress** is a feeling of tension in your body, your mind, or both. Your heart might beat faster, or your palms might get sweaty. "Butterflies" might flutter around in your stomach. Stress is your body's natural reaction to challenges.

A little stress can be helpful. Good stress can give you extra energy to play well in a game or do well on a test. However, when stress is too great or lasts too long, it can be harmful. Bad stress can harm your health and interfere with your life. Bad stress can be caused by:

- trying to do too much and leaving no time to relax.
- putting too much pressure on yourself.
- worrying about problems at home or at school.
- coping with the changes of puberty.
- keeping a problem inside instead of talking to someone.

To reduce the stress in your life, set realistic goals. Don't try to do too many things in a short time. Eating healthful foods, getting enough sleep, and getting enough exercise all help reduce stress. Be sure to allow time for fun, too.

Talk with a parent or other trusted adult about anything that's bothering you. He or she may be able to help you understand things in a way you had not thought of before.

CAUSE AND EFFECT **How can talking to a parent or another adult about a problem help you reduce stress?**

When to Get Help for Stress

If you feel any of the symptoms below, ask a parent for help.

frequent tiredness	trouble sleeping	frequent headaches
eating problems	trouble concentrating	

Lesson 4 Summary and Review

1 Summarize with Vocabulary

Use vocabulary and other terms from this lesson to complete the statements.

Our actions, words, and _____ show our feelings. When we have too much to do, we feel _____. Stress that helps you do well on a test is called _____. Stress that makes you feel sick is called _____.

2 Critical Thinking How can body language get in the way of communication?

3 What are two ways to manage stress?

4 (Focus Skill) COMPARE AND CONTRAST Draw and complete this graphic organizer to compare and contrast good stress and bad stress.

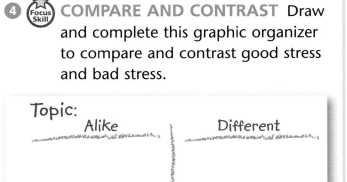

Topic:

Alike   Different

5 Writing to Inform—Narration

Write a story that tells how a fifth grader becomes stressed about something and then learns how to handle the stress.

Manage Stress
At School

Stress is part of everyday life. A little stress is OK, but too much can make you sick and unhappy. Fortunately, you can learn how to handle stress so it does not become a problem. Using the steps for **Managing Stress** can help you keep the stress in your life at a reasonable level.

Erin is starting her first day at a new school. She doesn't know anyone at the school, and she's worried about making new friends there. How can she manage the stress she's feeling?

1 **Know what stress feels like.**

2 **Try to determine the cause of the stress.**

As Erin waves goodbye to her father, her heart starts beating faster and she feels a little shaky. She knows these are symptoms of stress.

It's lunchtime, and Erin knows the cause of her stress—she's worried about fitting in. Should she sit by herself? Will others ask her to sit with them?

3 Do something that will help relieve you of stress.

Erin reduces her stress by taking a deep breath and relaxing her shoulders and other muscles.

4 Visualize yourself doing well in the stressful situation.

Erin pictures herself sitting with others from her class, talking with her new friends. After picturing that, she joins a group of students at a table.

Problem Solving

A. This morning it's Jacob's turn to present his oral book report. He enjoyed reading the book and has prepared a good report, but he feels a little sick in his stomach.

- Use the steps for **Managing Stress** to tell how Jacob can handle the stress he feels.

B. Mackenzie wants to be in the school play, but the thought of trying out for a part gives her a headache. Maybe she should forget trying to be in the play and just go see it when it's presented. No one would even know that she ever thought about trying out.

- Using what you know about stress and responsibility, explain what Mackenzie could do to handle her stress.

Resolving Conflicts

Dealing with Conflicts at School

Conflicts are struggles that result from people's differing needs and wants. It takes practice to resolve conflicts. Handling conflicts at school can be very hard. When groups of friends take sides, a conflict can quickly involve a large number of students. A problem that starts at school can become a conflict outside of school as well.

How should you deal with conflicts at school? If you find yourself too angry to talk about a problem, just walk away. Give yourself time to cool off. When you are calmer, you will be more in control. Then it will be easier to work toward a peaceful solution.

Did the soccer ball go out of bounds? These players learn how to resolve this conflict peacefully. ▶

Conflict resolution is a respectful way to solve problems. It helps people find solutions that everyone involved can accept. Using the five steps in conflict resolution can help you resolve disagreements in ways that respect each person's needs.

Conflict Resolution

1. As calmly as possible, tell what happened and how you feel about it.

2. Share your feelings without blaming or criticizing the other person.

3. Listen to the other person with an open mind. Respect his or her feelings.

4. Take responsibility for your actions. Ask what you can do to help solve the problem.

5. Find a solution that you and the other person can both accept.

ACTIVITY

Life Skills

Resolve Conflicts

You and Corey find a baseball lying on the ground. He thinks it's his ball, and you think it's yours. You both begin arguing and trying to grab the ball. Use the conflict resolution steps on this page to find a solution to this problem.

The first thing to do in conflict resolution is to stop arguing. Try to talk calmly about the problem. Allow each person to tell his or her side of the conflict without interruption. Use "I" messages, such as this one: "I feel angry because I did most of the work on our project. I had to write the whole report."

Listen respectfully to the other person's "I" message. He or she might say, "I feel angry, too, because I think I did my share. I worked hard on the map for the project, but it took a lot longer than I expected. I just didn't have enough time to finish it."

After everyone involved understands what the problem is, you can work together to find a solution. Perhaps you can help finish the map to meet the deadline for the project.

SEQUENCE **When you want to resolve a conflict, what should you do before you discuss the problem?**

Respect Cultural Differences

People from other cultures often speak different languages, celebrate different holidays, and wear various kinds of clothes. They may even look different. We should respect these differences, but sometimes they lead to conflicts.

For example, Joy wants to be friendly toward a new boy in class, so she asks him about his family. In his culture, questions about one's family are considered impolite, so he doesn't answer. Now Joy thinks the new student is unfriendly. She might even decide that all the people in his culture are unfriendly. A belief based on thinking that everyone in a certain group is the same is a **stereotype**.

Can you think of any group in which every member is exactly the same? All groups are made up of people with differences. This is why stereotypes are often incorrect and usually unfair.

Did You Know?

The word *stereotype* did not always refer to a judgment about a person or group. Long ago, printers made a mold for each letter of the alphabet. Many copies, or stereotypes, of a letter could be made from each mold. The printer put each letter in place by hand. If more stereotypes were needed for a letter, more could be made from one mold.

One result of being a nation of many cultures is the variety of delicious foods we have. ▶

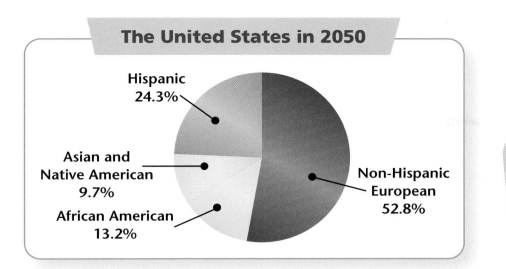

The United States in 2050

Hispanic 24.3%

Asian and Native American 9.7%

African American 13.2%

Non-Hispanic European 52.8%

Myth and Fact

Myth: The ancestors of most people in the United States came here from Europe.

Fact: By 2050 nearly half of the people will have ancestors who were not from Europe. They will have ancestors from South and Central America, Asia, Africa, India, and Pacific and Caribbean islands.

Because of Joy's misunderstanding, she may now have a prejudice against the boy's culture. A **prejudice** is an unfair negative attitude toward a whole group.

How can we avoid stereotypes and prejudice? We should look at people as individuals, too, not just as members of a group.

CAUSE AND EFFECT How can believing a stereotype lead to conflict?

Lesson 5 Summary and Review

1 Summarize with Vocabulary

Use vocabulary and other terms from this lesson to complete the sentences.

When people have different needs, they might have a _____. The steps of _____ can help them solve the problem peacefully. Expecting bad behavior from someone who belongs to a certain group is a _____. This can lead to _____ toward the entire group.

2 Critical Thinking What is a stereotype that some people have about teenagers? Why do you think this belief may be incorrect?

3 Why is it important to find a peaceful resolution to a conflict?

4 (Focus Skill) **COMPARE AND CONTRAST** Draw and complete this graphic organizer to show how a prejudice and a stereotype are alike and different.

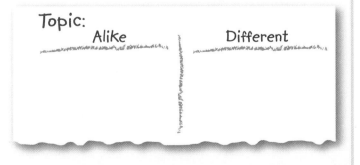

Topic:

Alike   Different

5 Write to Express— Solution to a Problem

Think of a stereotype that may cause conflicts in school. Describe this problem and suggest ways to avoid conflicts.

313

Uncomfortable Feelings

Dealing with Feelings

In this lesson, you will learn ways to deal with five uncomfortable feelings: boredom, anger, loneliness shyness, and grief. These feelings are not good or bad, right or wrong. They are simply feelings. You decide how to express them and how to deal with them.

Being in control of your feelings makes you strong and confident. Learning how to deal with your feelings is an important part of growing up.

MAIN IDEA AND DETAILS **What are some uncomfortable feelings?**

Boredom

When you are bored, you feel tired and restless. You might sit and stare into space. You might feel most bored when you are sick or when all your friends are busy.

Strategies: Exercise can help. So can finding something unusual to do by yourself or thinking of a way to help someone in your family or community. Doing something for someone else is an excellent way to fight boredom.

Anger

Anger can rage out of control, or it can stay bottled up inside you. You can be angry with other people or with yourself.

Strategies: Admit you are angry, and then calm down. Leave the situation, or count to ten. Take several deep breaths. Then express your feelings in an "I" message without blaming others or being critical. Just telling someone what is bothering you can help you feel better. If you're angry with someone, ask how he or she feels. Then listen carefully to the answer. Be ready to forgive someone who has hurt your feelings—and be ready to forgive yourself, too. If you are angry for a long time, talk to a parent.

Loneliness

Loneliness is a painful, empty feeling of isolation. It could be the result of an argument with a friend or a move to a new neighborhood. Having a negative self-concept can make loneliness seem worse. You may think that no one wants to be your friend, so there is no point in trying to find one.

Strategies: First, name your feeling. If you have argued with a friend, use the steps of conflict resolution to make peace. If you have just moved, remember that making new friends takes time. Joining an after-school activity might help you meet a new friend who shares one of your hobbies or interests. If your loneliness continues, talk to a parent or other trusted adult.

Shyness

If you are shy, you avoid talking to other people, especially in groups or in unfamiliar situations. At these times, your shyness may make you blush, give you sweaty hands, or make your heart beat faster. When you have to talk to someone new, you may end up with "butterflies" in your stomach.

Strategies: Remember that there is nothing wrong with you. Some people are naturally shy. To help overcome your shyness, ask another student how he or she feels about a situation that bothers you, such as giving an oral report. You may be surprised to learn that the same situations that bother you also bother other people!

Grief

Grief is a sad feeling that lasts for a long time. It may come after the death of a pet, a friend, or a family member or after a change in the family. You may cry often and find it hard to concentrate. Some people have trouble sleeping. You might not enjoy the things you used to.

Strategies: Grief can go on for a while, so be patient with yourself. Talking about your loss with a parent or other adult you trust can help you start to feel better. Writing about it can also help. The pain will lessen over time.

Personal Health Plan

Real-Life Situation
All people have feelings from time to time that make them uncomfortable. Suppose you have just moved to a new neighborhood.
Real-Life Plan
Write about how you feel. Make a list of ways you can deal with your feelings.

Dealing with Uncomfortable Feelings

Pretending that uncomfortable feelings do not exist will not make them go away. Instead, face those feelings and deal with them in positive ways. Change the situation if you can, or change the way you think about it. Try the tips listed below. You are in control!

SUMMARIZE Explain two or three of the most important tips in this list.

❶ Be aware of your feelings.

❷ Speak up. Ask a parent for help if the feeling lasts a long time or hurts too much.

❸ Tell a friend.

❹ Make a plan of action for changing the situation.

❺ Get some vigorous exercise.

❻ Get involved in a fun activity or group.

Lesson 6 Summary and Review

❶ Summarize with Vocabulary

Use the terms discussed in this lesson to complete the statements.

When you rage out of control, you are feeling _____. When you can't think of anything to do, you are feeling _____. When you feel sad about the death of a pet, you are feeling _____. When you can't bring yourself to speak to a new student, you are feeling _____. When you are sick in bed and wish someone would visit you, you are feeling _____.

❷ Name at least four ways to cope with anger. Explain which one works best for you.

❸ Critical Thinking How could you help someone who is feeling grief?

❹ (Focus Skill) COMPARE AND CONTRAST Draw and complete this graphic organizer to compare and contrast the feelings of shyness and loneliness.

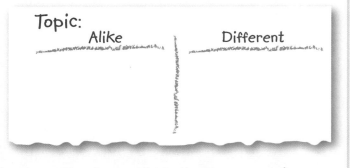

Topic:
Alike   Different

❺ Write to Inform—Explanation

Think of an uncomfortable feeling not discussed in this lesson, such as fear, or guilt. Explain what the feeling is like and some things that might cause it.

ACTIVITIES

Math

Spreading Smiles Let's say you smile at two people, and those two people each spread your smile to two more people. If those four each spread the smile to two more people, how many people are smiling?

Art

What Does a Friend Look Like? Draw a symbolic picture of an ideal friend. For example, an ideal friend might have large ears so he or she can be an excellent listener. An ideal friend might have super-strong muscles for playing basketball with you or have extra-long arms to give you big hugs when you need them. An ideal friend might have a large heart, also, to be able to forgive you if you hurt his or her feelings.

Technology Project

Laugh Graph For two days, keep a log of why you laughed while you were at school. Then make a bar graph of the results. Show how many times you laughed because you were happy and how many times you laughed because you were nervous. If you laughed for other reasons, show them, too.

 For more activities, visit **The Learning Site.**
www.harcourtschool.com/health

Home & Community

Posters for Peace Make a series of posters that will help other students at your school learn ways to resolve their conflicts peacefully. Display your posters in a hallway or the cafeteria.

Career Link

Martial Arts Instructor Imagine that you teach one of the martial arts, such as karate, kung fu, or tae kwon do. What would you teach your students about resolving conflicts? What would you tell them to do and not to do? What is the most important piece of advice you would give your students?

Reading Skill

COMPARE AND CONTRAST

Draw and then use this graphic organizer to answer questions 1 and 2.

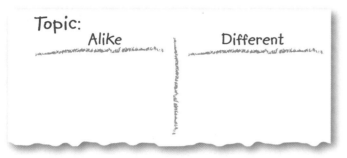

Topic:

Alike   Different

1 Write at least two ways that healthy and unhealthy relationships are alike.

2 Write at least two ways that healthy and unhealthy relationships are different.

Use Vocabulary

Match each term in Column B with its meaning in Column A.

Column A	Column B
3 A way to get what you want	**A** goal setting
4 How you see yourself	**B** clique
5 A way you show your feelings	**C** attitude
	D body language
6 A group that leaves others out	**E** self-concept
	F stereotype
7 How you feel about life	**G** prejudice
8 A belief based on thinking that everyone in a group is the same	
9 Bad feelings about people because they belong to a certain group	

Check Understanding

Choose the letter of the correct answer.

10 A state of good health is _____. (p. 294)
  A self-concept   **C** wellness
  B habit   **D** attitude

11 This boy is demonstrating one way to deal with _____. (p. 314)

one... two... three... four...

  F loneliness   **H** shyness
  G anger   **J** grief

12 Wanting to do a different project than the rest of the group is _____. (pp. 310–311)
  A prejudice   **C** a stereotype
  B a conflict   **D** body language

13 If your heart is pounding and your hands feel sweaty, you are probably experiencing _____. (pp. 308–309)
  F stress   **H** boredom
  G a habit   **J** loneliness

14 This girl's body language shows that she is _____. (pp. 304–305)

  A bored   **C** listening
  B angry   **D** prejudiced

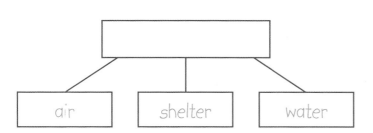

air   shelter   water

15 Which word belongs in the top box? (p. 294)

  F wants   **H** needs

  G habits   **J** goals

16 When you do something over and over, it becomes _____. (p. 290)

  A an attitude   **C** a goal

  B a habit   **D** a clique

17 An aggressive person is likely to _____. (p. 299)

  F push someone to get his or her own way

  G listen carefully to others

  H set goals that are difficult to reach

  J resolve conflicts peacefully

18 People who have a negative self-concept _____. (pp. 292–293)

  A can easily make changes in their lives

  B do not expect to meet their goals

  C can usually resist peer pressure

  D can't help how they feel

19 A so-called friend is trying to get you to steal a lunch from someone's backpack. This is an example of _____. (p. 300)

  F prejudice

  G peer pressure

  H a stereotype

  J managing stress

Think Critically

20 Audrey has set a goal of improving her grades. Explain why she should adjust her goal, and suggest one for her.

21 At lunchtime, a friend sighs and says, "I'm really having a bad day." Describe at least two ways you could use active listening to help this friend.

22 A neighbor your age wants you to take some of your uncle's cigarettes so you both can find out what smoking is like. The neighbor says, "If you're really my friend, you'll do this with me." How would you describe this relationship? What can you say to this person?

Apply Skills

23 **BUILDING GOOD CHARACTER**

  Respect A new girl at school has trouble saying certain words. You hear a student making fun of her. What can you do?

24 **LIFE SKILLS**

  Manage Stress Your science report is due tomorrow, so you go to the library to use a computer. When you get there, all five computers are being used. The library will close in an hour. You might not have time to finish your report—or even start it! Your stomach feels upset, and your hands are sweaty. How can you deal with this situation?

Write About Health

25 **Write to Inform** Explain why dealing with feelings is an important part of maintaining good health.

Supporting Your Family

Reading Skill

IDENTIFY MAIN IDEA AND DETAILS
The main idea is the most important thought in a reading passage. Details help you understand the main idea. They usually tell about *who*, *what*, *when*, *where*, *why*, and *how*. Use the Reading in Health Handbook on pages 372–383 and this graphic organizer to help you read the health facts in this chapter.

Identify Main Idea and Details

Main Idea:

Detail: Detail: Detail:

Health Graph

INTERPRET DATA In the past most American families with children had a father who worked and a mother who stayed home. Study the graph below to find out how things have changed. What trend is shown in the graph?

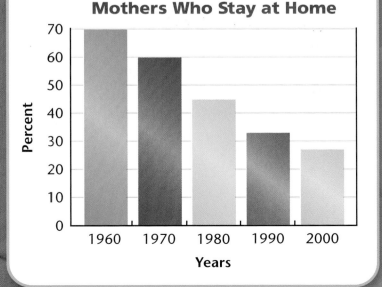

Mothers Who Stay at Home

Percent

70
60
50
40
30
20
10
0

1960   1970   1980   1990   2000

Years

Daily Physical Activity

Supporting your family includes helping with chores. Some chores, like washing windows and raking leaves, provide physical activity.

 Be Active!
Use the selection, Track 11, **Funky Flex**, to practice exercises you can share with your family.

1 Changing Families, Changing Roles

Lesson Focus

Family members can help and support each other during times of change.

Why Learn This?

Being a responsible member of your family will help you feel good about yourself.

Vocabulary

empathy
negotiate

Family Changes

Change is something that you can depend on happening regularly. Some changes happen with little or no effort on your part. You grow taller. A new student joins your class. You get a new soccer coach.

Other changes require your effort. If a new person joins your family, for example, you will need to do things in new ways. Some of the new ways will be challenging. You might have to share your room. Or you might have to do more chores. A new family member is a big change for the whole family.

Family members need to help each other when important changes happen. As you *mature*, or grow older, you become more responsible. You can be more helpful to your family. You can especially help younger brothers and sisters deal with big changes.

◄ Losing a pet can be a painful experience. A parent or other family member can help you deal with the loss.

Dealing with Change in Families

Change	Common Effects	Dealing with Change
Remarriage	Confusion about how to fit into a new family	Take time to adjust, and be patient with each other.
Birth of a baby	More responsibilities for parents; older children may feel jealous and left out	Find ways to help out so parents will have more time to spend with you.
Moving	Happiness about your new home but sadness about leaving old friends and old school	Make friends in your new neighborhood and school.
Death	Sadness, loneliness, and anger	Talk about your feelings; write about your feelings.

Sharing things with new family members helps them feel welcome. ▼

Pleasant Changes Many of the changes you experience through the years are pleasant. For example, you might discover that you enjoy singing, so you might become part of a choir. Your whole family may experience pleasant changes together. Your family may decide to take a special vacation, try new foods, or start a new activity that is fun for everyone. These changes can help your family grow closer.

Difficult Changes Families sometimes experience big changes that are hard to deal with. A new baby, divorce, remarriage, and death are all difficult changes. Such changes put stress on families. During these times, family members need to support each other.

(Focus Skill) **MAIN IDEA AND DETAILS** **Write about ways that changes affect families. Describe pleasant and difficult changes, and include details.**

323

Consumer Activity

Analyze Media Messages

TV families often argue. Watch one of your favorite shows. When family members argue, write down the cause. Then write how they settled the argument. Did they negotiate a solution that made both sides happy?

Family Responsibilities

When you were a baby, your parents took care of all your needs. They fed you, dressed you, and kept you safe. Now you are older. You are mature enough to be responsible for yourself and others in many ways.

You can help and support your family by being respectful. Listen respectfully to other people's ideas and opinions. If you disagree, do so without yelling or getting angry. You are also mature enough to feel **empathy** (EM•puh•thee), which means you can understand other people's feelings. When you have empathy, you are able to imagine that you are in someone else's place. You can relate to how the person feels. When you know how a person feels, you can treat him or her the way that you would like to be treated in the same situation.

You are also old enough to be able to negotiate (nih•GOH•shee•ayt). When you **negotiate**, you discuss and resolve a conflict with another person.

You'll never forget to do a chore if you make a list of what to do. Check off your chores as you do them. ▼

MY CHORES
Feed the cat.
Clean the litter box.
Take out the trash.
Set the table.

For example, if you and your sister both want to use the computer at the same time, you can negotiate a solution that both of you can accept.

As you become more responsible, your family begins to trust and depend on you. You do your regular chores without being reminded. You try to do your chores better, and you accept suggestions for improvement. Doing your chores well helps the whole family.

You even do things without being asked. For example, if you see a bike left in the driveway, you move it to a safe place. When someone is behind on chores, you offer to help. Sometimes you help the family by doing a special job, like cleaning up the kitchen after a party.

As a responsible family member, you are a good model for younger brothers and sisters. For example, when you make a mistake, you are mature enough to take responsibility for it. You also learn from your mistakes.

▲ Caring about his older sister is one way this boy shows he is a responsible family member.

DRAW CONCLUSIONS **Why is it important to feel empathy?**

Quick Activity

List Responsibilities
Think about the types of jobs you do for your family now. Could you have done these jobs five years ago? What types of jobs will you be able to do in a few years? Write your answers in a chart.

◀ This furry family member depends on other family members to feed him.

Volunteering in the Community

Some families do *volunteer* work. Volunteers give their time to good causes without being paid. Many families collect food for people who don't have enough. Some families help clean up parks or lakes. Still others read to people in nursing homes.

Volunteering has many benefits. It meets needs in your community. It is also a way to spend time with your family. Working together toward a common goal can be very satisfying for all of you. Volunteer work also helps you as you mature by showing you how to care for others. As a volunteer, you become a more responsible person.

SUMMARIZE List several types of volunteer work that families can do.

◀ **Families often help community or religious organizations collect food.**

Lesson 1 Summary and Review

1 Summarize with Vocabulary

Use vocabulary and other terms from this lesson to complete the statements.

As you _____, or grow older, you can become more _____ and helpful in your family. As you continue to grow, you can feel _____, which is an understanding of other people's feelings. You are also able to _____. This means that you can help resolve conflicts through discussion. Some families _____, or help out in their neighborhoods.

2 What are two pleasant and two difficult changes that a family can experience?

3 Critical Thinking How can you become a more responsible member of your family?

4 (Focus Skill) MAIN IDEA AND DETAILS Draw and complete this graphic organizer to show three details related to the main idea described in the box.

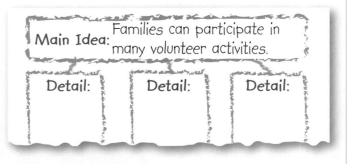

Main Idea: Families can participate in many volunteer activities.

| Detail: | Detail: | Detail: |

5 Write to Entertain—Poem

Write an eight-line poem that is titled "I'm Nearly Grown Up Now."

Caring

Support Family Members

Changes in the makeup of your family can be stressful. This is especially true for a new family member or a family member who moves away. A new family member may not feel welcome or accepted. A family member who moves away, such as a grandparent who moves to a nursing home, needs your support more than ever. Here are a few simple ways to show these family members that you really care about them:

- **Include all family members in family traditions.**
- **Do something special for a family member.**
- **Show family members things you think might interest them. For example, you can show a grandparent photos or movies on a computer.**
- **Be a good listener.**
- **Respect the opinions of all family members, even though you might disagree with them.**
- **Be responsible by doing your chores and helping out, even when you're not asked to.**
- **Be understanding.**

Activity

With a classmate, write a short skit for the class. You can play the role of a boy or girl whose family has just adopted a twelve-year-old. Your classmate can play the role of the adopted child. Write a dialogue for the two children. The adopted child should express his or her fears about joining the new family. You should show how to welcome him or her through words and actions.

Communication in Families

How Families Communicate

Why are some families close? They're close because they communicate (kuh•MYOO•nih•kayt) well. Family members **communicate** by sharing views, thoughts, and feelings with each other. They also listen carefully. As a result, the family stays close during bad times as well as good.

A family's well-being depends on good communication. When you are happy, tell your family why. If you hit a home run or get a good grade in school, let everybody know about it. You should also let family members know when you are sad. Tell them what is troubling you. They will listen to you and let you know they care. They may even have a solution to your problem. If not, they can help you work on one. Just talking about a problem with a parent or another family member is helpful.

Good communication isn't only about you. It includes showing you care about others. Find ways to

Busy families can communicate while they prepare meals together. ▶

Quick Activity

Communicate Good Things Write three good things that have happened to you in the last week. Share your list with your family.

tell family members how much you love them. Saying something nice helps spread good feelings through the whole family. Also, listen respectfully when other family members talk to you. Listening carefully is another way to show you care.

Many families have busy schedules. How do they find time to communicate? Many families talk things over at mealtimes. Some families even make it a point to cook dinner together.

Sometimes, schedules do not allow regular family meals. In this case, work with your family to find a time when all of you can be together. Maybe you can plan an activity you'll all enjoy, such as playing a game together or going to a park or beach.

You can even communicate with family members in writing. Writing letters is a way for family members to stay in touch when they might be apart. Try writing a note to say you are sorry for something you said or did. You can also use a note to tell a parent where you are and when you will be home. Such notes show that you care about and respect your family.

You don't always need words to communicate. Doing something special for a family member also shows you care.

CAUSE AND EFFECT **What is the effect of telling people you are proud of them?**

PersoNaL HeaLth PlaN ▶

Real Life Situation
You realize that you should communicate better with your family members. You want to take action immediately.

Real-Life Plan
Make a list of some of the good things you like about each family member. Share your list with your family.

One way families communicate is by planning a vacation together, even if everyone isn't happy with the plan. ▼

Resolving Family Conflicts

Conflicts happen in every family. They often result from misunderstandings. Failure to communicate also causes conflicts. You might argue with a brother about the use of a game or toy. You might disagree with a parent about how late you can stay outdoors after dinner. Such conflicts are normal, but they should be resolved before they grow.

Family members need to work together to resolve conflicts. Understanding the other person's point of view is important. If you have a conflict with someone, listen carefully and quietly to what that person is saying. To be sure you understand the person's thinking, ask questions. Then calmly give your point of view. Clearly tell your wants, needs, and feelings with "I" messages, such as "I feel badly when I can't watch my favorite TV show about animals. Someday I want to be a vet."

Being a responsible family member means thinking how your actions will affect others. ▶

After you and the other person give your points of view, work toward a solution. It should be one that makes both of you happy. Giving in on some points, or *compromising*, is part of becoming a mature person. But sometimes a compromise is not possible. The differences between the people are too great. In those cases, a parent or another family member may suggest a fair solution.

At times, your parents may tell you that you can't do something you'd like to do because it isn't safe. You should accept their decision. They probably have good reasons for making it. Accepting a decision you can't change shows that you are mature.

Some families resolve conflicts by holding family meetings. These meetings give all family members the chance to tell their points of view. This may help avoid more serious conflicts by settling disagreements before they go too far. Good communication helps keep families happy and strong.

SUMMARIZE **What are three things you can do to resolve small disagreements before they grow into larger ones?**

▲ Many families like to keep a note board in the kitchen. They write schedules and dates on the board. They may also leave important messages there.

ACTIVITY

Life Skills

Resolve Conflicts

Bill says it's his sister Jo's turn to walk the dog, but she tells him she wants to play a computer game first. Write down two ways to help them resolve this conflict. How can writing possible solutions help you resolve your own conflicts?

Abuse and Neglect

Myth and Fact

Myth: **You should never talk to a stranger.**

Fact: **You may need to ask a stranger for help in an emergency. Always remember to use common sense. If you feel uncomfortable with a stranger, leave immediately and ask someone else for help.**

Bad things can happen in all types of families. These bad things may include abuse. *Abuse* is the harmful treatment of another person.

Abuse can be physical or verbal. Physical abuse may include hitting, shaking, kicking, and biting. Even tickling can be physical abuse. It's abuse when the person who is doing the tickling does not stop when asked.

Sexual abuse is another form of physical abuse. It's an act of touching a person in a way that makes the person feel uncomfortable or confused. Sexual exploitation (ex•ploy•TAY•shuhn) is a form of sexual abuse. **Exploitation** means "taking advantage of someone." Sexual exploitation is taking advantage of someone in a sexual way.

Verbal abuse may include yelling, threatening, and name-calling. This type of abuse can hurt a person just as much as physical abuse. People who are verbally abused often lose self-esteem.

Neglect is another form of abuse. **Neglect** is failure to take care of a person's basic needs, such as food and clothing. Sometimes family members are guilty of neglect of another family member.

◀ Your school counselor can help you learn about forms of abuse.

Abuse, exploitation, and neglect are against the law. If someone is doing something to you against your will or is doing something to you that you don't like, tell the person "No!" in a firm voice. Then get away from the person as quickly as you can. As soon as possible, tell a parent or another trusted adult about the abuse.

COMPARE AND CONTRAST **What is the difference between good tickling and bad tickling?**

Having your fingerprints on file can help police if you become lost or are kidnapped. ▶

Lesson 2 Summary and Review

❶ Summarize with Vocabulary

Use vocabulary and other terms from this lesson to complete the statements. Families stay close when they _____. When conflicts arise, it is important to be able to _____, or give in on some points. Bad things sometimes happen in families. One of these is _____, which is a failure to take care of a person's basic needs. Another bad thing is sexual _____.

❷ Critical Thinking What are some ways family members can communicate good feelings without using words?

❸ How can families resolve small conflicts before they get worse?

❹ MAIN IDEA AND DETAILS Draw and complete this graphic organizer to show details related to the main idea described in the box.

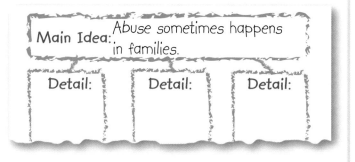

Main Idea: Abuse sometimes happens in families.

| Detail: | Detail: | Detail: |

❺ Write to Inform—Explanation

You and your sister can't agree on which TV program to watch. Explain how to resolve this disagreement so that each of you is happy.

333

Communicate
with Your Family

Communicating with other people is not always easy, but it is important. Communication skills help you express your feelings in healthful ways. Using the steps for **Communicating** can help you build better relationships with the people in your family.

Kendra's mom has just taken a job. Kendra wonders about coming home to an empty house after school. Her older brother gets home an hour after Kendra arrives. She worries about who will drive her to dance lessons and help her with her homework. How can Kendra use communication skills to help her talk to her parents?

 Understand your audience.

Kendra knows that her mom will be away from home more often, so her mom will need help from the whole family.

2 **Give a clear message.**

After dinner Kendra talks to her parents. "I'm worried about being home alone after school. Who will help me with my homework?"

③ Listen actively.

Rusty can keep me company.

You could do homework after supper.

I think those are good ideas.

The family listens, and everyone makes suggestions. They agree that Kendra can let the dog in to keep her company and do her homework after supper.

④ Gather feedback.

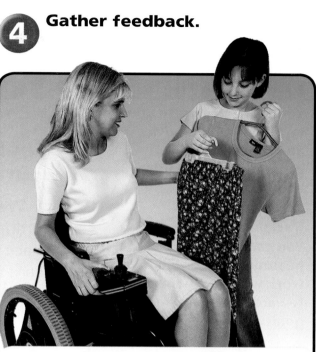

Kendra realizes that her family cares about her and will help her adjust to the changes.

Problem Solving

A. Mandy shares a computer with her older brother. She is upset because he seems to want to use the computer whenever she wants to. She must finish a research paper in two days, and she needs to use the computer for at least three or four hours.
   • Use the steps for **Communicating** to help resolve Mandy's problem. Be sure the resolution is fair.

B. Julio often forgets to do things he promises. As a result, his older sister usually has to do more chores around the house.
   • How can Julio's older sister be fair while helping her brother learn not to be forgetful?

Families Working Together

LESSON 3

Lesson Focus

Your family can give you information and advice about health and can promote good health within the family.

Why Learn This?

You can live a happier, healthier, longer life if you work with your family toward achieving health goals.

Vocabulary

health maintenance

Myth and Fact

Myth: You should play through pain.

Fact: If you feel pain while you are exercising or playing, you should stop immediately. Pain tells you that the activity is hurting you. If you ignore the pain, you may seriously injure yourself.

Seeking Health Advice from Family Members

We all have questions about our health from time to time. For example, have you ever wondered if a new snack food is bad for you? Or have you ever wanted to learn more about exercising to keep a healthful weight? Information about these and many other health topics can often be found at home.

Your parents may not be doctors or nurses, but they can probably answer many of your health questions. When they decided to raise a family, your parents may have read books about family health. They probably have also asked your family doctor many questions.

Parents should be the first people you talk to about health matters. They can help you decide what exercises to do. They can also help you choose the right foods to eat. They can even give you medicines for a cold or a fever.

▲ If you injure yourself, tell a parent or another trusted adult right away.

336

Your parents may not have all the answers. But they can help you look for them, and they know when to ask a doctor. Together with your parents you might find health information by searching the Internet. Your local library also has books, magazines, and other health-related resources you can use together.

Some health questions that you have might be personal. You should never be embarrassed to ask your parents these types of questions. They care for you and understand your feelings because they were once your age, too. Not asking these types of questions may be putting your health at risk.

 MAIN IDEA AND DETAILS
Your parents can help you find health information. Name two places where you might find this type of information.

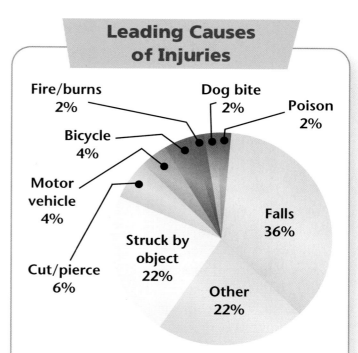

Leading Causes of Injuries

Fire/burns 2%
Dog bite 2%
Poison 2%
Bicycle 4%
Motor vehicle 4%
Cut/pierce 6%
Struck by object 22%
Falls 36%
Other 22%

Quick Activity

According to the graph, what is the leading cause of injuries? List the causes in order, from most common to least common.

Each year one out of every five children is treated for an injury. ▼

Promoting Health Within the Family

You and your family can meet many challenges if you work together. Staying healthy is a big challenge. However, it is a challenge that is worth the effort to meet. Families that promote health are usually happier and more likely to live long, active lives.

Families can do many things to promote health in the home. The problem, however, is finding time. Families today are very busy. Often, both moms and dads have jobs. Older brothers and sisters may have jobs or activities after school. You probably have many activities, too. On the next page are ways a family can promote health.

Families who take walks together get good exercise. Walks also provide a time for families to communicate. ▶

◀ Picking fresh vegetables or fruit with your family is good exercise and fun. Fresh foods also taste great and add variety to your diet.

Make time for healthful activities

Talk about healthful activities that family members can enjoy together. Making time for family activities may be hard. If one person is always busy, offer to do one or more of his or her chores. If the jobs are divided evenly, your family will have a better chance to find time for things that are healthful and fun.

Eat more meals as a family

Eating meals with your family helps you develop good eating habits. Children who have regular family meals usually eat foods that are more healthful than do children who eat alone. They usually eat fewer snacks, too. Eating together also gives everyone a chance to suggest family activities.

Exercise and play together

Regular exercise helps keep you healthy. Your family can enjoy exercising and playing together. Walking, biking, hiking, swimming, and just playing ball in the park are activities that can be enjoyed by the whole family.

SEQUENCE Make a list of three things that your family can do to promote health within the family. List your ideas in order of importance to you.

Consumer Activity

Access Valid Health Information Eating healthful, balanced meals is important. With a parent, use the Internet or the library to research the nutritional value of different foods. Then use your research to plan and write out a healthful menu for your family for a week.

339

Real-Life Situation
You realize you may not be doing everything you can for your health.
Real-Life Plan
Make a weekly chart with a personal health maintenance program. Provide spaces where you can check off each completed item.

Developing a Family Health Plan

When you set goals, you make a plan containing the steps that will lead you to the goals. That is why families that want to maintain, or keep, their health need a plan. A **health maintenance** (MAYNT·uhn·uhns) plan includes the steps to take to achieve goals for good health. A typical family health maintenance plan might include the following:

1. Exercise at least 30 minutes each day.

2. Eat a variety of foods.

3. Learn basic first-aid techniques.

4. Get enough sleep.

5. Brush and floss your teeth regularly.

DRAW CONCLUSIONS Can a family be healthy without developing a health maintenance plan?

Lesson 3 Summary and Review

1 **Summarize with Vocabulary**

Use vocabulary and other terms from this lesson to complete the statements.

Family meetings provide an opportunity for a family to _____, or share feelings and opinions about family health. Every family should develop a _____ plan. Such a plan lays out the steps the family should take to achieve its health goals.

2 Who are the first people you should talk with when you have questions about health matters?

3 **Critical Thinking** Why is it often difficult for families to promote health in the home?

4 (Focus Skill) **MAIN IDEA AND DETAILS** Draw and complete this graphic organizer to show the missing details of a health maintenance plan.

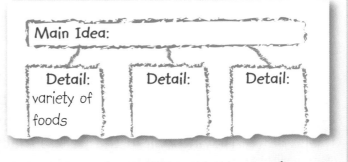

Main Idea:

Detail: variety of foods | Detail: | Detail:

5 **Write to Inform—Explanation**
Explain how to change a health maintenance plan as a family changes.

ACTIVITIES

 Math

Survey Friends and Classmates Survey your friends and classmates to find out how many times their families have moved in the last ten years. Show your results in a bar graph. Then find the average number of times your classmates and friends have moved in the last five years.

 **Science**

Observe Animal Communication

Observe pets, such as dogs and cats, or wild animals, such as birds and squirrels. Notice how they communicate with other animals of their kind and with animals of different kinds. What parts of their bodies do they use? What do you think they are trying to communicate? Write a short report describing your observations.

Technology Project

Make a Leaflet Families can grow stronger when they volunteer to help people in the community. Find three or four activities in your community that a family could volunteer to do. Using a computer, make a leaflet that lists and briefly describes these activities. If a computer is not available, use construction paper and markers to make your leaflet.

 For more activities, visit The Learning Site. www.harcourtschool.com/health

 Home & Community

Order Activities Ask your classmates what activities their families do together. Summarize the answers in a list showing the activities in order from the most common to the least common. Share your list with your classmates and teacher.

Career Link

Social Worker Social workers help families deal with difficult changes. Suppose you are a social worker. You have an appointment with a family of people who are stressed because of a new baby. Prepare a list of five suggestions that you think will help them deal with this change in their family.

Reading Skill

IDENTIFY MAIN IDEA AND DETAILS

Draw and then use this graphic organizer to answer questions 1 and 2.

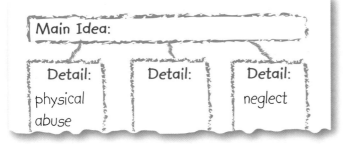

Main Idea:

Detail: physical abuse

Detail:

Detail: neglect

1 What main idea belongs in the graphic organizer above?

2 What detail is missing?

Use Vocabulary

Match each term in Column B with its meaning in Column A.

Column A	Column B
3 Understanding of others' feelings	**A** mature
	B negotiate
4 To resolve conflicts through discussion	**C** communicate
	D volunteer
5 To work for a cause without being paid	**E** neglect
	F empathy
6 To become more responsible and helpful	
7 To share thoughts, opinions, and feelings	
8 To fail to provide someone with basic needs, such as food or clothing	

Check Understanding

Choose the letter of the correct answer.

9 Which of these changes is **NOT** a difficult change that families sometimes face? (pp. 322–333)
  A a death   **C** a new baby
  B a move   **D** a new teacher

10 Change is something that happens _____. (p. 322)
  F once in a while   **H** regularly
  G hardly ever   **J** never

11 Which of these actions is **NOT** a form of abuse?
  A hitting   **C** name-calling
  B disagreeing   **D** neglect

12 Being able to compromise is part of being a(n) _____ person. (p. 331)
  F mature   **H** old
  G young   **J** unreasonable

13 Which of these changes requires some effort on your part? (p. 322)
  A getting older
  B getting taller
  C getting good grades
  D getting a new teacher

14 Which of the following items is **NOT** a basic need? (p. 332)

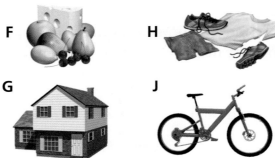

F   H

G   J

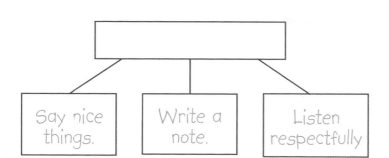

```
┌─────────────────┐
│                 │
└─────────────────┘
    ╱      │      ╲
┌────────┐┌────────┐┌────────────┐
│Say nice││Write a ││  Listen    │
│things. ││ note.  ││respectfully│
└────────┘└────────┘└────────────┘
```

15 Which is the main idea of the graphic organizer above? (p. 328–329)

   A compromise   **C** negotiation

   B communication **D** disagreement

16 Misunderstandings and poor communication can lead to _____. (p. 330)

   F conflicts   **H** exploitation

   G solutions   **J** compromises

17 Which of these actions would probably **NOT** be a good idea if you are abused? (pp. 332–333)

   A saying "No!" in a firm voice

   B quickly getting away from the abuser

   C telling no one about the abuse

   D calling an abuse hotline

18 People who are verbally abused often lose _____. (p. 332)

   F self-esteem   **H** weight

   G their patience **J** their temper

19 The picture on page 330 is an example of _____. (p. 330)

   A politeness   **C** caring

   B rudeness   **D** sharing

Think Critically

20 What are some signs that you are becoming more mature?

21 Why is it important for family members to communicate with each other on a regular basis?

22 What role does listening play when you are trying to resolve a conflict with someone?

Apply Skills

23   **BUILDING GOOD CHARACTER**

   Caring Your grandmother has just told you that she will be moving to a nursing home on the other side of town. She is very sad and confused. What can you do or say to show her that you care about her?

24   **LIFE SKILLS**

   Communicate Your parents are very special to you. Despite some disagreements, you respect them and the judgments they have made. What are some of the ways you can show your parents how much you appreciate them?

Write About Health

25 **Write to Inform—Explanation** Explain why it is important to support your family during good times as well as bad times.

Working Toward a Healthful Community

Reading Skill

SUMMARIZE A summary is a short statement that includes the main idea and the most important details in a passage. Use the Reading in Health Handbook on pages 372–383 and this graphic organizer to help you summarize the health facts in this chapter.

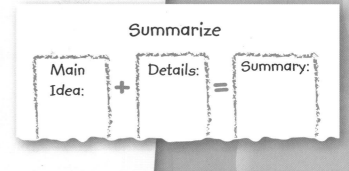

Summarize

| Main Idea: | + | Details: | = | Summary: |

Health Graph

INTERPRET DATA Bike helmets protect bike riders against head injuries. Many states have passed laws that require bike riders to wear helmets. What is the total percentage of bike riders that use helmets more than half of the time?

Survey of Helmet Use by Cyclists Age 16 and Under

Always use helmets 59%

Use helmets more than half the time 10%

Never or almost never use helmets 19%

Use helmets less than half the time 12%

Daily Physical Activity

Picking up trash in your neighborhood or at school is a great way to get some exercise and improve your community.

🎵 *Be Active!*
Use the selection, Track 12, **Broadway Bound**, to share some exercise time with your classroom community.

Groups That Protect Public Health

Lesson Focus

Both government and private groups work to protect public health.

Why Learn This?

You will know what information and services these groups can give you.

Vocabulary

public health
sanitation

Government Protects Public Health

People living in a community often catch each other's colds. Catching a cold from someone usually isn't serious. However, the spread of a serious disease, such as West Nile virus, is a public health problem. **Public health** is the health of all the people in a community. Government agencies and private groups work to keep communities healthy.

In the federal government three agencies of the Department of Health and Human Services (DHHS) protect public health.

- The National Institutes of Health (NIH) carries out and supports medical research.
- The Food and Drug Administration (FDA) makes sure that medicines work and are safe. The FDA also makes sure that foods are safe and that packaged foods are labeled with nutritional values.
- The Centers for Disease Control and Prevention (CDC) gathers information about communicable diseases. It tells doctors and other health-care workers what diseases to look for in communities where people are ill.

Focus Skill **SUMMARIZE How does the federal government protect public health?**

◄ Researchers at the CDC study communicable diseases. They share their findings with hospitals, doctors, and other health-care workers.

346

Private Groups Protect Public Health

There are several large private groups in this country that help promote public health. They do this by educating the public and raising money for research. Many of these groups depend on unpaid workers, or *volunteers,* to do much of their work.

- The American Cancer Society (ACS) researches the causes and effects of all types of cancer. It also helps cancer patients get the information and treatment they need.
- The aim of the American Heart Association (AHA) is to reduce illness and death from heart disease and stroke by educating people about these problems.
- The American Diabetes Association (ADA) helps people with diabetes manage their disease.
- The purpose of the American Lung Association (ALA) is to help people with chronic lung diseases, such as asthma.

COMPARE AND CONTRAST How are the ACS and the AHA alike and different?

▲ A private group sponsored this race as a fundraising event. The money raised will be used for research to find a cure for cancer.

Consumer Activity

Access Information About Health You have read about a few large private groups that focus on particular diseases. Find out more about similar but smaller groups. Make a chart showing the names of the groups and the diseases they focus on.

Myth & Fact

Myth: **Everybody in the world gets fresh water from a tap in his or her home.**

Fact: **In some places in the world, people walk for hours every day just to get water to drink.**

WHO works with governments and private groups throughout the world to make clean water and good sanitation available to more people. ▼

The World Health Organization

The World Health Organization (WHO) provides public health services worldwide. One important goal of WHO is to make sure all children in the world are immunized against deadly diseases such as diphtheria, measles, polio, tetanus, typhoid, and whooping cough.

WHO also performs other important services around the world. It trains health-care workers and educates people about diseases. WHO also helps mothers and children get healthful food and good medical care. In addition, it makes sure that medicines sent between countries are pure. As the CDC does in the United States, WHO tracks the spread of communicable diseases worldwide.

Another aim of WHO is to improve water supplies and sanitation in parts of the world that do not have clean running water. **Sanitation** (sa•nuh•TAY•shuhn) is the safe disposal of human wastes. Diseases can spread quickly in places where water isn't clean and where human wastes aren't disposed of properly. Today almost two and a half billion people in the world have no sanitation facilities. Many of these people also lack clean water for drinking and cooking. WHO is working to change this.

WHO is also concerned about the rapid rise in tobacco use in many countries. In 2003 WHO sponsored the Framework Convention on Tobacco Control. This is a public health treaty that encourages countries around the world to work toward stopping the spread of tobacco use.

 SUMMARIZE **What jobs does the World Health Organization do?**

WHO has held international conferences on smoking and health to discuss problems and look for solutions. ▼

Lesson 1 Summary and Review

❶ Summarize with Vocabulary

Use vocabulary and other terms from this lesson to complete the statements.

Both government and private groups work to protect _____ health. Some workers are paid, and others are _____. Some groups work to prevent the spread of dangerous _____ , such as typhoid. Many people in the world do not have clean water or _____ facilities.

❷ Which public agencies track the spread of diseases?

❸ Critical Thinking Why do you think educating people about diseases is a main goal of many public health groups?

❹ SUMMARIZE Draw and complete this graphic organizer to summarize how government agencies and private groups protect public health.

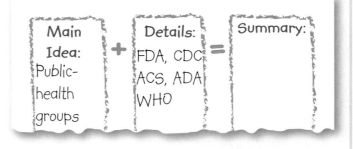

Main Idea: Public-health groups **+** Details: FDA, CDC ACS, ADA WHO **=** Summary:

❺ Write to Inform — Description

Write a news story about one of the public-health groups in this lesson.

LESSON

2

Community Health Needs

Lesson Focus
Each community has a system for taking care of its public health needs.

Why Learn This?
Health issues in your community can affect your life and the lives of your family members.

Vocabulary
sewage
septic tank
sanitary landfills

Medical Care and Health Records

Suppose you go for a hike in a nearby park. When you finish the hike, you find a deer tick on your leg. Deer ticks can carry Lyme disease, which makes people feel weak. What would you do?

Lyme disease is curable, but you would need prompt medical treatment. You might go to your doctor or see a doctor at a local health department clinic. The doctor would review records of all the tests, treatments, and illnesses you have had and any allergies you have. This information would help the doctor decide how best to treat you.

Doctors inform the local health department about illnesses that might affect the community. The health department keeps records of these illnesses. It uses the records to decide if an illness is spreading and threatening the public health. The records can also help other agencies study certain diseases.

 SUMMARIZE **Summarize how private doctors and public clinics meet community health needs.**

The bacteria that cause Lyme disease are carried by deer ticks. Ticks spread the bacteria when they bite. ▶

◀ Hikers should cover arms and legs to prevent tick bites.

◀ Often, raccoons and other wild mammals carry diseases. One of the most dangerous is *rabies*. Rabies is spread when an infected mammal bites another mammal.

Disease Control and Prevention

Health information that doctors send to local health departments is sometimes shared with state health departments and the CDC. The CDC tells health-care workers about where certain disease outbreaks are occurring. The CDC also tells health-care workers how to recognize certain diseases in their patients. With this information, workers can stop some communicable diseases before they spread very far.

The best way to control disease is to prevent it. Doctors and local health departments work to prevent the spread of disease by:

- vaccinating children against serious diseases.

- vaccinating older people and others against the flu.

- inspecting restaurants and food stores to ensure they are clean and that food is handled properly.

SEQUENCE **What happens after a doctor gathers medical records about a patient who has a communicable disease?**

Information Alert!

Smallpox Smallpox is a communicable disease that was eliminated in 1977. Recently, people began to fear that smallpox might be spread by terrorists. Now the United States has enough vaccine for everyone in the country.

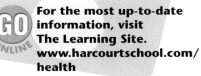

For the most up-to-date information, visit The Learning Site. www.harcourtschool.com/ health

351

Protecting the Environment

The water you drink starts out in wells, lakes, rivers, or reservoirs. It is cleaned, treated, and tested for bacteria at a water treatment plant. Finally, it is piped to homes and businesses.

Much of the water we use simply goes down the drain. Some of it is flushed down the toilet. The mixture of wastewater and human wastes that leaves homes and businesses is called sewage. Sewage flows through pipes to a treatment plant. There it is cleaned and treated before being released into rivers, lakes, or oceans.

The sewage from some homes is sent into septic tanks. A septic tank is a concrete or steel tank buried in the ground. Bacteria in the tank change most of the human wastes into harmless substances that flow slowly out of the tank and into the soil.

Your local sanitation department collects garbage, or *solid waste,* and hauls it away to be burned or to be buried in sanitary landfills. **Sanitary landfills** (SAN•uh•tair•ee LAND•filz) are large holes dug in the

Workers record information gathered by water-sampling machines. They make sure wastewater is safe to release into the environment. ▼

▲ When a sanitary landfill is full, it can be covered and used for new purposes.

ground to hold trash. The holes are usually lined with plastic or clay. This keeps harmful materials in solid waste from polluting the land or the water that flows underground. Each day, the collected waste is covered with dirt to keep birds and other animals from spreading diseases to nearby communities.

MAIN IDEA AND DETAILS What are two types of community wastes? How do communities get rid of each type?

Lesson 2 Summary and Review

❶ Summarize with Vocabulary

Use vocabulary and other terms from this lesson to complete the statements.

Before we drink water from the tap, it is cleaned at a _____. The mixture of wastewater and human wastes that leaves our homes is called _____. Some homes collect this matter in a _____, where _____ change most of the human wastes into harmless substances. Sanitation departments often bury trash in _____.

❷ How does the CDC work to control disease?

❸ Critical Thinking If a landfill does not have a protective lining of clay or plastic, what effect might it have on public health?

❹ (Focus Skill) **SUMMARIZE** Draw and complete this graphic organizer to summarize how communities control and prevent disease.

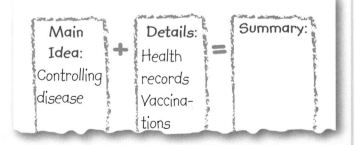

Main Idea: Controlling disease + Details: Health records Vaccinations = Summary:

❺ Write to Inform—How-To

Write a short pamphlet about what people should do to avoid getting Lyme disease. Research the subject. Include what people should do in areas that have deer ticks.

Handling Community Emergencies

Lesson Focus

A number of kinds of emergencies may affect your community, and many agencies can help your community handle them.

Why Learn This?

Knowing about possible emergencies can help you be prepared for an emergency in your community.

Vocabulary

evacuation

Disasters like floods can strike without warning. Often, however, people and communities have time to prepare for them. ▼

Floods

When streams, lakes, or rivers overflow with water, there is a flood. Floods usually occur when rain falls or snow melts faster than it can be soaked up by the soil or carried away by rivers. Floods can cause great damage. In farming areas, for example, a flood can destroy crops. In towns, floods can fill houses and businesses with water and mud, damaging furniture and machinery. In all areas, floodwater can pollute drinking water.

Sometimes, floods can be predicted. This gives communities time to get ready. The picture on the next page shows young people helping prepare for a flood by filling bags with sand. The sandbags will be stacked high along a river to keep the rising water from flooding the surrounding land.

For a disaster such as a flood, local government agencies and private groups like the Red Cross organize volunteers who want to help.

What if the sandbags do not protect the community from the flood? It may be necessary for the local emergency manager to organize an evacuation. An **evacuation** (ee•vak•yoo•AY•shuhn) is the removal of people from their homes to safer places.

If the flood causes a great amount of damage, the state's governor and local officials may ask the President to declare the region a disaster area. The Federal Emergency Management Agency (FEMA) will then help the community. FEMA helps organize federal, state, and local agencies to:

- restore public services and power.
- provide transportation and communication.
- assist with medical care.
- ensure a supply of food in the disaster area.
- help people apply for money to rebuild.

 SUMMARIZE How can a community prepare for and respond to a flood?

Personal Health Plan ▶

Real-Life Situation
Your family has decided to prepare a family emergency plan.
Real-Life Plan
Ask your parents to go to the FEMA website or the Department of Homeland Security website. Using the information there, help organize and write your family's emergency plan.

Life Skills

Communicate

Communicating clearly and quickly with emergency workers can save lives. You can prepare for this kind of communication. Make sure you know your community's emergency phone number. Keep important information, such as your address and nearby cross streets, near the phone.

Robots can be used in fires that are too dangerous for humans, such as fires in warehouses filled with chemicals. ▼

Fires

The fire shown in the picture on this page broke out in an empty warehouse. People in the area smelled smoke and called the fire department. What happened next?

1. Firefighters rushed to the scene. They sprayed the warehouse with water. They also sprayed the buildings next to the warehouse to keep them from catching fire. Firefighters evacuated nearby apartment buildings.

2. Red Cross volunteers set up an emergency shelter and mobile feeding units for firefighters and for people whose homes were damaged by the fire.

3. After the fire was out, officials from the fire department and police department dug through the rubble. They looked for evidence of the cause of the fire. Local businesses, churches, and schools raised money to help people affected by the fire.

This device helps firefighters see through dense smoke, enabling them to find trapped people. ▼

Interpret Graphs Look at the bar graph at the right. Which caused more fires from 1990 to 1994—lightning or humans?

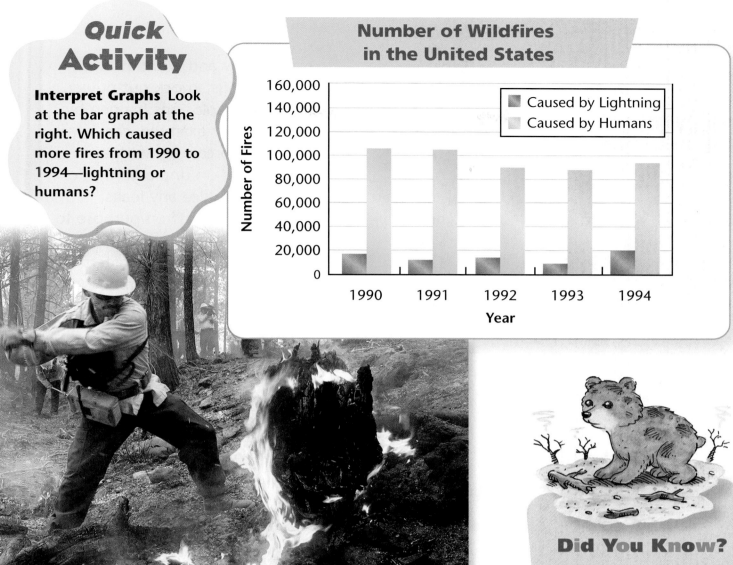

Number of Wildfires in the United States

- Caused by Lightning
- Caused by Humans

Number of Fires: 160,000 / 140,000 / 120,000 / 100,000 / 80,000 / 60,000 / 40,000 / 20,000 / 0

Year: 1990 / 1991 / 1992 / 1993 / 1994

▲ To put out a forest fire, firefighters may set backfires, which burn up fuel needed for a fire to spread.

Forest fires are handled differently from fires in towns and cities. If local firefighters need help with a forest fire, specially trained firefighters from the United States Forest Service respond.

SEQUENCE In order, list steps that people threatened by fire can take to respond to the threat.

Did You Know?

The Real Smokey Bear In 1950 a careless person started a forest fire in New Mexico. This fire injured a black-bear cub. The cub was rescued by firefighters and later given to the chief of the U.S. Forest Service to use in its forest fire prevention program. The bear was named Smokey Bear. When he "retired" from the Forest Service, Smokey Bear moved to the National Zoo, where he lived until 1975.

Explosions

Explosions usually occur quickly and without much warning. They can destroy buildings, knock out power, and injure and kill people. Many explosions happen by accident. Natural gas explosions, for example, can happen when leaking gas comes in contact with a flame or spark. Gas companies add an unpleasant odor to natural gas so that people will notice any leaks.

Some explosions, however, are set off on purpose to hurt people or destroy property. Federal, state, and local governments all work hard to prevent disasters like these. Many police departments have bomb squads trained to stop explosives from going off.

COMPARE AND CONTRAST **How are accidental disasters and deliberate disasters alike? How are they different?**

◀ In 1995 an explosion destroyed part of a government building in Oklahoma City, Oklahoma. The Oklahoma City National Memorial honors the 168 people who died.

Lesson 3 Summary and Review

❶ Summarize with Vocabulary

Use vocabulary and other terms from this lesson to complete the statements.

There are several kinds of emergencies. Too much rain can cause a _____. If this threatens homes, the local emergency manager will organize an _____. Specially trained teams from the U.S. Forest Service deal with _____ by setting _____. A bomb or a gas leak can cause an _____.

❷ What types of groups work together to help communities handle emergencies?

❸ Critical Thinking Why is FEMA helpful when a disaster affects a large area or several states?

❹ (Focus Skill) SUMMARIZE Draw and complete this graphic organizer to show a community's reaction to a gas explosion.

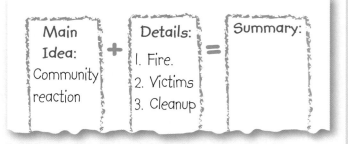

| Main Idea: Community reaction | + | Details: 1. Fire. 2. Victims 3. Cleanup | = | Summary: |

❺ Write to Inform—Narration

Write about how you and your family might help during a local emergency.

Citizenship

Taking Pride in Your Community

Your community is your neighborhood. You see it every day. You can probably think of some great ideas for how to make it a better place. One example might be helping out with a community garden. Here are some steps to get you started in improving your community. You can make a difference!

- **Look around. Ask yourself, "What would make my community a better place?"**

- **Write down your ideas. Include the locations of the improvements and what you think needs to be done.**

- **Show your list to a parent or another adult, such as a teacher. Work with that person to choose your best idea.**

- **Write up a plan. Say what you want to do and how you think it can happen. List any special equipment that will be needed. In your plan, show that you know all the safety rules for working with the equipment.**

- **If your plan involves fixing something, find out who owns it. You will need the owner's permission to carry out your plan.**

Activity

With your family or class, discuss your plan and others' plans for improving your community. As people share ideas, write each one down. At the end of the discussion, decide on something you can all do together as a family or class to show pride in your community.

Developing a garden is one way to take pride in your community. ▶

Protecting Land, Water, and Air

Protecting Land

Land, water, and air are important natural resources and need to be protected. **Natural resources** are materials that people use from the environment. How can we protect these resources?

We need land to grow crops and feed animals. We also need land for our homes, schools, factories, and businesses. We use landfills for disposing of our trash. However, land is limited. One way we can protect the land is by producing less trash. To do this, follow the three R's—*reduce, reuse,* and *recycle.* Here are some things to do at home and at school:

- Reduce the amount of paper you use.
- Reuse paper or plastic bags the next time you shop.
- Recycle aluminum cans, paper, plastic, and glass.

Focus Skill **SUMMARIZE** **What can people do to protect the land?**

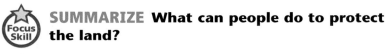

One way to protect the land is by recycling. ▼

There are many ways to conserve water. You can take showers instead of baths. You can also use a water-saving attachment on a garden hose.

Protecting Water

You can protect your community water supply by conserving water. You **conserve** (kuhn•SERV) when you save something or use it carefully. There are many ways you can conserve water at home and school:

- Don't let the water run when it's not in use. For example, turn off the faucet while you brush your teeth.
- Use low-flow shower heads to conserve water. These cut in half the amount of water you would use with other shower heads.
- Fix leaky pipes and faucets. A leak big enough to fill a cup in 10 minutes wastes more than 3,000 gallons a year.
- Cut back on activities that use water. For example, use a broom instead of a hose to clean the sidewalk. Water the lawn only when it looks dry.

DRAW CONCLUSIONS Why might people in dry areas want to grow plants that grow well in dry soil?

ACTIVITY

Building Good Character

Respect Moira's research on saving water has shown her that small actions add up. She wants to tell her parents about ways to save water. However, she doesn't want to act as if she's telling them what to do. Write two ways that Moira can try to get her message across with respect.

Protecting Air

Factories make most of the products we use every day. Unfortunately, some factories release pollution into the air. Motor vehicles and other gasoline-powered equipment also pollute the air.

People who breathe polluted air are more likely to have colds, flu, asthma, eye irritation, some kinds of cancer, and even heart attacks. Polluted air also damages grass, trees, flowers, and crops.

People have developed ways to cut down on air pollution. Many factory smokestacks now have devices that "scrub" the smoke by removing solids and harmful gases. The federal government has passed laws controlling the gases allowed in car exhaust. Cars built today produce far less pollution than cars built twenty years ago.

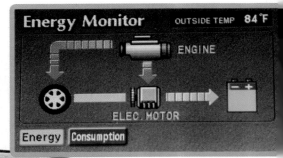

Cars and trucks cause most air pollution. The engines of hybrid cars burn fuel only part of the time they run. They use electric power the rest of the time. Hybrid cars burn less fuel and produce less pollution than regular cars. ▼

What can you and your classmates do to reduce air pollution? One way is to bike, walk, or use public transportation when you need to get around. Another is to follow the three *R's*. Less use of new products means less air pollution from factories.

CAUSE AND EFFECT **For the desired effect of having clean air, what are some possible causes?**

Clean air helps us enjoy outdoor activities.

Quick Activity

Identify Resources for Recreation Make a list of outdoor activities that require clean land, clean water, or clean air. Describe the resources needed for each activity. Then explain why clean resources are important for good health.

Lesson 4 Summary and Review

❶ Summarize with Vocabulary

Use vocabulary and other terms from this lesson to complete the statements.

Land, water, and air are _____. We must _____, or save them, by using them carefully. If we practice the three *R's*, _____, _____, and _____, we will help protect the environment.

❷ Give an example of each of the three *R's*.

❸ Critical Thinking Who do you think has the main responsibility for protecting land, water, and air—individual citizens or government agencies? Give reasons to support your answer.

❹ (Focus Skill) SUMMARIZE Draw and complete this graphic organizer to show how to protect our water resources.

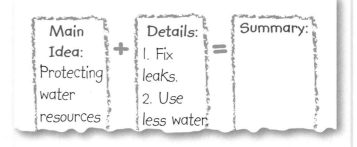

Main Idea: Protecting water resources + Details: 1. Fix leaks. 2. Use less water = Summary:

❺ Write to Inform—Narration

Write a brief story about a family of people whose lives change when they start following the three *R's*. Your story can be humorous or serious.

363

Set Goals
to Protect Resources

All of us can help protect important resources. Using the steps for **Setting Goals** can make the job easier. You can use these steps to help protect resources such as land, water, and air.

Carla and her family recycle many things at home. However, people at her school seem to be less careful. She wonders if there is anything she can do about it.

1 Set a goal. In this case, it is to get more people to recycle.

Carla sets a goal. She wants her schoolmates to do more recycling.

2 List and plan steps to meet the goal. Determine whether you will need help.

Carla decides to make posters about recycling. She asks the principal for permission to hang the posters in the cafeteria.

3 Check your progress as you work toward the goal.

4 Reflect on and evaluate the results of your work.

Carla makes one poster and then asks some friends to help her make and hang the other posters.

After a few days, Carla notices that the recycling bins are being used more often. She feels good about her success.

Problem Solving

A. José's father complains about the size of the water bill. José says that in school he has learned some simple ways to conserve water. His father asks for José's suggestions.
   • Use the steps for **Setting Goals** to help José and his father make a plan for conserving water.

B. Fatima packs her own lunch for school. She realizes that she throws away a lot of the packing materials. She wants to use the three *R*'s to be more responsible about the environment.
   • Suggest some steps Fatima can take to achieve her goal of making less trash.

Protecting Consumers

Government Works to Protect Consumers

Whenever you pay for a product or service, you're a consumer. For example, you're a consumer when you buy a bike helmet at a store or get a checkup at the doctor's office. Some states have laws that help protect consumers. State licensing boards also help by making sure that health-care workers, such as doctors and nurses, are properly trained.

The federal government also protects consumers, through a number of agencies that make sure products and services are safe and effective. One such agency, the Food and Drug Administration (FDA), makes sure that foods, medicines, and cosmetics sold in the United

Seals like the one on this bottle help protect food from tampering. ▶

The FDA makes and enforces rules to ensure that meat is safe to eat. ▶

Not suitable for children under 8 years. May contain small parts and sharp points.

▲ The CPSC requires toys and games with tiny parts to have warning labels. These labels warn that small children could choke on the parts.

Quick Activity

Analyze Labels In your classroom or at home, find a product with a warning label. Write about how this label might affect the use of the product.

States are safe. It also decides what information must be on the labels of these products.

Another government agency that protects consumers is the Consumer Product Safety Commission (CPSC). It works to reduce the risk of injury by doing things such as:

- setting safety standards for products.
- informing the public about unsafe products.
- working with manufacturers to fix unsafe products.

SUMMARIZE Summarize the things that government agencies do to protect consumers.

Myth and Fact

Myth: **All products for sale at a store are safe to use.**

Fact: During an average year, the CPSC finds hundreds of unsafe products. These products have to be recalled, or returned to the manufacturers.

Consumer Activity

Research What You Buy Suppose you want to buy a piece of safety equipment, such as a bike helmet. Look for an article about it in a consumer magazine or on a website. Then use this information to help decide which helmet to buy.

Many private groups, also, work to protect consumers. Several of these groups test products and publish their findings in consumer magazines or on consumer websites. They also check to make sure that businesses provide the services they promise to consumers.

Another kind of consumer group is the Better Business Bureau (BBB) in your community. If you want to know whether to trust a local business, you can ask the BBB whether there are any complaints against the business. If you have your own complaint about a business, you can send it to the BBB. The complaint will be kept on file to help other consumers.

DRAW CONCLUSIONS **What kinds of things might happen if consumer groups did not exist?**

Lesson 5 Summary and Review

1 Summarize with Vocabulary

Use terms from this lesson to complete the statements.

Whenever you buy goods or services, you are a _____. Governments protect health consumers through state _____ boards. A government agency that makes sure foods and medicines are safe is the _____. A government agency that monitors product safety is the _____. You can find information about the safety and quality of products in _____ magazines.

2 Name two ways the Food and Drug Administration protects consumers.

3 Critical Thinking How do consumer groups, like the CPSC, help consumers?

4 (Focus Skill) SUMMARIZE Draw and complete this graphic organizer.

Main Idea: Government and private groups	+	Details: Set safety standards and test products	=	Summary:

5 Write to Express—Business Letter

Imagine that you have a complaint against a local business. Write a letter that might be sent to the Better Business Bureau to explain the problem and to ask for an investigation.

ACTIVITIES

Math

Calculate Water Savings A person taking a shower uses about 5 gallons of water per minute. If a person shortens his or her daily shower by one minute, how much water could be saved in one week? In one month?

Science

Wasted Water Fill a gallon jug with water, and put it in the refrigerator for an hour. Measure the water's temperature with a thermometer. Then gather a few more gallon jugs. Turn on the cold-water tap. Let the water run into the jugs until it is cold enough to enjoy as a drink. Measure the temperature. Is it warmer or colder than the refrigerated water? How much water was wasted before the tap water got cold enough to drink?

Technology Project

Make a Video With a partner, write a skit about steps to take during a community emergency, such as a severe storm. Act out the skit with your partner or classmates, and videotape the performance.

For more activities, visit The Learning Site.
www.harcourtschool.com/health

Home & Community

Be Aware Design and prepare a reference card that people can keep near the phone. List the names and numbers of emergency agencies. Include a sentence about what each agency does. If possible, distribute copies of the card to other students so they can take them home.

Career Link

Industrial Hygienist Suppose you are an industrial hygienist. You look for health hazards that might affect workers in their jobs. Make a checklist that an industrial hygienist could use while inspecting your school. List any places, things, and activities that could be health hazards. You might ask a teacher for ideas.

Chapter Review and Test Preparation

Focus Skill Reading Skill

SUMMARIZE

Draw and then use this graphic organizer to answer questions 1 and 2.

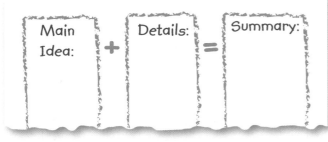

1 Write a summary sentence about groups that protect community health.

2 Write details about ways to conserve natural resources.

Use Vocabulary

Decide whether each statement is true or false. If it is false, replace the underlined part with a term that makes the statement true.

3 People who work without pay are called <u>consumers</u>.

4 <u>Sewage</u> contains water and human wastes.

5 An <u>emergency</u> is the removal of people from their homes to safe places.

6 To <u>conserve</u> something is to save it.

7 Materials that people use from the environment are called <u>natural resources</u>.

8 The safe disposal of human wastes is called <u>recycling</u>.

9 <u>The environment</u> is the health of all the people in the community.

10 Bacteria in <u>septic tanks</u> change wastes into harmless substances.

Check Understanding

Choose the letter of the correct answer.

11 The _____ is a United States government group that carries out and supports health research. (p. 346)
  A American Diabetes Association
  B National Institutes of Health
  C American Heart Association
  D World Health Organization

12 Which group does **NOT** work to prevent and control disease? (p. 368)
  F WHO   H ACS
  G CDC   J BBB

13 Which of the following is the correct place to dispose of solid trash? (pp. 352–353)
  A septic tank
  B reservoir
  C treatment plant
  D sanitary landfill

14 Which of these terms refers to using fewer things so that you don't have as much to throw out? (p. 360)
  F reduce   H recycle
  G reuse   J receive

15 Which of these is **NOT** usually sent to community recycling centers? (p. 360)

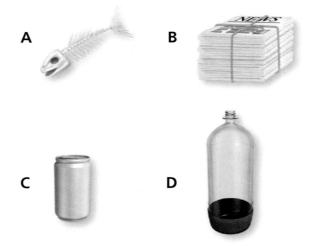

A   B

C   D

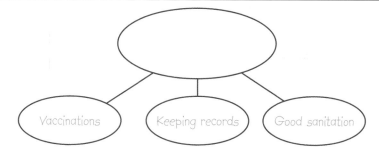

Vaccinations   Keeping records   Good sanitation

16 Which best states the main idea of this web? (pp. 350–353)
  F preventing disease
  G Lyme disease
  H state licensing board
  J consumer magazine

17 Low-flow shower heads limit
_____. (p. 361)
  A ozone   **C** water use
  B land use   **D** water pollution

18 Of the four listed, which is the most important method of disease prevention? (pp. 348–349)
  F vaccinations   **H** disease tracking
  G sanitation   **J** smoking prevention

19 Which of the following does the World Health Organization **NOT** do? (p. 348)
  A checks food for safety
  B trains health-care workers
  C vaccinates children
  D improves water supplies

20 Which agency requires labels like this? (p. 367)

> **Not suitable for children under 8 years. May contain small parts and sharp points.**

  F Better Business Bureau
  G Department of Homeland Security
  H Centers for Disease Control
  J Consumer Product Safety Commission

Think Critically

21 If you had to choose between a car that uses very little gas but costs a lot and a car that uses a lot of gas but costs less, which would you choose? Explain your choice.

22 In what ways can a flood affect a community's public health facilities?

Apply Skills

23 **BUILDING GOOD CHARACTER**
Citizenship Suppose community officials predict that a flood will strike your community within a day or two. Describe what you could do to help prepare for the flood.

24 **LIFE SKILLS**
Set Goals All of your family members use a lot of paper for schoolwork and other work. The paper is made mostly from trees and often ends up in a landfill. State some steps for setting and reaching the goal of reducing your use of paper.

Write About Health

25 **Write to Express—Solution to a Problem** Suppose air pollution is a problem in your city. Write a short speech in which you try to persuade people to take steps to reduce air pollution.

⭐ Compare and Contrast

Learning how to compare and contrast information can help you understand what you read. You can use a graphic organizer like this one to show information that you want to compare and contrast.

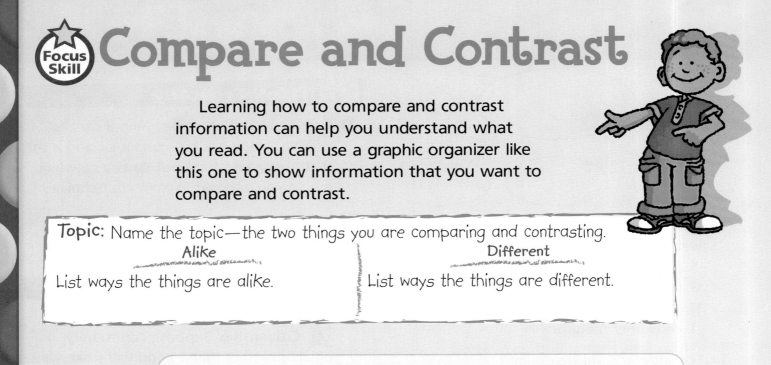

Topic: Name the topic—the two things you are comparing and contrasting.

Alike	Different
List ways the things are alike.	List ways the things are different.

Tips for Comparing and Contrasting

- To compare, ask: *How are people, places, objects, ideas, or events alike?*
- To contrast, ask: *How are people, places, objects, ideas, or events different?*
- When you compare, look for signal words and phrases such as *similar*, *both*, *too*, and *also*.
- When you contrast, look for signal words and phrases such as *unlike*, *however*, *yet*, and *but*.

Here's an example.

Compare →

Contrast

Maria sees herself as being honest, good at sports, and friendly. Sheila also thinks of herself as honest. However, her negative self-concept leads her to believe that she is clumsy and that Maria is her only friend. Both girls have a great sense of humor, which helps them stick together.

Here's what you could record in the graphic organizer.

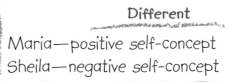

Topic: Sheila and Maria

Alike	Different
Both—honest	Maria—positive self-concept
Both—good sense of humor	Sheila—negative self-concept

More About Comparing and Contrasting

Identifying how things are alike and how they're different can help you understand new information. Use the graphic organizer on page 372 to sort the following new information about Maria and Sheila.

Sometimes a paragraph compares and contrasts more than one topic. In the following paragraph, one topic of comparison is underlined. Find a second topic for comparison or contrast.

Justin and Zach are great friends. Zach loves basketball and Justin loves football. They take turns choosing which sport to play. Steven and Ben live next door to each other. Ben loves hockey and Steven loves kickball. They argue about which sport to play. The two don't get along well.

Skill Practice

Read the following paragraph. Use the Tips for Comparing and Contrasting to answer the questions.

Vitamins and minerals are nutrients. They help keep parts of your body strong and healthy. For example, vitamin A helps keep your skin and eyes healthy. Calcium is a mineral that helps build strong bones and teeth.

1. What are two ways vitamins and minerals are alike?
2. Explain a difference between vitamins and minerals.
3. Name two signal words that helped you identify likenesses or differences in this paragraph.

⭐ Draw Conclusions

You draw conclusions by using information from the text and your own experience. This can help you understand what you read. You can use a graphic organizer like this one to help you draw conclusions.

What I Read		What I Know		Conclusion:
List facts from the text.	+	List related ideas from your own experience.	=	Combine facts from the text with your own experience.

Tips for Drawing Conclusions

- Ask: *What story information do I need to think about?*
- Ask: *What do I know from my own experience that could help me draw a conclusion?*
- Pay close attention to the information the author gives and to your experience to be sure your conclusion is valid, or makes sense.

Here's an example.

> Matt thought he could get ready for school faster if he eliminated things in his morning routine. He decided his hair looked neat and didn't need to be brushed. Matt went downstairs to eat breakfast. As he walked into the kitchen, his older sister started laughing. Matt went back upstairs.

Here's what you could record in the graphic organizer:

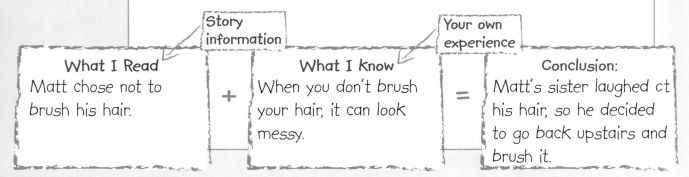

	Story information			Your own experience	
What I Read Matt chose not to brush his hair.	+	**What I Know** When you don't brush your hair, it can look messy.	=	**Conclusion:** Matt's sister laughed at his hair, so he decided to go back upstairs and brush it.	

More About Drawing Conclusions

Sensible conclusions based on the facts you read and on your experience are valid. For example, suppose the paragraph on page 374 had ended with the sentence *Matt glared at his sister and stormed out the door.* You might have come to a different conclusion about Matt's decision to brush his hair.

What I Read		What I Know		Conclusion:
Matt glared at his sister.	**+**	A glaring person is usually unhappy with another person.	**=**	Matt decided he didn't care what his sister thought about his hair.

Sometimes a paragraph might not contain enough information for drawing a valid conclusion. Read the paragraph below. Think of one valid conclusion you could draw. Then think of one invalid conclusion someone might draw from the given information.

David was about to go swimming with his friends. His mom asked him to be sure to reapply sunscreen throughout the day. David rolled his eyes as the door slammed behind him. That evening a sunburned David couldn't go to the movies with his friends. His mom was unhappy with his behavior.

Skill Practice

Read the following paragraph. Use the Tips for Drawing Conclusions to answer the questions.

Stephanie was afraid that her older sister, Alexa, had picked up a harmful habit. She noticed that her sister's hair and clothes smelled like smoke. She also smelled smoke on Alexa's breath. Stephanie wondered if she should tell her parents about the smell.

1. What conclusion did you draw about Alexa?
2. What information from your personal experience did you use to draw the conclusion?
3. What story information did you use?

Focus Skill

Identify Cause and Effect

Learning how to identify cause and effect can help you understand what you read. You can use a graphic organizer like this one to show cause and effect.

Cause:

A cause is an action or event that makes something happen.

Effect:

An effect is what happens as a result of an action or event.

Tips for Identifying Cause and Effect

- To find an effect, ask: *What happened?*
- To find a cause, ask: *Why did this happen?*
- Remember that events can have more than one cause or effect.
- Look for signal words and phrases, such as *because* and *as a result*, to help you identify causes and effects.

Here's an example.

Randy and Albert were in a conflict *because* Randy tripped over Albert's jacket and it got dirty. The boys listened to each other. Randy said he didn't *see* the jacket *because* it was on the floor. Albert said he understood that it was an accident. Albert agreed to be more careful about hanging up his jacket. He said he was glad Randy hadn't *been* hurt.

Here's what you could record in the graphic organizer.

Cause:
Randy tripped over Albert's jacket.

Effect:
Albert's jacket got dirty.

More About Cause and Effect

Events can have more than one cause or effect. For example, suppose the paragraph on page 376 included the sentence *Randy sprained his ankle.* You could then identify two effects of Randy's tripping.

Cause: Randy tripped over Albert's jacket.

→ **Effect:** Albert's jacket got dirty.

→ **Effect:** Randy sprained his ankle.

Some paragraphs contain more than one cause and effect. In the paragraph, one cause and its effect are underlined. Find a second cause and its effect.

Nick and Emma were playing soccer at lunchtime. As Nick turned to look for the ball, <u>it hit him in the head and he fell.</u> Nick looked angrily at Emma. He got up to hurl the ball at her. She pleaded that hitting him was an accident. Nick wanted Emma to promise to be more careful. Emma said she would practice kicking straighter. Emma and Nick agreed on a solution that worked for both of them.

Skill Practice

Read this paragraph. Use the Tips for Identifying Cause and Effect to help you answer the questions.

Illegal drugs have many harmful effects. As a result of using illegal drugs, a person can be harmed or even die. Marijuana can cause memory loss and lung problems. Cocaine or crack can make the heart beat so fast that the user may have a heart attack and die.

1. What can cause a person to have memory loss?
2. What are three other effects of illegal drugs?
3. What two signal words or phrases helped you identify the causes and effects in this paragraph?

Identify Main Idea and Details

Focus Skill

Being able to identify the main idea and details can help you understand what you read. You can use a graphic organizer like this one to show the main idea and details.

Main Idea: The most important idea of a paragraph, several paragraphs, or a selection

| **Detail:** Information that tells more about the main idea | **Detail:** Information that tells more about the main idea | **Detail:** Information that tells more about the main idea |

Tips for Identifying Main Idea and Details

- To identify the main idea, ask: *What is this mostly about?*
- Remember that the main idea is not always stated in the first sentence.
- Be sure to look for details that help you answer questions such as *Who?*, *What?*, *Where?*, *When?*, *Why?*, and *How?*
- Use pictures as clues to help you figure out the main idea.

Here's an example.

> Main Idea
>
> Getting enough exercise is a key to good health. Daily physical activity helps you manage stress and maintain a healthful weight. It strengthens your body systems and boosts overall fitness. Doing a variety of activities helps, too.
>
> Detail

You could record this in the graphic organizer.

Main Idea: Exercise is important to good health.

| **Detail:** Exercise helps you manage stress and maintain a healthful weight. | **Detail:** Exercise helps you keep your body systems strong. | **Detail:** Doing a variety of activities is important. |

More About Main Idea and Details

Sometimes the main idea of a passage is at the end instead of the beginning. The main idea may not even be stated. However, it can be understood from the details. Look at the following graphic organizer. What do you think the main idea is?

Main Idea: ?

| Detail: Warm up your body before exercise. | Detail: Do aerobic exercise that lasts at least twenty to thirty minutes. | Detail: After exercise, give your body time to return to normal by doing low-level activity. |

A passage can contain details of different types. In the following paragraph, identify each detail as a reason, an example, a fact, a step, or a description.

Some kinds of exercise do not build cardiovascular fitness. Activities that use oxygen faster than it can be replaced are anaerobic. For example, sprinting as fast as you can is anaerobic. So is carrying a heavy load. Anaerobic activities build strength, but they don't help your heart.

Skill Practice

Read this paragraph. Use the Tips for Identifying Main Idea and Details to answer the questions.

Being a responsible family member means people depend on you. You may have jobs to do, such as walking the dog. Doing your jobs sets a good example for younger brothers or sisters. As you mature, your responsibilities grow.

1. What is the main idea of the paragraph?
2. What supporting details give more information?
3. What details answer any of the questions *Who?*, *What?*, *Where?*, *When?*, *Why?*, and *How?*

Sequence

Paying attention to the sequence of events, or the order in which things happen, can help you understand what you read. You can use a graphic organizer like this one to show sequence.

| 1. The first thing that happened | ➤ | 2. The next thing that happened | ➤ | 3. The last thing that happened |

Tips for Understanding Sequence

- Pay attention to the order in which events happen.
- Remember dates and times to help you understand the sequence.
- Look for signal words such as *first*, *next*, *then*, *last*, and *finally*.
- Sometimes it's helpful to add your own time-order words to help you understand the sequence.

Here's an example.

Time-order words

How does blood move in your heart? The atria *squeeze* after blood has moved into them from the body and lungs. *Next*, blood moves into the ventricles. *Finally*, the ventricles squeeze and blood goes back through the body and lungs.

You could record this in the graphic organizer.

| 1. Blood moves into the atria from the body and lungs, and the atria *squeeze*. | ➤ | 2. Blood moves into the ventricles, and the ventricles squeeze. | ➤ | 3. Blood moves to the lungs and the body. |

More About Sequence

Sometimes information is sequenced by dates or times. For example, in an emergency, authorities often need to know the exact times at which events occurred. Use the graphic organizer to sequence events that occurred during an emergency you experienced or read about.

1. My grandfather started getting chest pains at about 7:15 P.M.	2. My mom called 911 at about 7:17 P.M.	3. The ambulance arrived at 7:23 P.M, and my grandfather received CPR.

When time-order words are not given, add your own words to help you understand the sequence. In the paragraph below, one time-order word has been included and underlined. What other time-order words can you add to help understand the paragraph's sequence?

Last week I saw my cousin Diane crash her bike into a tree. First, I performed a ten-second survey. I realized that Diane needed immediate help, so I quickly called 911. I made sure that Diane didn't move until the ambulance arrived. I tried to stay calm and confident so that I could help Diane.

Skill Practice

Read the following paragraph. Use the Tips for Understanding Sequence to answer the questions.

One day at camp, Amy fell off her horse. First, I surveyed the situation. Next, I saw that she might have broken a bone, so I quickly dialed 911. Then, because of the possible broken bone, I told Amy to lie still. Finally, I calmly talked to Amy until the ambulance arrived.

1. What was the first thing Amy's friend did after Amy fell off the horse?
2. What might have happened if Amy's friend had left out the second step in the sequence of these events?
3. What four signal words helped you identify the sequence of events in this paragraph?

Focus Skill ★ Summarize

Learning how to summarize helps you identify the most important parts in a passage. This can help you understand what you read. You can use a graphic organizer like this one to help you summarize.

Main Idea:		Details:		Summary:
Tell about the most important information you have read.	+	Add details that answer the questions *Who?, What?, Where?, When?, Why?,* and *How?*	=	Retell what you have just read, including only the most important details.

Tips for Summarizing

- To write a summary, ask: *What is the most important information in the paragraph?*
- To include details with your summary, ask: *Who, what, when, where, why, and how?*
- Remember to use fewer words than the original has.
- Don't forget to use your own words when you summarize.

Here's an example.

> Making healthful choices reduces your risk of getting some diseases. Reduce your risk of heart disease and lung cancer by not using tobacco. Exercise regularly and eat healthful, low-fat foods to help prevent heart disease.

Main Idea

Detail

Here's what you could record in your graphic organizer.

Main Idea:		Details:		Summary:
Healthful choices reduce your risk of disease.	+	Exercise regularly, eat low-fat foods, and don't smoke.	=	Make healthful choices to live a longer life.

More About Summarizing

Sometimes a paragraph includes information that would not be included in a summary. For example, suppose the paragraph on page 382 included a sentence about the number of people who die of lung cancer each year. The graphic organizer would remain the same, because that detail is not important to understanding the paragraph's main idea.

Main Idea:
Healthful choices reduce your risk of disease.

+

Details:
Exercise regularly, eat low-fat foods, and don't smoke.

=

Summary:
Make healthful choices to live a longer life.

Sometimes the main idea of a paragraph is not in the first sentence. In the following paragraph, two important details are underlined. What is the main idea?

Did you ever wonder how you "catch" an illness from someone else? <u>Infectious diseases are caused by pathogens.</u> Pathogens cause infection when they grow and multiply. <u>They spread disease when they are passed from one person to another.</u>

Skill Practice

Read the following paragraph. Use the Tips for Summarizing to answer the questions.

One important task of a local health department is to inspect restaurants. Restaurants must be clean. The foods must be handled properly and kept at proper temperatures. If the health department finds too many problems, it can close down a restaurant until the problems are corrected.

1. If a friend asked you what this paragraph is about, what information would you include? What would you leave out?
2. What is the main idea of the paragraph?
3. What two details would you include in a summary?

First Aid

384

Health and Safety

For Bleeding–Universal Precautions

Y ou can get some diseases from a person's blood. Avoid touching anyone's blood. Wear protective gloves if possible. To treat an injury, follow the steps.

If someone else is bleeding

1

Wash your hands with soap if possible.

2

Put on protective gloves, if available.

3

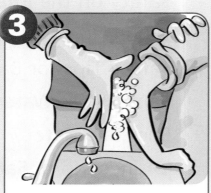

Wash small wounds with soap and water. Do not wash serious wounds.

4

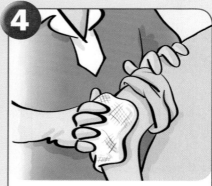

Place a clean gauze pad or cloth over the wound. Press firmly for ten minutes. Don't lift the gauze during this time.

5

If you don't have gloves, have the injured person hold the gauze or cloth in place with his or her hand for ten minutes.

6

If after ten minutes the bleeding has stopped, bandage the wound. If the bleeding has not stopped, continue pressing on the wound and get help.

If you are bleeding

Follow the steps above. You do not need to avoid touching your own blood.

For Choking

If someone else is choking

1

Recognize the Universal Choking Sign—grasping the throat with both hands. This sign means a person is choking and needs help.

2

Stand behind the person, and put your arms around his or her waist. Place your fist above the person's belly button.

3

Grab your fist with your other hand. Pull your hands toward yourself, and give five quick, hard, upward thrusts on the person's stomach.

If you are choking when alone

1 Make a fist, and place it above your belly button. Grab your fist with your other hand. Pull your hands up with a quick, hard thrust.

2 Or keep your hands on your belly, lean your body over the back of a chair or over a counter, and shove your fist in and up.

387

For Burns

- Minor burns are called first-degree burns and involve only the top layer of skin. The skin is red and dry, and the burn is painful.

- Second-degree burns cause deeper damage. The burns cause blisters, redness, swelling, and pain.

- Third-degree burns are the most serious because they damage all layers of the skin. The skin is usually white or charred black. The area may feel numb because the nerve endings have been destroyed.

All burns need immediate first aid.

Minor Burns
- Run cool water over the burn, or soak it for at least five minutes.
- Cover the burn with a clean, dry bandage.
- Do not put lotion or ointment on the burn.

More Serious Burns
- Cover the burn with a cool, wet bandage or clean cloth. Do not break any blisters.
- Do not put lotion or ointment on the burn.
- Get help from an adult right away.

For Nosebleeds

- Sit down, and tilt your head forward. Pinch your nostrils together for at least ten minutes.

- You can also put a cloth-covered cold pack on the bridge of your nose.

- If your nose continues to bleed, get help from an adult.

For Insect Bites and Stings

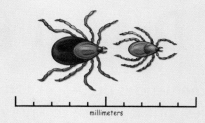

millimeters

- Always tell an adult about bites and stings.

- Scrape out the stinger with your fingernail.

- Wash the area with soap and water.

- A wrapped ice cube or cold pack will usually take away the pain from insect bites. A paste made from baking soda and water also helps.

- If the bite or sting is more serious and is on an arm or leg, keep the leg or arm dangling down. Apply a cold, wet cloth. Get help immediately.

- If you find a tick on your skin, remove it. Protect your fingers with a tissue or cloth to prevent contact with infectious tick fluids. If you must touch the tick with your bare hands, wash your hands right away.

- If the tick has already bitten you, ask an adult to remove it. Using tweezers, an adult should grab the tick as close to your skin as possible and pull the tick out in one steady motion. Do not use petroleum jelly or oil of any kind because it may cause the tick to struggle, releasing its infectious fluids. Thoroughly wash the area of the bite.

For Skin Rashes from Plants

Many poisonous plants have three leaves. Remember, "Leaves of three, let them be." If you touch a poisonous plant, wash the area and your hands. Change clothes, and wash the ones the plant touched. If a rash develops, follow these tips.

- Apply calamine lotion or a paste of baking soda and water. Try not to scratch. Tell an adult.

- If you get blisters, do not pop them. If they burst, keep the area clean and dry. Cover the area with a bandage.

- If your rash does not go away in two weeks or if the rash is on your face or in your eyes, see your doctor.

For Dental Emergencies

Dental emergencies occur less often than other health emergencies, but it is wise to know how to handle them.

Broken Tooth

- Rinse your mouth with warm water. Wrap a cloth around a cold pack, and place it on the injured area. Save any parts of the broken tooth. Call your dentist immediately.

Bitten Tongue or Lip

- Apply direct pressure to the bleeding area with a cloth. Use a wrapped cold pack to stop swelling. If the bleeding doesn't stop within fifteen minutes, go to a hospital emergency room.

Knocked-Out Permanent Tooth

- Find the tooth, and clean it gently and carefully. Handle it by the top (crown), not the root. Put it back into the socket if you can. Hold it in place by biting on a piece of clean cloth. If the tooth cannot be put back in, place it in a cup with milk or water. See a dentist immediately because time is very important in saving the tooth.

Food or Object Caught Between Teeth

- Use dental floss to gently take out the food or object. Never use anything sharp to remove what is stuck between your teeth. If it cannot be removed, call your dentist.

Remember that many dental injuries can be prevented if you

- wear a mouth guard while playing sports.

- wear a safety belt while riding in a car.

- inspect your home and get rid of hazards that might cause falls and injuries.

- see your dentist regularly for preventive care.

Food Safety Tips

Tips for Preparing Food

- Wash your hands thoroughly before preparing food. Also wash your hands after preparing each dish.

- Defrost meat in a microwave or the refrigerator. Do NOT defrost meat on the kitchen counter.

- Keep raw meat, poultry, and fish and their juices away from other foods.

- Wash cutting boards, knives, and countertops immediately after cutting up meat, poultry, or fish. Never use the same cutting board for meats and vegetables without thoroughly washing the board first.

Tips for Cooking

- Cook all food thoroughly, especially meat. This will kill bacteria that can make you ill.

- Red meats should be cooked to a temperature of 160°F. Poultry should be cooked to 180°F. When fish is safely cooked, it flakes easily with a fork.

- Eggs should be cooked until the yolks are firm. Never eat foods or drink anything containing raw eggs. Never eat uncooked cookie dough made with raw eggs.

Tips for Cleaning Up the Kitchen

- Wash all dishes, utensils, and countertops with hot, soapy water.

- Store leftovers in small containers that will cool quickly in the refrigerator. Don't leave leftovers on the counter to cool.

- Your refrigerator should be 40°F or colder.

- Write the date on leftovers. Don't store them for more than five days.

Kitchen Safety

Sometimes you may cook a meal or prepare a snack for yourself. Be careful—kitchens can be dangerous. You need to follow safety rules to avoid burns, cuts, and other accidental injuries. You should be especially careful if you're home by yourself.

General Rules

- Follow rules for preparing and storing food safely (page 391).

- Be sure a responsible adult knows what you plan to cook and which kitchen tools you will use.

- Learn fire safety rules for the home.

- To avoid the risk of burns and fires, use the stove or oven as little as possible.

- Clean up after yourself. Turn off all appliances before you leave the kitchen.

Stoves and Ovens

- Get an adult's permission to use the stove or oven. If possible, use a microwave.

- Keep clothing away from burners. Avoid clothes with sleeves or laces that hang down. They could catch fire.

- Keep pot handles turned in toward the center of the stove.

- Use an oven mitt to handle hot trays or metal pot handles. A mitt covers your whole hand.

- Be sure you have a firm grip before you lift a container of hot food.

Microwaves

Always follow the directions on the food labels. Remember these rules:

- Be careful when you take food out of a microwave. Even if the container isn't hot, steam can burn you.

- Never use metal containers, dishes with gold or silver decoration, or aluminum foil in a microwave. The metal can cause sparks or even start a fire.

- Never use a microwave to heat only water. When heating water, always place a non-metal object such as a wooden stirrer in the container.

Appliances and Kitchen Tools

- Check with an adult to find out which appliances you are allowed to use.

- Never turn an appliance off or on while your hands are wet.

- Kitchen knives are sharp and very dangerous. You should use knives and other sharp kitchen tools only with an adult's permission.

Good Posture at the Computer

Good posture is very important when using the computer. To help prevent eyestrain, muscle fatigue, and injuries, follow the posture tips shown below. Remember to grasp your mouse lightly, keep your back straight, avoid facing your monitor toward a window, and take frequent breaks for stretching.

top of screen at or just below eye level

shoulders in line with ears and hips

neck and shoulders relaxed

arms at sides bent as shown

wrists straight

feet flat on floor

Safety on the Internet

The Internet is a remarkable tool. You can use it for fun, education, research, and more. However, like anything else, it has some downsides. Some people compare the Internet to a city—not all the people there are people you want to meet, and not all the places you can go are places you want to be. On the Internet, as in a real city, you have to use common sense and follow safety guidelines to protect yourself. Below are some easy rules you can follow to stay safe online.

Rules for Online Safety

- Talk with an adult family member to set up rules for going online. Decide when you can go online, how long you can be online, and what kinds of places you can visit. Do not break the rules you agree to follow.

- Don't give out personal information such as your name, address, and telephone number or information about your family. Don't give the name or location of your school.

- If you find anything online that makes you uncomfortable, tell an adult family member right away.

- Never agree to meet with anyone in person. If you want to get together with someone you have met online, check with an adult family member first. If a meeting is approved, arrange to meet in a public place, and bring an adult with you.

- Don't send your picture or anything else to a person you meet online without first checking with an adult.

- Don't respond to any messages that are mean or make you uncomfortable. If you receive a message like that, tell an adult right away.

When Home Alone

Everyone stays home alone sometimes. When you stay home alone, it's important to know how to take care of yourself. Here are some easy rules to follow that will help keep you safe when you are home by yourself.

Do These Things

- Lock all the doors and windows. Be sure you know how to lock and unlock all the locks.

- If someone who is nasty or mean calls, say nothing and hang up immediately. Tell an adult about the call when he or she gets home. Your parents may not want you to answer the phone at all.

- If you have an emergency, call 911. Be prepared to describe the problem and to give your full name, address, and telephone number. Follow all instructions given to you. Do not hang up the phone until you are told to do so.

- If you see anyone hanging around outside your home, call a neighbor or the police.

- If you see or smell smoke, go outside right away. If you live in an apartment, do not take the elevator. Go to a neighbor's house, and call 911 immediately.

- Entertain yourself. Time will pass more quickly if you are not bored. Work on a hobby, read a book or magazine, do your homework, or clean your room. Before you know it, an adult will be home.

Do NOT Do These Things

- Do NOT use the stove, microwave, or oven unless an adult family member has given you permission and you know how to use these appliances.

- Do NOT open the door to anyone you don't know or to anyone who is not supposed to be in your home.

- Do NOT talk to strangers on the telephone. Do not tell anyone that you are home alone. If the call is for an adult family member, say that he or she can't come to the phone right now and take a message.

- Do NOT have friends over unless an adult family member has given you permission to do so.

A caller ID display can help you decide whether to answer the phone.

Safety Tips for Babysitters

Being a babysitter is a very important job. As a sitter you are responsible for the safety of the children in your care. Adults depend on you to make good decisions. Here are some tips to help you be a successful and safe babysitter.

When you accept a job as a babysitter, ask

- what time you should arrive.
- how long the adults will be away.
- what your responsibilities will be.
- the amount of pay you will receive.
- what arrangements will be made for your transportation to and from the home.

When you arrive to start a job, you should

- arrive several minutes early so that the adults have time to give you information about caring for the child.
- write down the name and phone number of the place the adults are going and what time they will be home.
- find out where emergency phone numbers are listed. The list should have numbers for the police, the fire department, and the children's doctor.
- find out where first-aid supplies are kept. You should be prepared to give first aid in an emergency.
- ask what and when the children should eat.
- ask what activities the children may do.
- ask when the children should go to bed and what their bedtime routine is.

While you are caring for children, you should

- never leave a baby alone on a changing table, sofa, or bed.
- never leave a child alone, even for a short time.
- check children often when they are sleeping.
- never leave a child alone near a pool or in the bathtub.
- never let a child play with a plastic bag.
- keep dangerous items out of a child's reach.

- know where all the doors are, and keep them locked. Do not let anyone in without permission from the adults.
- take a message if the phone rings. Do not tell the caller that you are the babysitter or that the adults are out.
- call the adults if there is an injury or illness. If you can't reach them, call the emergency numbers on the list.

Never leave children playing alone.

Never leave a child to eat alone.

Never leave children alone near a pool or in the bathtub.

Safety near Water

Water can be dangerous—a person can drown in five minutes or less. The best way to be safe near water is to learn how to swim. You should also follow these rules:

- Never swim without a lifeguard or a responsible adult present.

- If you can't swim, stay in shallow water. Don't rely on an inflatable raft.

- Know the rules for the beach or pool, and obey them. Don't run or play roughly near water.

- Do not dive in head-first until you know the water is deep enough. Jump in feet-first the first time.

- Watch the weather. Get out of the water at once if you see lightning or hear thunder.

- Protect your skin with sunscreen and your eyes with sunglasses.

- Wear a Coast Guard–approved life jacket anytime you are in a boat.

- Know what to do in an emergency.

Backpack Safety

Carrying a backpack that is too heavy can injure your back. Carrying one incorrectly also can hurt you.

Safe Use

- Choose a backpack with wide, padded shoulder straps and a padded back.

- Lighten your load. Leave unnecessary items at home.

- Pack heavier items so that they will be closest to your back.

- Always use both shoulder straps to carry the backpack.

- Never wear a backpack while riding a bicycle. The weight makes it harder to stay balanced. Use the bicycle's basket or saddlebags instead.

This is the right way to carry a backpack.

This is the wrong way to carry a backpack.

Safe Weight

A full backpack should weigh no more than 10 to 15 percent of your body weight. Less is better. To find 10 percent, divide your body weight by 10. Here are some examples:

Your Weight (pounds)	Maximum Backpack Weight (pounds)
70	7
80	8
90	9

Thunderstorm Safety

Thunderstorms are severe storms. Lightning can injure or kill people, cause fires, and damage property. Here are thunderstorm safety tips.

- **If you are inside**, **stay there.** The safest place to be is inside a building.

- **If you are outside**, **try to take shelter.** If possible, get into a closed car or truck. If you can't take shelter, get into a ditch or another low area.

- **If you are outside**, **don't be near any tall objects.** Don't stand in an open field, on a beach, on a hilltop, or near a lone tree. Find a low place and crouch down, with only your feet touching the ground.

- **Stay away from water.** Lightning is attracted to water, and water conducts electricity.

- **Listen for weather bulletins.** Storms that produce lightning may also produce tornadoes. Be ready to take shelter in a basement or in a hallway or other room without windows.

Earthquake Safety

An earthquake is a strong shaking of the ground. The tips below, many for adults, can help you and your family stay safe.

Before an Earthquake

- Bolt tall, heavy furniture, such as bookcases, to the wall. Store the heaviest items on the lowest shelves.
- To prevent fires, bolt down gas appliances and use flexible hose and connections for both gas and water lines.
- Firmly anchor overhead light fixtures to the ceiling to keep them from falling.

During an Earthquake

- If you are outdoors, stay there. Move away from buildings and electric wires.
- If you are indoors, stay under heavy furniture or in a doorway. Stay away from glass doors and windows and heavy objects that might fall.
- If you are in a car, go to an open area away from buildings and overpasses.

After an Earthquake

- Continue to watch for falling objects as aftershocks shake the area.
- Have the building checked for hidden structural problems.
- Check for broken gas, electric, and water lines. If you smell gas, shut off the gas main and leave the area. Report the leak.

Blizzard Safety

A blizzard is a dangerous snowstorm with strong winds and heavy snowfall. It may last for 12 to 36 hours, with snowfall greater than 6 inches in 24 hours and winds gusting higher than 35 miles per hour. Visibility may be less than 1/4 mile. The following tips can help you and your family stay safe during a blizzard.

Your home should have

- a working flashlight with extra batteries.

- a battery-powered NOAA weather radio, radio, or TV.

- extra food and water, plus medicines and baby items if needed.

- first-aid supplies.

- heating fuel such as propane, kerosene, or fuel oil.

- an emergency heating source.

- a smoke detector and a fire extinguisher.

If traveling by car or truck, your family should

- keep the gas tank nearly full. The vehicle should be fully checked and properly prepared for winter use.

- always let a friend or relative know the family's travel plans.

- keep a blizzard survival kit in the vehicle. It should contain blankets; a flashlight with extra batteries; a can and waterproof matches to melt snow for drinking; and high-calorie, nonperishable food.

- remain in the vehicle in a blizzard, and tie something bright to the antenna. Run the motor for short times for heat. Use the inside light only while running the motor.

Glossary

Numbers in parentheses indicate the pages
on which the words are defined in context.

PRONUNCIATION RESPELLING KEY

Sound	As in	Phonetic Respelling	Sound	As in	Phonetic Respelling	Sound	As in	Phonetic Respelling
a	bat	(BAT)	eye	idea	(eye•DEE•uh)	th	thin	(THIN)
ah	lock	(LAHK)	i	bit	(BIT)	u	pull	(PUL)
air	rare	(RAIR)	ing	going	(GOH•ing)	uh	medal	(MED•uhl)
ar	argue	(AR•gyoo)	k	card	(KARD)		talent	(TAL•uhnt)
aw	law	(LAW)		kite	(KYT)		pencil	(PEN•suhl)
ay	face	(FAYS)	ngk	bank	(BANGK)		onion	(UHN•yuhn)
ch	chapel	(CHAP•uhl)	oh	over	(OH•ver)		playful	(PLAY•fuhl)
e	test	(TEST)	oo	pool	(POOL)		dull	(DUHL)
	metric	(MEH•trik)	ow	out	(OWT)	y	yes	(YES)
ee	eat	(EET)	oy	foil	(FOYL)		ripe	(RYP)
	feet	(FEET)	s	cell	(SEL)	z	bags	(BAGZ)
	ski	(SKEE)		sit	(SIT)	zh	treasure	(TREZH•er)
er	paper	(PAY•per)	sh	sheep	(SHEEP)			
	fern	(FERN)	th	that	(THAT)			

abstinence (AB•stuh•nuhns): Avoiding behavior that puts your health at risk (*197*)

abstract thinking (ab•STRAKT THING•king): A complex kind of thinking that involves imagining different solutions to problems (*27*)

acute (uh•KYOOT): Describes the kind of illness that doesn't last for a long time (*212*)

addiction (uh•DIK•shuhn): A constant need for and use of a substance even though the user knows it is harmful (*236*)

additives (AD•uh•tivz): Things that food manufacturers add to foods; some are nutrients, such as vitamins or minerals, and some simply improve taste (*97*)

adolescence (ad•uh•LES•uhnts): A period of rapid growth and development from age ten to age nineteen (*22*)

aerobic exercise (air•OH•bik EK•ser•syz): Exercise that strengthens the heart and lungs and helps build cardiovascular fitness (*121*)

aggressive (uh•GREH•siv): Describes forceful behavior that could harm someone physically or emotionally (*299*)

alcoholism (AL•kuh•hawl•iz•uhm): Addiction to alcohol (*270*)

alveoli (al•VEE•uh•ly): The lungs' air sacs, in which oxygen and carbon dioxide are exchanged (*7*)

anabolic steroids (a•nuh•BAH•lik STIR•oydz): Prescription medicines that treat health problems but are abused by people who want to increase the size of their muscles (*237*)

anaerobic exercise (an•er•OH•bik EK•ser•syz): Brief, intense activity that helps build muscle strength (*121*)

anorexia (an•uh•REKS•ee•uh): An eating disorder in which a person diets too much or even starves himself or herself (*85*)

antibiotic (an•ty•by•AHT•ik): A medicine that kills certain bacteria, fungi, or protozoa (*203*)

antibodies (AN•tih•bahd•eez): Substances made by white blood cells to help fight disease (*202*)

astigmatism (uh•STIG•muh•tiz•uhm): A condition in which the lens of the eye is curved unevenly and everything looks blurry (*53*)

attitude (A•tuh•tood): The way you feel about something (*290*)

bacteria (bak•TIR•ee•uh): One-celled pathogens that can, but do not always, cause disease by producing harmful wastes (*196*)

blood alcohol level (or BAL) (BLUHD AL•kuh•hawl LEH•vuhl): The amount of alcohol in a person's blood (*266*)

body image (BAH•dee IM•ij): The way you think your body looks (*23*)

body language (BAH•dee LANG•gwij): The way you use your body to express your feelings (*304*)

bully (BUL•ee): Someone who hurts or frightens others (*177*)

C

calories (KAL•uh•reez): The units used for measuring the amount of energy in a food (*86*)

capillaries (KAP•uh•lair•eez): Very small blood vessels that connect arteries with veins (*6*)

carbohydrates (kar•boh•HY•drayts): The starches and sugars that supply most of the body's energy (*74*)

carbon monoxide (KAR•buhn muh•NAHK•syd): A poisonous gas in tobacco smoke; takes the place of oxygen in the blood (*261*)

carcinogens (kar•SIN•uh•juhnz): Substances that cause cancer (*261*)

cardiovascular fitness (kar•dee•oh•VAS•kyoo•ler FIT•nuhs): Good health of the circulatory system, including a strong heart (*120*)

cartilage (KAR•tuhl•ij): Soft, rubbery material that forms part of the skeleton (*10, 18*)

cell (SEL): The basic unit of structure of all living things (*4*)

chronic (KRAHN•ik): Describes the kind of illness or condition that affects a person for a long time (*212*)

cilia (SIL•ee•uh): Tiny, hairlike structures that line many of the breathing passages (*201*)

clique (KLIK): A group that keeps other people out (*302*)

communicable disease (kuh•MYOO•nih•kuh•buhl dih•ZEEZ): A disease that can be spread from person to person (*190*)

communicate (kuh•MYOO•nih•kayt): To share views, thoughts, and feelings with others and to listen to them (*328*)

concrete thinking (KAHN•kreet THING•king): Solving problems involving real objects that you can see and touch (*27*)

concussion (kuhn•KUHSH•uhn): A brain injury caused by a strong blow to the head (*143*)

conflicts (KAHN•flikts): Struggles over different needs and wants (*310*)

conserve (kuhn•SERV): To save something or use it carefully so it will last (*361*)

decibels (DES•uh•buhlz): The units used for measuring the loudness of sounds (*57*)

digested (dy•JEST•uhd): Broken down (*8*)

dosage (DOH•sij): The correct amount of medicine to take (*235*)

drug (DRUHG): A substance, other than food, that affects the way the body or mind works (*228*)

emergency (ee•MER•juhn•see): A situation that calls for quick action (*140*)

empathy (EM•puh•thee): Understanding of other people's needs and feelings (*324*)

energy balance: Taking in the same number of calories you use (*86*)

environment (en•VY•ruhn•muhnt): All the things that surround you every day (*15*)

environmental tobacco smoke (or ETS) (en•vy•ruhn•MEN•tuhl tuh•BA•koh SMOHK): Tobacco smoke in the air; can harm nonsmokers (*263*)

enzyme (EN•zym): A chemical, found in saliva, that helps change food into a form the body can use (*73*)

esophagus (ih•SAHF•uh•guhs): The long tube that leads to the stomach (*8*)

evacuation (ee•vak•yoo•AY•shuhn): The removal of people from their homes to safer places because of a disaster (*355*)

expiration date (ek•spuh•RAY•shuhn DAYT): The date after which a medicine should not be used (*235*)

exploitation (eks•ploy•TAY•shuhn): Taking advantage of someone (*332*)

farsighted (FAR•syt•uhd): Able to see faraway objects clearly, while nearby objects look blurry (*53*)

fats (FATS): The nutrients that contain the most energy (*74*)

first aid (FERST AYD): Immediate care given to an injured person (*142*)

flammable (FLAM•uh•buhl): Relating to materials that will burn if exposed to enough heat (*159*)

flexibility (flek•suh•BIL•uh•tee): The ability to bend and twist your body comfortably (*128*)

food allergy (FOOD AL•er•jee): A bad reaction to a food that most other people can eat without becoming ill (*93*)

Food Guide Pyramid (FOOD GYD PIR•uh•mid): A diagram that helps people choose a balanced diet (*79*)

food poisoning (FOOD POY•zuhn•ing): An illness caused by eating or drinking something that contains harmful germs (*102*)

fungi (FUHN•jy): Small, simple living things such as yeasts and molds; they can invade the skin or respiratory system as pathogens (*196*)

gang (GANG): A group that uses violence; members commit crimes, use and sell drugs, and carry weapons (*178*)

gingivitis (jin•juh•VYT•is): A gum disease that occurs when plaque hardens on the teeth and irritates the gums (*50*)

glands (GLANDZ): Groups of specialized cells that produce hormones (*16*)

goal setting (GOHL SEH•ting): The process of choosing a goal and working toward it (*295*)

growth spurt (GROHTH SPERT): A period of rapid growth (*20*)

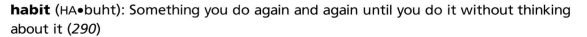

habit (HA•buht): Something you do again and again until you do it without thinking about it (*290*)

hair follicle (HAIR FAHL•ih•kuhl): A pitlike structure, in the skin, from which hair grows (*44*)

hazard (HA•zerd): Something in the environment or something a person does that can cause harm or injury (*139*)

health consumer (HELTH kuhn•SOOM•er): A person who buys and uses health products or services (*60*)

health maintenance (HELTH MAYNT•uhn•uhns): Describes a plan that involves laying out steps that need to be taken to reach health goals (*340*)

heredity (huh•RED•ih•tee): The passing of traits from parents to children (*14*)

hormones (HAWR•mohnz): Chemicals, produced by glands, that regulate many body functions (*16*)

hygiene (HY•jeen): Cleanliness (*34*)

illegal drugs (ih•LEE•guhl DRUHGZ): Drugs that are not medicines and that are against the law to sell, buy, have, or use (*238*)

immunity (ih•MYOON•uh•tee): The body's ability to "remember" how to make antibodies to a disease (*202*)

immunization (im•yoo•nuh•ZAY•shuhn): Giving a vaccine to people to make them immune to a disease (*208*)

infection (in•FEK•shuhn): The rapid growth of pathogens in the body (*195*)

ingredients (in•GREE•dee•uhnts): Substances that are in a product (*62, 96*)

inhalants (in•HAYL•uhnts): Substances that people abuse by breathing in their fumes (*244*)

insulin (IN•suh•lin): A chemical that helps body cells take in sugar from the blood (215)

intoxicated (in•TAHK•sih•kay•tuhd): Strongly affected by a drug (*267*)

joint (JOYNT): A place where two or more bones fit together (*10*)

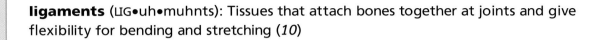

ligaments (LIG•uh•muhnts): Tissues that attach bones together at joints and give flexibility for bending and stretching (*10*)

M

medicine (MED•uh•suhn): A drug used to treat illness or disease (*228*)

medicine abuse (MED•uh•suhn uh•BYOOS): The taking of medicine to do something other than treat an illness (*236*)

medicine misuse (MED•uh•suhn mis•YOOS): The taking of medicine without following directions exactly (*236*)

minerals (MIN•uhr•uhlz): Nutrients that help your body grow and work (*76*)

mucus (MYOO•kuhs): A thick, sticky substance that traps pathogens and keeps them from getting any farther into your body (*201*)

muscular endurance (MUHS•kyuh•ler in•DUR•uhnts): The ability to use your muscles for a long time without getting tired (*129*)

muscular strength (MUHS•kyuh•ler STRENGTH): The ability to use your muscles to lift, push, or pull heavy objects (*128*)

myth (MITH): An idea that is thought to be true by some people, but is actually false (*60*)

N

natural disasters (NACH•er•uhl dih•ZAS•terz): Events in nature so powerful that they often result in the destruction of buildings and other structures; they include earthquakes, tornadoes, hurricanes, floods, and volcanic eruptions (*164*)

natural resources (NACH•er•uhl REE•sawrs•uhz): Materials from the environment that people use (*360*)

nearsighted (NIR•syt•uhd): Able to see nearby objects clearly, while faraway objects look blurry (*53*)

neglect (nih•GLEKT): Failure to take care of a person's basic needs, such as food and clothing (*332*)

negotiate (nih•GOH•shee•ayt): To discuss and resolve conflicts with another person (*324*)

nephrons (NEF•rahnz): Filters, in the kidneys, that remove waste and extract water from the blood (*9*)

neurons (NOOR•ahnz): Nerve cells; they receive signals from and send signals to other neurons (*12*)

nicotine (NIK•uh•teen): A drug, found in tobacco, that makes the heart work harder (*261*)

noncommunicable disease (nahn•kuh•MYOO•nih•kuh•buhl dih•ZEEZ): A disease that does not spread from person to person (*190*)

nutrients (NOO•tree•uhnts): Substances in food that provide the body with energy and building materials (*72*)

nutritionist (noo•TRISH•uhn•ist): A scientist who studies ways to prepare healthful diets (*79*)

oil gland (OYL GLAND): A gland that releases oil which coats the hair and spreads over the skin (*44*)

organ (AWR•guhn): A group of tissues that work together to perform a particular job (*5*)

orthodontia (awr•thuh•DAHN•shuh): The correction of crooked teeth (*51*)

overdose (OH•ver•dohs): A dangerously large drug dose that can cause illness or death (*239*)

over-the-counter medicines (or OTC medicines) (OH•ver•thuh•KOWN•ter MED•uh•suhnz): Medicines that can be bought without a prescription (*231*)

pathogens (PATH•uh•juhnz): Organisms or viruses that cause communicable diseases (*195*)

pedestrians (pih•DES•tree•uhnz): People who are walking (*154*)

peer pressure (PIR PRESH•er): The influence a group has over your actions and decisions (*300*)

physical activity (FIZ•ih•kuhl ak•TIV•uh•tee): Any movement of muscles that uses energy (*113*)

plaque (PLAK): A sticky substance formed on the teeth by bacteria (*50*)

portion control (PAWR•shuhn kuhn•TROHL): A limit on the number and sizes of the servings you eat (*84*)

prejudice (PREH•juh•duhs): An unfair negative attitude toward a whole group (*313*)

prenatal (pree•NAYT•uhl): Before birth (*20*)

prescription medicines (pree•SKRIP•shuhn MED•uh•suhnz): Medicines that can be bought only with an order from a doctor (*230*)

preservatives (pree•ZERV•uh•tivz): Chemicals added to foods to keep them from spoiling (*97*)

proteins (PROH•teenz): The building blocks of the body (*75*)

protozoa (proh•tuh•ZOH•uh): One-celled organisms that are larger than bacteria and often cause serious diseases (*196*)

puberty (PYOO•ber•tee): The physical changing that a person experiences during adolescence (*22*)

public health (PUH•blik HELTH): The health of all the people in a community (*346*)

recycle (ree•SY•kuhl): To make something old into something new (*360*)

reduce (ree•DOOS): To use less (*360*)

reflex action (REE•fleks AK•shuhn): An automatic response in which information from the senses is received and acted on by the spinal cord without first traveling to the brain (*13*)

refuse (rih•FYOOZ): To say *no* to something (*246*)

resistance (rih•ZIS•tuhns): Your body's natural ability to fight off diseases on its own (*204*)

reuse (ree•YOOZ): To use again (*360*)

sanitary landfills (SAN•uh•tair•ee LAND•filz): Large holes dug in the ground and lined with clay or plastic to contain trash and to keep wastes from seeping into the soil (*352*)

sanitation (sa•nuh•TAY•shuhn): The safe disposal of human wastes (*348*)

seizure (SEE•zher): A sudden attack of unconsciousness or uncontrolled body movement (*218*)

self-concept (self•KAHN•sept): The way you see yourself most of the time (*290*)

self-medication (self•med•ih•KAY•shuhn): The process of deciding on your own what medicine to take (*236*)

septic tank (SEP•tik TANGK): A concrete or steel tank buried in the ground outside a house to handle wastewater (*352*)

serving (SER•ving): The measured amount of food that is recommended for a meal or a snack (*79*)

sewage (SOO•ij): The mixture of wastewater and human waste that leaves homes and businesses (*352*)

side effects (SYD ih•FEKTS): Unwanted reactions to medicines (*232*)

SPF (Sun Protection Factor): A sunscreen rating that indicates about how much longer the sunscreen enables you to be in the sun without getting a sunburn, compared with no protection at all (*42*)

stereotype (STAIR•ee•uh•typ): A belief based on the idea that everyone in a certain group is the same (*312*)

stress (STRES): A feeling of tension in your body, your mind, or both (*306*)

symptoms (SIMP•tuhmz): Signs and feelings of a disease (*194*)

system (SIS•tuhm): A group of organs that work together to do a job (*5*)

tar (TAR): In tobacco a sticky, dark paste that builds up in the lungs and makes breathing difficult (*261*)

tendons (TEN•duhnz): Strong, flexible bands of tissue that attach muscles to bones, near the joints (*11*)

terrorism (TAIR•er•iz•uhm): The use of force or violence against people or property for a political or social goal (*173*)

tissue (TISH•oo): A group of cells of the same kind that work together (*4*)

ultraviolet rays (uhl•truh•VY•uh•lit RAYZ): The invisible light waves given off by the sun that cause sunburn and tanning (*41*)

vaccine (vak•SEEN): A medicine that can give immunity to a disease (*203*)

violence (VY•uh•luhns): Any act that harms or injures someone (*172*)

viruses (VY•ruh•suhz): The pathogens that are the smallest and cause the most disease (*196*)

vitamins (VYT•uh•minz): Nutrients that help the body do certain things (*76*)

volunteers (vahl•uhn•TIRZ): People who work without pay (*347*)

weapon (WEH•puhn): Anything that can be used to harm someone (*176*)

wellness (WEL•nuhs): A state of good health (*294*)

withdrawal (with•DRAW•uhl): The painful reaction that occurs when an addicted person suddenly stops using a drug (*239*)

zero-tolerance policy (ZIR•oh TAHL•er•uhns PAHL•uh•see): A plan in which no violence, weapons, or threats of any kind are allowed in a school and students who don't follow the plan are punished (*183*)

Index

CREDITS

Cover Design: Bill Smith Studio

Photographs:

KEY: (t) top, (b) bottom, (l) left, (r) right, (c) center, (bg) background, (fg) foreground;

Cover Photographer: Brian Fraunfelter

5 The Granger Collection, New York; 12 (l) Scott Camazine/Photo Researchers; 15 (t) Custom Medical Stock Photos; 18 (t) Science Photo Library/Photo Researchers; 19 Michael Heller/911 Pictures; 21 Getty Images; 33 Robin Rudd/Unicorn Stock Photos; 44 (r) Custom Medical Stock Photo; 50 Phototake; 54 (b) John Easley/Deep Sea Images; 55 George Hall/Corbis; 60 (l) Spencer Grant/PhotoEdit; 64 Peter Byron/PhotoEdit; 66 (inset) Center for Disease Control; 67 Bob Daemmrich/The Image Works; 87 Doug Pensinger/Getty Images; 89 (l) Bender - StockFood Munich/StockFood; 89 (r) FoodPix; 98 (l) Michael Newman/PhotoEdit; 98 (r) Creatas Royalty Free Stock Resources; 113 (b) Custom Medical Stock Photos; 115 Hub Willson/Robertstock.com; 116 Reuters NewMedia/Corbis; 118 David Madison; 121 Mary Lagenfeld Photo; 122 (t) Dennis MacDonald/PhotoEdit; 122 (tl) Index Stock Imagery; 122 (cl) Getty Images; 122 (bl) Creatas Royalty Free Stock Resources; 122 (bc) Cindy Charles/PhotoEdit; 122 (br) Mary Kate Denny/PhotoEdit; 127 Todd Rosenberg/Getty Images; 138 (l) Getty Images; 141 Dwayne Newton/PhotoEdit; 142 C. Bradley Simmons/Bruce Coleman, Inc.; 143 (t) Dung Vo Trung/Corbis Sygma; 145 Myrleen Ferguson Cate/PhotoEdit; 151 Brian Bahr/Getty Images; 164 (tr) David Pollack/Corbis; 164 (cl) Aaron Horowitz/Corbis; 167 Michael Newman/PhotoEdit; 173 Brett Coomer/AP/Wide World Photos; 184 Department of Homeland Security/AP/Wide World Photos; 185 Richard Patterson/AP/Wide World Photos; 191 (c) Microworks/Phototake; 191 (b) Walter Reinhart/Phototake; 193 Bruce Coleman, Inc.; 196 (t) CNRI/Science Photo Library/Photo Researchers; 196 (c) A. Pasieka/Photo Researchers; 196 (b) Custom Medical Stock Photo; 197 (l) Rick Poley/Visuals Unlimited; 197 (r) Dr. Linda Stannard, UCT/Science Photo Libary/Photo Researchers; 200 (l) Custom Medical Stock Photo; 202 Dennis Kunkel/Phototake; 203 (l) Science Photo Library/Photo Researchers; 203 (r) Hulton-Deutsch Collection/Corbis; 208 Eric Kamp/Index Stock Imagery; 215 (t) Cygnus; 223 Thinkstock/PictureQuest; 225 (tr) FoodPix; 225 (br) FoodPix; 228 Wolfgang Kaehler/Corbis; 229 (l) Alison Wright/Corbis; 229 (r) Ariel Skelley/Corbis; 237 Kevin Dodge/Masterfile; 238 Joe Klein/Corbis Sygma; 240 (t) Ivan Polunin/Bruce Coleman, Inc./PictureQuest; 242 (b) Getty Images; 243 (t) Dan Lamont/Corbis; 247 (l) Adam Woolfitt/Corbis; 261 (l) Science Photo Library/Photo Researchers; 261 (r) Phototake; 263 (l) James A. Finley/AP/Wide World Photos; 263 (r) Science Photo Library/Photo Researchers; 267 Bill Bachmann/PhotoEdit; 268 (l) Science Photo Library/ Photo Researchers; 268 (r) Science Photo Library/ Photo Researchers; 270 Tony Freeman/PhotoEdit; 271 (l) Robert Brenner/PhotoEdit; 271 (c) Gary Conner/ PhotoEdit; 271 (r) Bill Aron/PhotoEdit; 273 Richard Hutchings/PhotoEdit; 279 Donald Miralle/Getty Images; 284 Guy Cali/Stock Connection/PictureQuest; 294 (t) Renee Comet Photography/StockFood; 294 (b) Getty Images; 298 Dana White/PhotoEdit; 312 (t) Royalty-free/Corbis; 333 Bob Daemmrich/Stock, Boston/PictureQuest; 339 (t) Cleo Photography/ PhotoEdit; 346 Paul A. Souders/Corbis; 347 D.J. Peters, Tyler Morning Telegraph/AP/Wide World Photos; 348 Bert Wiklund; 349 Courtesy of World Health Organization; 350 (r) David M. Phillips/Photo Researchers; 351 D. Robert & Lorri Franz/Corbis; 352 (t) Rick Strobel; 352 (b) John Zoiner; 353 PhotoEdit; 354 AP/Wide World Photos; 355 Susan Day/Daybreak Imagery; 356 (l) Mark Richards/PhotoEdit; 356 (r) Michael Heller/911 Pictures; 357 Justin Sullivan/Getty Images; 358 (t) David Longstreath/AP/Wide World Photos; 358 (c) Wendell Metzen/Bruce Coleman, Inc.; 359 David Young-Wolff/PhotoEdit; 361 Getty Images; 363 Dennis MacDonald/PhotoEdit; 366 (r) Getty Images; 369 Kurt Thorson;

All other photos © Harcourt School Publishers. Harcourt photos provided by the Harcourt Index, Harcourt IPR, and Harcourt photographers; Weronica Ankarorn, Victoria Bowen, Eric Camden, Annette Coolidge, Doug Dukane, Ken Kinzie, Brian Minnich, and Steve Williams.

Illustrations:

David Brooks, 372, 374, 376, 378, 380, 382; Maggie Flavhan, 239; Patrick Gnan, 36, 68, 108, 134, 168, 286, 342, 370; Chris Jagmin, X, XI, 7,13, 28, 29, 48, 58, 65, 85, 93, 100, 124, 125, 140, 141, 146, 158, 177, 186, 198, 199, 210, 211, 250, 266, 276, 280, 295, 302, 308, 309, 314, 315, 330, 334, 361, 364, 365; Joe Lemonnier, 228; Fran Milner, 386, 387, 388, 389, 390, 391, 392, 393, 394, 395, 396, 397, 398, 399, 400, 401, 402, 403; Phil Scheuer, 17, 34, 35, 41, 45, 62, 67, 104, 107, 121, 142, 150, 152, 160, 163, 165, 167, 185, 133, 202, 212, 223, 233, 232, 240, 255, 262, 263, 265, 267, 263, 282, 285, 296, 301, 307, 313, 316, 318, 336, 341, 348, 357, 362, 369; Bart Vallecoccia, 4, 5, 6, 7, 8, 9, 10, 11, 12, 16, 18, 20, 43, 44, 48, 49, 50, 52, 53, 55, 73, 119, 120, 195, 197, 217, 241, 262, 269